Worship across the Racial Divide

ALSO BY GERARDO MARTI

A Mosaic of Believers
Diversity and Innovation in a Multiethnic Church

Hollywood Faith
Holiness, Prosperity, and Ambition in a Los Angeles Church

Worship across the Racial Divide

Religious Music and the Multiracial Congregation

GERARDO MARTI

OXFORD
UNIVERSITY PRESS

OXFORD
UNIVERSITY PRESS

Oxford University Press, Inc., publishes works that further
Oxford University's objective of excellence
in research, scholarship, and education.

Oxford New York
Auckland Cape Town Dar es Salaam Hong Kong Karachi
Kuala Lumpur Madrid Melbourne Mexico City Nairobi
New Delhi Shanghai Taipei Toronto

With offices in
Argentina Austria Brazil Chile Czech Republic France Greece
Guatemala Hungary Italy Japan Poland Portugal Singapore
South Korea Switzerland Thailand Turkey Ukraine Vietnam

Published by Oxford University Press, Inc.
198 Madison Avenue, New York, New York 10016

www.oup.com

Library of Congress Cataloging-in-Publication Data
Marti, Gerardo, 1965–
Worship across the racial divide : religious music and
the multiracial congregation / Gerardo Marti.
p. cm.
Includes bibliographical references (p.) and index.
ISBN 978-0-19-539297-5
1. Music—Religious aspects. 2. Music and race.
3. Multiculturalism—Religious aspects. I. Title.
ML3921.M37 2012
264'.2089—dc23 2011018782

1 3 5 7 9 8 6 4 2

Printed in the United States of America
on acid-free paper

For Laura, and our children,
Miranda, Zachary, Nathan, and Genevieve

Nothing unites beings more immediately and intimately, however, than the common worship and adoration of the 'holy'... it lies in the essence of the intention toward the holy to unite and join together. All possible divisions are based solely on symbols and techniques, not on the holy itself.

—MAX SCHELER,
Formalism in Ethics and Non-formal Ethics of Values

If the social scientist is able to point out that traditional and customary social policies do not have the results, intended or pretended by those who champion them, honest social intentions will find more adequate instruments for the attainment of their ends, and dishonest pretentions will be unmasked.

—REINHOLD NIEBUHR,
Moral Man and Immoral Society

See how elastic our stiff prejudices grow when love once comes to bend them.

—HERMAN MELVILLE, *Moby-Dick*

Contents

Preface

THANKS FIRST AND FOREMOST to the pastors and administrators, worship leaders and music directors, singers and musicians, as well as long-time members and first-time visitors of the twelve racially and ethnically diverse churches studied for this book. Any insight available is made possible by the gracious cooperation of clergy, staff, members, and visitors of these churches as they generously shared their worship experiences. Their openness and candor not only makes this research possible but also allows knowledge gained from their experiences to be shared with others who hope to achieve their success. Any errors committed in my sincere attempt to accurately describe the dynamics inherent to these churches are solely my own.

I am also grateful for grant support from the Louisville Institute that allowed for extensive data gathering in the multiracial churches included in this study. Executive Director Jim Lewis provided enthusiastic support for this research well after the funding period ended. The project was also enriched through my involvement as a Congregational Studies Team Fellow as part of the Engaged Scholars Project funded through the Lilly Endowment in the company of outstanding social scientists of religion, including Steve Warner, Nancy Ammerman, Bill McKinney, Jim Nieman, Penny Edgell, Larry Mamiya, Jackson Carroll, Carl Dudley, Nancy Eiesland, Robert Schreiter, and Jack Wertheimer. Special thanks especially to Bill McKinney, who during his tenure as President of the Pacific School of Religion took time both during and after my sojourn as a Fellow for timely feedback and ongoing encouragement.

During my research, I also benefited from a unique opportunity to review recent transformations in Christian worship through the Seminars in Christian Scholarship program at Calvin College in 2006 under the leadership of John Witvliet, Director of the Institute for the Study of Christian Worship. John, who deserves great respect for his mastery of worship history and contemporary practices, was also instrumental in making my time the following summer as a *Communitas* scholar extremely productive, and Calvin College provided time, resources, office space, and quite a bit of free food to fuel the writing for the initial framework of this book. Sociologist and friend Steve Warner also deserves thanks for his leadership in directing an intensive summer seminar surrounded by scholars of race and religion on "Congregations and Religious Diversity in Contemporary America" in 2008 through the Seminars in Christian Scholarship program. During that time, Nancy Ammerman, Michael Emerson, and Joy Charlton contributed feedback and their expertise. Greg Scheer, Bert Polman, and Marilyn Rottman also from Calvin College each contributed assistance to the project at several key moments.

Professors Don Miller and Jon Miller graciously received me as a Visiting Research Associate in the Center for Religion and Civic Culture at the University of Southern California during summers 2005 and 2006 to think and write. Don and Jon are outstanding scholars and equally outstanding mentors.

At Davidson College, a very special thanks goes to Candace Coleman and Sarah Coffey for outstanding research assistance. Also, thanks to Jane Reid, Katie Hamilton, and Rachel Kiselewich for transcription assistance and Austin Raymond, Joe McGinley, and Allie Christ for formatting assistance. LuAnne Sledge was invaluable in managing grant accounts, and Gayle Kaufman always offered a listening ear.

Davidson College provided funding for a sabbatical 2008–2009. During this time, I accepted an External Faculty Fellowship through the Humanities Research Center at Rice University as the Lynette S. Autrey Visiting Professor of Religious Studies (which carried a joint connection to the Department of Sociology). I especially thank Michael Emerson, Co-Director of the Kinder Institute for Urban Research at Rice, for wonderful feedback and camaraderie. My gratitude extends to Jeff Kripal, Tony Pinn, and Michael Lindsey as well as Uwe Steiner and Hank Hancock who each contributed to a friendly and productive time in Houston. Lauren Henderson was a truly fabulous research assistant during my stay.

Cynthia Read, Executive Editor at Oxford University Press, expressed quick interest in this project, and Charlotte Steinhardt ushered the book through publication.

In finalizing the manuscript, William G. Roy, Professor of Sociology at the University of California, Los Angeles, provided timely encouragement in casual conversation at the annual meetings of the American Sociological Association and took time to review the opening chapter. In addition, Douglas Harrison, Associate Professor of English at Florida Gulf Coast University graciously read draft chapters on music and African

Americans and provided additional references in relation to the history of gospel music.

From beginning to end, Jon Johnston (Pepperdine University), Kevin D. Dougherty (Baylor University), Ed Ransford (University of Southern California), and Samuel Sánchez y Sánchez (Davidson College) provided unfailing support. I really cannot thank you all enough.

Finally, I dedicate this book to my wife Laura for her support of my scholarship. I also dedicate this book to her and our children Genevieve, Nathan, Zachary, and Miranda.

Worship across the Racial Divide

1

Introduction

THE DREAM OF DIVERSITY AND THE DILEMMA OF MUSIC

I don't know. Maybe it's the music.
—BRENDA, MIXED ANCESTRY, volunteer staff

WHEN MARTIN LUTHER King, Jr., took his first pastorate at Dexter Avenue Baptist Church in 1954, one of his first priorities was to diversify the congregation. "I was convinced that worship at its best is a social experience with people of all levels of life coming together to realize their oneness and unity under God," he wrote in *Stride Toward Freedom.* King believed the mission of the church was to actualize the universality of God's kingdom on earth. And that means churches would also become integrated. "The church must remove the yoke of segregation from its own body," he wrote, as an expression of the unified "colony of heaven" who owe their "ultimate allegiance to God." He lamented that "the church has a schism in its own soul." Although King in his day remarked, "here and there churches are courageously making attacks on segregation, and actually integrating their congregations," church leaders today are tired of bearing the embarrassment of having mono-racial fellowships in an increasingly multiracial world.[1] His pioneering insistence on diversity is now a growing value among all American church leaders.

Stimulated by demographic changes in the United States that are rapidly transforming schools and neighborhoods across the country, there has been a tremendous rise since the 1990s in the desire for racial and ethnic diversity across our nation's churches.[2] Pastors and church leaders are rejecting their mono-racial past and embracing a multiracial future. The bridging of racial-ethnic divides through liturgical structures is an increasingly shared value because the Sunday at eleven o'clock racial segregation of the American church is no longer acceptable. Their growing conviction is that if the gospel is to remain valid as a means toward establishing peace not only within ourselves but between both neighbors and nations, churches must openly and directly work through all aspects of their ministry to confront proactively whatever may be perpetuating the persistent racial divide. Many denominational bodies have initiated programs for racial reconciliation. Interdenominational networks like Intervarsity Christian Fellowship incorporate racial diversity as core to their organizational mission. And in seminary courses, conferences, and workshops discussing race and the local church, Christian leaders increasingly talk about racial homogeneity as a form of racism such that single-race churches are viewed as "unbiblical" and "unspiritual." Healthy churches are supposed to be able to cross all racial and ethnic divides.

Integrated worship is fundamental to the vision of a truly multiracial church. My own research in integrated congregations over the past decade seems to point to the critical importance of worship music in cultivating racially diverse churches. When I looked back through notes from my studies of Mosaic and Oasis (two churches that successfully integrate people from at least four dominant ethnic-racial groups), I found that church members remained in congregations that reflect their musical tastes and desires.[3] Church leaders in both churches believed this was true and consequently focused much attention on the construction and performance of music in hopes of attracting and keeping diverse congregants. And so I began to suspect that music might be the single greatest determinant of a congregation's racial composition. Could sacred music be the gateway for stimulating integrated congregations?

The Dream of Diversity and the Dilemma of Music

In a time of iPods, satellite radio, and internet databases, musical preferences can be personally arranged, and individuals seldom need to listen to music they do not like. People are able to create personal soundtracks for their lives. But not at church. When coming to church, individuals are "forced" to listen to a range of music they have no choice in selecting. This means that attenders can accommodate their musical tastes only by choosing among entire church services rather than particular Christian songs. Because individuals make choices "with their feet," churches in turn have been "forced" to accommodate the consumer-oriented listening audience of potential church members by carefully considering the type and style of music they play.

Nearly every congregation in America is characterized by an almost complete absence of racial and ethnic diversity. The increased sensitivity to racial dynamics and the greater consideration of musical tastes combine to produce new challenges for local church leaders. Church leaders make choices about musical content and style in order to influence the ethnic and racial composition of their congregation. These leaders believe music matters; at the same time, they are not sure just quite how it matters, to what extent, and what to change if it really does. Amid this ambiguity, congregational worship leaders face enormous challenges. For example, in a recent United Methodist publication, the composer and church music director Craig Courtney describes how diversity of musical styles practiced in churches has broadly expanded. Training has shifted from classics and chorals to drums and electric guitar. Acoustics and amplification have altered the expectations and arrangements for sound. And, "worst of all, we are told that it is now worship style that attracts or repels visitors. And so, conversely, the success or failure of church growth has been placed squarely on our shoulders."[4] If churches are going to become diverse, and therefore "successful," it will be up to worship leaders and music directors to lead the way.

The reasons for writing this book came to me forcefully during a worship seminar at Calvin College in 2006 when a music director talked openly about the immense pressure he experienced to become more "multicultural" in worship. He was told by his leadership, "We need to become 'blacker.'" In pursuit of a "quick fix," he introduced gospel choir music with a few Negro spirituals "thrown in" somewhere in the services. Although the almost entirely white congregation experienced the music as "cool" saying that it had "a great beat" and even prompted reflection on what it meant to hear music that expressed survival and liberation, this "quick fix" approach ended up reinforcing stereotypes of what African Americans are "supposed to be" overall. So-called "black music" intended to expand diversity in this white congregation effectively deepened racial divides already embedded and remained unchallenged.

The demand for music that appeals across racial and ethnic cultures has prompted great speculation, producing fights amid values, assumptions, theological convictions, and cherished practices. A book focusing explicitly on worship in multiracial churches—churches that successfully integrate two or more racial-ethnic groups in the same worship service—is now critical. Several "advice books" fail to fill this gap by depending on either anecdotal evidence (what happened to me) or exegetical bible study (what the Bible tells us to do). Church leaders believe worship is key to bringing racial and ethnic groups together yet have varying opinions on how worship can and should be conducted to accomplish diversity—regardless of their own experiences of success, and indeed, even in spite of continual failure. But misguided worship practices based on faulty racial assumptions are dangerous in that they can accentuate rather than relieve the pervasive racial tensions in American Christianity. Many sweeping notions of "race" and "worship" influence the practical activity of members and attenders in multiracial churches. Congregational leaders and attenders vary widely in the manner in which ideas about race and worship affect their church's ministries. The lack of consistency between churches provokes more deeply analytical considerations. Indeed, the talk about worship in any particular multiracial church often masks rather than highlights the core racial dynamics of a congregation.

The Diversity of Diverse Worship

I will let you in on a secret now—based on the research to be presented in this book, there is no single worship style of music that successfully determines the likelihood of achieving a multiracial church. If I had initially believed that music was a "magic bullet" leaders could use to manipulate the style and therefore manipulate the racial and ethnic composition of a congregation, that belief was shown to be seriously flawed. Such a simplistic, deterministic view on the nature of American congregations and the place of music within them is inadequate for coming to terms with the dynamic structures of music and race in any multiracial church.

In my observations of churches it is the *practice* of music that is more important than the *singing* or *hearing* of music. Understanding how music and worship structure diverse relationships is more important than simplistic notions of "racial worship experiences" or "intentional integrative leadership." Diversity does happen through worship music—aside from (and even in spite of) the varying beliefs and practices and even without the intention to diversify—because music and worship create spaces of interaction where cross-racial bonds are formed. Practical activity, not mystical notions of worship, determines the successful cultivation of multiracial churches. So music does matter, but not in ways typically believed. And it is accomplished in a variety of liturgical settings. By revealing how notions of race shape actual musical worship practices, this book illuminates core processes in the successful racial integration of multiracial churches that go largely unnoticed by both scholars and church participants.

For this research, I spent time observing successfully diverse Protestant congregations from a broad range of denominational and non-denominational backgrounds and talking with their members.[5] My first realization was recognizing the diversity of diverse worship. For one of my first visits, I drove away from the Pacific Ocean toward the high desert and wound my way through the outer edges of metropolitan Los Angeles to attend the evening service of a very large church located at the center of several new suburban housing developments. These and other developments were built to serve ex-Angelinos who shifted eastward for a more affordable lifestyle while keeping the attractions of the big city within reach. I pass an alternating pattern of empty fields, storefront malls, and gated communities until I finally find the church. The building is brand new, the lines of the black-topped parking lot recently painted, and the mall-like architecture indicated plenty of room for children's classrooms, recreational play areas, staff offices, and a sizeable, two-tiered worship auditorium. The outstanding racial diversity of the church is the main reason I am here.

I park the car and find my way inside, saying "hello" to a few people I had met last week, and immediately notice the mix of whites, blacks, and Latinos making their way into the evening service with me. Coming through the doors I see the stage brightly lit, find a place among plush theater-style seating on the bottom level, and wait for the service to begin. People around me are talking and smiling with hugs and handshakes going around easily. The worship director, an African American, appears onstage at the piano with a shout into the microphone to welcome the milling crowd and announces the start of the service. Behind the worship director, long lines of men and women file onto rows of bleachers to the left. This is the "inspiration choir" I had heard about whose membership is almost half black, another one-third white, and the rest Hispanic. Lights go down, the atmosphere changes, and the music starts. We are ready to worship.

The sound is loud, more gospel-ish, a bit funky, with enthusiastic trills from the worship director and solos from the choir. The choir sways, the rhythm is deep and steady, as the worship director both plays and directs, bringing the choir on the stage and the congregation on the floor together in song. Everyone around me is soon on their feet, clapping, singing, guided by words displayed on big screens overhead. As the first song fades, other musicians emerge on stage. Following a shift of finger-play on the piano, the new instruments strike a Latin beat. Electric guitar, acoustic drums, and conga drums weave into the new song. People begin to whoop and yell both on and off stage. Both the choir and the crowd bounce up and down, keeping pace with a faster rhythm as the worship director smiles with affirmation. Then, another transition—a quieter song this time—and the bright lights on the platform focus on the piano playing a smooth melody with a contemporary beat I know is popular in many evangelical churches. The leader finishes the song with a quiet grace. The first worship set is over, and the teaching pastor for the night jumps into the spotlight to continue the service.

The immersive experience of worship in this successfully multiracial church led me to write pages of notes speculating how this must be the way worship happens in order for diversity to occur. My confidence in such a knee-jerk conclusion was quickly undermined by other church experiences. The following week, I went to another multiracial congregation, this time in downtown L.A.

Housed in a neo-gothic church building whose stone-façade architecture sharply contrasts with the steel-and-concrete block structures on either side, I walked through the main entrance. Beneath a stone archway, the wooden front doors swing open to reveal dark paneling, rich-red carpeting, and a short foyer before the inner sanctuary. Whites, blacks, and Latinos talk in hushed tones as they enter, and I take a seat near the middle as the service begins. The high ceiling within accentuates several classically designed stained glass windows on either side of the building. Rows of straight pews all face a raised altar with choir loft, elevated pulpit, and a grand organ whose golden pipes draw my eyes upward toward a mosaic glass window of Jesus with arms outstretched toward the congregation.

Sitting and absorbing the grandeur of this historic building, I hear a surge of fugue-like music from the organ swell to announce the start of the service. The sound reverberates throughout the church. A procession of long-robed choir members carrying a tall, bronze cross steadily make their way down the center aisle. About half are white and half black with a few brown-skinned, dark-haired Latinos mixed among them. They gather in staggered lines at the front of the altar as the organ quiets and the lead pastor, dressed in a long, white robe, raises her hands to welcome those gathered. The music director turns away from the organ for a moment to tell the congregation to take their hymnals for the first congregational song. With a pause creating a dramatic silence that fills the room, the music director pounds the first notes and grandly signals to both choir and congregation to join together in song. A new melody echoes through the sanctuary as people find the correct page. We musically march together through a subdued anthem punctuated at key points by the organ to accentuate key phrases and keep vocalists at the front and in the pews unified through several stanzas. The song ends with a rousing flourish. The music director then waves for the congregation to sit down before turning to the organ again and leading the now assembled choir in special music. The gorgeous harmonies elicit a sense of the majesty embedded in the architecture and evoke profound connections between the faithful of yesterday and today. The song ends, the choir sits down, and the preaching pastor takes her place at the pulpit to present today's scripture reading before giving her sermon.

Both of these churches have outstanding levels of diversity, yet both invoke musical rituals of worship in very different ways. Musical style and participation are qualitatively different, provoking questions in me that are being asked by many church leaders: How does the music and worship in these churches relate to the diversity achieved in these congregations? More broadly, what is the relationship between sacred music and racial diversity amidst the overwhelming segregation of American congregations? This question is producing an intellectual scramble among worship leaders, choir directors, and music publishers to find a ground for understanding how sacred music might unify believers across racial and ethnic cultures. The current literature on worship is filled with programmatic suggestions as writers on worship present prescriptive approaches that insist on a particular way of accomplishing worship through music.

The findings of my research surprised me, and I believe this book will surprise many readers. After hundreds of conversations with people at lectures, seminars, and workshops around the country, I see how pious church members find it disconcerting that the nature of worship varies widely—even within their own specific religious tradition. Any hope for a productive dialogue on the nature of worship amid diversity must avoid the tendency to universalize familiar experiences or to project our ideal images into necessary forms of worship. There are thousands of ecclesiastical communities just in the United States, each with their own histories and controversies, and sociologists (along with growing numbers of church leaders) who regularly observe worship practices become highly sensitized to the contextual specificity of what happens in various localities. And as churches are working through incorporation of racial and ethnic diversity, they are growing to understand the need to grapple with careful observations of worship from a variety of congregations, whether those churches are distinguished by history, geography, or denominational orientation.

No sociologist could ever answer the question of what should be in any church's worship service. But what that sociologist can do with confidence is discover the consistent patterns of thought and behavior found in racially diverse worship services and see how these patterns affect the congregation as a whole. More than merely cataloging a simple survey of occurrences, the power of sociological paradigms is how they reveal inherent and often unseen social dynamics—including racial and ethnic dynamics—involved in the ongoing production and reproduction of worship services. This book takes seriously that "worship is a social act, embedded in cultures and societies, rather than an individual alone."[6] So rather than focusing on seemingly unchanging aspects of church tradition, *Worship across the Racial Divide* eagerly looks at the ways in which churches are addressing a historically new set of challenges in achieving racial reconciliation and unity.

The Significance of Worship and Music in the Christian Tradition

In this study, worship is acknowledged to include far more than the music of the service. Worship is defined "as a public ritual event, an assembly usually conceived as an occasion for a kind of divine-human gift exchange."[7] Worship is not solely an individual process; worship is a shared, social activity (implied in the term "ritual").[8] Worship is a social process with profound interactions—spoken and unspoken, overt and covert—between those gathered together. Indeed, it is the emphasis on remembering the social aspect of worship that provides avenues of grasping a more expansive understanding of multiracial worship. And while there are various elements of worship (prayer, scripture reading, preaching, baptism, communion, healing, testimony, offerings, etc.), this book focuses on congregational musical performance and response. Music is common in Christian liturgy and considered absolutely necessary to the worship of God. Whether Gregorian chant, Lenten Kantakion, metrical versions of the Psalms, or contemporary Christian rock, church leaders believe in the power of sacred music to accomplish unity among people of different races and ethnicities. Music has always been considered a powerful influence on belief and behavior in the Christian tradition through the words of music as well as by the practice of singing together.

Hymns and canticles are implicit to the Jewish and Christian traditions as the use of songs is evident through the practices of the two communities as well as through the incorporation of songs in the texts of their scriptures. The Psalms comprise the largest single collection of music in the scriptures. In the first Christian communities, the apostle Paul instructs churches to include music as a core activity in the assembling of the local church (1 Corinthians 14:26; Ephesians 5:19–20; Colossians 3:19). And numerous outbreaks of songs are scattered throughout the New Testament including the prologue of the Gospel of John (1:1–18), a hymn of Christ in Philippians (2:6–11), and another song in 1 Timothy (3:16).[9] Although music from non-biblical sources is evident as early as the second century, it is assumed that this music did not only include "singing" verses from scriptural text but also the creation of new music, new hymns, new lyrics.

Yet, the fear of heresy provoked early church leaders to restrict congregational music from the days of the early church. It may seem strange to us now, but congregational singing is a very recent practice in church history. In the first centuries of Christianity, music was used to promote controversial new ideas and contributed to the development of Gnosticism and other non-orthodox teachings.[10] In the year 364, the 15th canon of the Council of Laodicea not only restricted musical content to singing psalms, but also, and more importantly, restricted musical performance and participation by establishing a designated, authorized group to sing. A choir of psalm-singers was officially entrusted with the public singing of psalms while others gathered in the assembly were not to sing. Even more, the 59th canon explicitly forbids using privately composed psalms and non-canonical writings in worship. So, the Council of Laodicea explicitly prohibited congregational singing and individual singing.[11] These musical prohibitions reveal deep convictions regarding the power of music to shape doctrinal faith, encourage fidelity to doctrinal truth, and foster growth in Christian character.[12]

Since the time of the Reformation, church leaders have been far less concerned about music's power to affect wrong beliefs and instead enthusiastic about its power to acculturate and reinforce the right ones. Music (mostly within Protestant traditions) is an important adjunct to the preaching of the service, a way of preparing and reinforcing the essential message proclaimed from the pulpit. The Word of God (*logos*) is given greater importance than the music, particularly within the Reformed tradition, leading to an emphasis on the words that are sung over merely hearing instrumental music in Protestant congregations. Words convey meaning and reinforce the proper teaching of the church, something instrumental music cannot do.[13] The composition of new sacred music with extra-biblical lyrics are composed with the specific intent to convey particular messages. Music is therefore harnessed by church leaders to foster unity as a shaper of doctrine and spiritual practice.

In addition to the use of music for teaching through the message of the words, sacred music is also intended to promote unity among believers simply through the act of expressing devotion and adoration together. Here the belief in the power of music is not so much in the particular doctrine being proclaimed but in the mere corporate act of singing together. Despite criticism in some Christian circles about the "thin" theological content of contemporary church music (leading to a preference for the doctrinally "thick" hymns of the eighteenth and nineteenth centuries), the intent of contemporary music is less to cognitively teach through words than it is to accomplish a corporate unity before the divine, even a corporate ushering in of the gathered assembly into the literal presence of the living God. Singing a chorus of "Jesus, Jesus, Jesus," then, may be theologically "thin," but can be quite "thick" in providing a corporate worship experience in which the focus is less on the words of the song and more on the sense of union in the hearing and singing together.

Within the Christian church, music has always been seen as a force to shape the beliefs and attitudes of people. Throughout the centuries, music has not been viewed as a neutral accessory, but a powerful force determinative of the shape of Christian community. And because the Christian church always sustained a vital interest in the manner of its worship, there is great attention on the nature of music and worship necessary for stimulating and sustaining ethno-racial diversity in congregations. The conversation among church leaders increasingly becomes the manner in which worship contributes to the formation of attitudes and practices that promote racial diversity. When does the worship of a church adequately help shape the character of people within the believing community? Indeed, as the imperative for racial diversity grows, it is inevitable that profound reconsiderations of the role of sacred music will become even more prominent.

The Supposed Miraculous Power of Worship for Racial Integration

Today, the emphasis on worship and music in the cultivation of racial diversity is embedded within a profound belief in the importance of worship and music for cultivating congregational unity. Church leaders from both Protestant and Catholic traditions readily indicate their desire to structure multicultural and multiethnic liturgical celebrations. The expansion of these pastoral concerns in the early twenty-first century involves a conscious inclusion of multiple languages in multilingual celebrations and the incorporation of indigenous cultural signs and symbols while maintaining Christian orthodoxy. Nearly all the books currently available that connect race and worship are written primarily for clergy and church practitioners who believe in "the miraculous power of worship."[14] Finding suitable music becomes an immediate priority.

New sources for diverse worship are continually being created to fulfill the desire for diversity-affirming worship. For example, Proskuneo, an online resource for "multilingual multicultural worship," distributes practice and accompaniment CDs along with a variety of additional multimedia materials in "out of the box" readily accessible packages (see http://www.proskuneo.info). Lyrics and PowerPoint slides are visually attractive, available in different languages, and highly affordable. The ministry offers conferences, retreats, seminars, workshops, one-on-one mentoring, internships, consulting, and a month-long "Proskuneo Worship Institute" and has even created a musical production with complete scripts, songs, sound tracks, and production notes along with a DVD to illustrate choreography, staging, and set design.

Another guide to "multicultural worship" comes from Mark R. Francis, an ordained priest and former professor of liturgy at Catholic Theological Union in Chicago. In his pamphlet, created through the Federation of Diocesan Liturgical Commissions and published in both Spanish and English, Father Francis insists on the importance of various musical forms, saying, "It is a romantic hangover to presuppose that music is a universal language and that it communicates the same thing to everyone." Rather, he proposes the "full multicultural" model in which a congregation brings together all cultural groups in the same liturgical service. The booklet reflects the Roman Catholic Church's concern with "inculturation," which is the way "the church makes the Gospel incarnate in different cultures and at the same time introduces peoples, together with their cultures, into her own community." For him, this "presupposes that the parish is consciously aware of being about the creation of 'something new' together: that all are working toward a respectful amalgamation of the various cultural elements of the parish into a way of worshiping God in Christ that is both faithful to the Catholic tradition and to the particular cultural gifts of every member of the assembly."[15]

Even more, a new "field of study" is developing in regard to race and worship labeled "ethnodoxology," defined by the International Council of Ethnodoxologists as "the theological and anthropological study, and practical application, of how every cultural group might use its unique and diverse artistic expressions appropriately to worship the God of the Bible."[16] The concern of "ethnodoxologists" is entirely with the study of music and worship in an explicitly Christian context. Teaching notes, training opportunities, lists of organizational partners and network associates, and an online journal, *Ethnodoxology*, all reinforce the vision and values of attaining appropriate worship for diverse peoples and resourcing the cultivation of multiracial congregations.

The growing literature on racially diverse churches always assumes racism must be removed through the discipleship of the church (a conviction that was greatly furthered by Martin Luther King, Jr., and civil rights religious leaders). Worship is increasingly evaluated for its potential for removing racism in the church. For example, George Yancey describes the "important asset of diverse worship": that "it lends itself to creating an attitude of racial acceptance." Music affects minds, which affects behaviors. The church must exemplify "openness through inclusive worship."[17] Indeed, the trend among those who believe that music is inherently connected to the racial-ethnic heritage of people is a belief that the practice of singing music from various traditions is important in and of itself for the cultivation of corporate unity. For example, the goal of connecting whites and Hispanics in a common congregation can be accomplished by singing a familiar hymn with a Latin flair. The meaning of the words is far less significant than the musical style of the music to which the congregation is exposed. Frameworks like that found in the highly influential book *United by Faith* also assert that the presence of different racial groups in a common assembly is indicative of proper spiritual formation in a congregation.[18] Because congregations should be sites of human liberation rather than oppression, racism is an evil to be confronted, and churches should become properly equipped to do so. Sheryl A. Kujawa-Holbrook asserts, "Racism is a profoundly spiritual concern and central to the proclamation of the gospel." She and others assume that worship music is part of what allows the reduction of racism to happen. "Congregations can be sources of both change and authentic racial reconciliation on the personal, interpersonal, institutional, and cultural levels of human society."[19] Worship is always viewed as one of the primary components that must be addressed in congregations if leaders are to reduce racism and accomplish diversification.

At times, the optimism of such congregational diversity projects is overwhelming. For Brenda Salter McNeil and Rick Richardson, worship music is a spiritual weapon taken up in the battle against racism. "As Christians, we must use spiritual weapons that have divine power to demolish strongholds of racism, hatred, oppression, injustice, and fear." They believe, "It takes the Holy Spirit to melt down the inner barriers we have erected and to create in us a desire for God and for other people." Through worship, "*soul change* leads to *social change*."[20] But not everyone shares the optimism of bringing ethnoracial groups together through worship.

Michael Emerson and Christian Smith's groundbreaking book *Divided by Faith* is one of the most thoughtful statements on the possibility of congregational diversity in America. Despite saying that "religion has tremendous potential for mitigating racial division and inequality," Emerson and Smith also assert "religion, as structured in America, is unable to make a great impact on the racialized society. In fact, far from knocking down racial barriers, religion generally serves to maintain these historical divides and helps to develop new ones.... In short, religion in the United States can serve as a moral force in freeing people, but not in bringing them together as equals across racial lines."[21] The American religious context overwhelmingly favors racial homogeneity. In the context of personal religious choice, churchgoers overwhelmingly choose to attend churches with people who are just like them. Emerson and Smith conclude that churches do little to promote racial unity and instead reinforce the racial differences that pervade American society.

Worship across the Racial Divide addresses such a pessimistic view while challenging the uninformed optimism of those who believe in the "power of worship." While religion as an abstract social force is not capable of eliminating racial divisions, particular elements of religious life can be and certainly are used as tools to accomplish specific religious imperatives that can alleviate racial and ethnic tensions.[22] Worship music in all its varied complexity is indeed utilized within Christian churches to help accomplish their goal of racial diversification—but not in ways that are consciously intended. Rather than see religious activity as a mystical force or as a mere reflection of the overwhelming forces of racial prejudice and discrimination, it is possible to see in practice how churches accomplish their ecclesiastical tasks of extending, supporting, and vitalizing their religious imperatives of integration by means of the use of music and worship. Despite reinforcing ethnic and racial differences through assumptions and stereotypes, this book reveals how churches indeed do—often inadvertently—promote racial diversity in their churches.

Entering the Practice of Worship

I undertook this research in 2005 to look at worship and music already practiced within the rare phenomena of multiracial churches and to examine *in practice* what is occurring within churches that are already successfully diverse. By generalizing from a sample of multiracial churches while incorporating the scattered findings of other scholars, I offer this book as a way to provide knowledge in place of rhetoric and stimulate a more informed discussion at the intersection of race, religion, and music. Poring over the literature on contemporary worship music and participating in many dialogues across the United States on the nature of multiracial worship in our world today, I am confident in saying no one knows what manner of worship is best for stimulating and accelerating racial and ethnic diversity in churches. None of the growing stream of studies on multiracial churches has explored music and worship in depth as scholars have neglected to follow up on the few insights available to explain what truly happens when diverse racial-ethnic groups worship together.

The study of multiethnic/multiracial congregations is quite new.[23] Religious scholars and congregational leaders are discovering the inherent processes involved in congregational diversification, that is, the integration of two or more ethnic/racial groups into shared ritual processes in a local church. We understand the rarity of multiracial churches, the appropriation of theology in promoting integration, the nature of identity negotiation within such churches, and the perceived costs and benefits of membership, yet we do not know much about how multiracial congregations emerge.[24] I want to move away from assumption and speculation to examine the worship and music already being practiced among the rare percentage of existing multiracial churches.

With generous funding, I spent 2005–2006 participating in twelve successfully multiracial churches from a wide variety of Protestant traditions in Southern California and interviewed over 170 of their members—including church leaders, church musicians, and regular attendees who have no clue how worship is planned or organized—about worship in their congregations.[25] These churches have already achieved the dream sought for by so many other churches, namely a racially integrated congregation. While diversity is to some degree dependent on extra-organizational factors such as the changing demographics of a geographic region, this study highlights a factor that is within control of church leaders: the construction of participation through worship music. By collecting data from a broader group of churches while pursuing in-depth understanding of the specific racial and ethnic dynamics within each church, I pursued this study with the confidence that ethnographic sociological research enables researchers like myself to understand the use of music in certain space and among certain populations.[26] My observations are supplemented by the preliminary data on worship gathered from my previous ethnographies on Mosaic and Oasis.[27] In looking through all of these observations and interviews, the persistent question guiding me was, "How do music and worship 'work' in successfully diverse congregations?"[28]

The following chapters reveal how my naïve expectations about the relationship between race and worship mirror those I found pervasive among scholars and practitioners. Music is important to achieving diversity—but not in the way I expected. By articulating my findings, I hope to enlighten those interested in truly understanding multiracial churches—rather than simply fantasizing about the romance of racial diversity—and show how we must fundamentally correct our expectations and reorient our observations to uncover the essential processes responsible for bridging the racial divide. And rather than only continuing to accumulate even more observations, the book articulates an approach for understanding music and worship that simultaneously accounts for individual worship experiences, leadership intentionality, and the broader constraints on actualizing diverse congregational worship.

To understand the dynamics of worship music in racially diverse churches, it became important to grasp music as a social rather than an acoustic phenomenon. I was guilty of "phonocentrism" when I began my study. I conducted church service observations with a digital tape recorder and strained to hear all elements of the music, attempting to spontaneously classify sounds and make sense of the total noise of the service. I naïvely walked into this research project expecting that there would be very few, very clear musical preferences among racial groups, that leaders catered to those preferences, and that as a result the congregation diversified as expected. In the course of my study, I came to see such a hope to be ridiculously overstated.

My growing observations forced me to attune less to what I "heard" in the service. Because ethnographic research enables an understanding of music in actual space and among specific populations, I found that paying attention to sound was far less important than the more challenging attempt to pay attention to the complex of practices of the worshiping community in the production and absorption of music. I focused on the musical styles in church services until I came to a growing recognition of music as a social practice, as occurring in an interactive process, and as creating opportunities for shared identity in a common community. Musical practice creates opportunity for formulating particular social bonds that transcend racial differences. With this shift in perspective, it became possible to draw out mechanisms within successfully diverse churches by which the practice of worship music *supports* rather than *deters* the creation of interracial connections, cross-racial bonds, and multiracial community.

In emphasizing practice as fundamental to how worship music "works," I deeply resonate with the work of Tia DeNora, who views music as "a powerful medium of social order."[29] In her book *Music in Everyday Life*, she writes, "To understand how music works as a device of social ordering, how its effects are reflexively achieved, we need actually to look at musical practice."[30] There are multiple layers of music in practice, from the personal-emotional to the structural-organizational. Nevertheless, in the scope of understanding the workings of music in congregational life, I emphasize how worship music provides an opportunity to exercise a form of "aesthetic agency" that compliments religiously motivated desire for racial and ethnic diversity. And while I had inherently privileged sound (like style, genre, pacing, and variety of music), I realized that what I had been observing was a complex of practices both embedded in and constitutive of social structures in all congregations. Sound is always embedded within practice.[31]

My "turn" toward social practices led me to a different set of observations and a search for a more adequate way of approaching the relationship between church music and racial-ethnic diversity that would account for individual experience, organizational structures, and greater social-structural contexts simultaneously. The unshakable center of my research decisively shifted toward the actual practices of worship found in a broad range of multiracial churches. In other words, because worship music happens in a particular space with particular practices, it became important to specify that the power of music (if there is any "power" to it at all) had to be discussed within the scope of a particular set of practices rather than a free-floating, merely auditory phenomena. This is what DeNora called "the interactionist critique of semiotics." In contrast with musicology, DeNora asserts the need for considering "musical forms as devices for the organization of experience, as referents for action, feeling and knowledge formulation."[32] What does this mean for understanding worship music?

DeNora's understanding of how music "works" is tied to an interpretive sociological approach that "agents attach connotations to things and orient to things on the basis of perceived meanings."[33] For the development of understanding music, this involves a shift from looking at the content of music and its supposedly static base of meanings to a more dynamic understanding of the cultural practices by which music, as an aesthetic material of culture, is appropriated and used in the production of social life.[34] To understand music, then, is not to perform a type of content analysis but rather to observe the manner in which music is enacted through behavior with all its attendant effects—whether they are intentional or not. Again, I am not merely interested in what people "think" about specific forms of music. Rather, the importance is to see the appropriation of cultural materials in action what worship music "does" in the context of congregational participation for racially diverse churches.

When church worship music is viewed as a means to accomplish congregational diversity, when music becomes "instrumental" (pardon my pun) for catalyzing and sustaining diversity, then the attempt to use music as an active element of social structure becomes clear. Church leaders, music directors, and worship pastors do not use such social-scientifically laden language; however, their belief that music is a central component to the cultivation of racial diversity speaks to their belief that music inherently makes certain types of social structures possible. For them, worship music enables, that is makes possible, the diversification of a congregation. Worship music is a resource that is harnessed to heighten awareness and simulate action to produce and accentuate attitudes and behaviors they believe will lead to racial and ethnic diversity.

Of course, church leaders may be wrong. How they think music "works" may actually be not at all the manner of its operation in the scope of activity within a congregation. The sociological phenomena of music may be operating in ways that are not planned or anticipated. I entered this research with an orientation similar to DeNora, who writes that "a sociology of musical affect cannot presume to know what music causes, or what semiotic force it will convey, at the level of reception, action, experience." This perspective motivates researchers like myself to pay attention to the way in which congregational members describe music and worship and racial and ethnic dynamics in relation to the practices observed in their congregation. Combining interviews and observations of both church musical leaders and church members, we can pursue "an empirical investigation of how music is actually read and pressed into use by others, how music actually comes to work in specific situations and moments of appropriation." We are "observing music appropriation in situ because . . . music's semiotic force cannot be derived from the music itself." DeNora's framework encourages us to move away from a purely emotional approach to music and its "powers" over human beings. Even more, DeNora is insistent that music's "powers" cannot be abstracted from their context. She argues for the need for an analysis that does not ignore music's properties but rather "considers how particular aspects of the music come to be significant in relation to particular recipients at particular moments, and under particular circumstances." Music has no power in and of itself, yet particular contexts can make music a salient, perhaps even determinative, aspect of social life. So she focuses on music "in action" as a "dynamic material of structuration."[35]

DeNora's corrective to semiotic analysis—a corrective with which this research resonates—is to pay attention to "situated actors" in that music involves particular audiences or recipients. Paying attention to the content of religious music fails to reveal the manner in which such music is produced, distributed, or consumed, all aspects of music's enactment in a social setting. In other words, analysis of the role of worship music in the life of a congregation will depend upon particularizing the significance and effect of music in actual congregational settings.

DeNora does not focus on *worship* music, yet the application of her framework to the operation of music in congregational settings is readily apparent. Following DeNora, this book is not concerned with sociology of music per se; rather, it acknowledges that music is being used in particular ways that accentuate the agency of human beings attempting to create particular worlds. Following works such as Paul Willis's *Profane Culture* and Simon Frith's *Sound Effects* and *The Sociology of Rock*, DeNora and I both see music as "a resource in and through which agency and identity are produced."[36] Music allows a space for people to develop their own selves in the presence of other selves. The capacity for music to create a space for self-development in congregational life is particularly evident in the experience of personal worship in a corporate setting. The aesthetic environment allows a means for understanding and demonstrating oneself through an aesthetic medium, something that is not possible for individual worshipers when they are all alone. In other words, the corporate worship experience allows the cultivation of a self that one cannot accomplish on one's own. Thus, the corporate setting of worship creates a unique and powerful setting for the cultivation of a particular type of self. While there is a bias in the literature that speaks to music in its ability to create a sense of "ontological security" or psychological comfort, this is a limited understanding of music that neglects the distinctively sociological dimension.[37] More than merely regulating moods or a sense of reality, music is a resource for creating and sustaining a self.[38]

Although my findings frame the use of music differently than these other theorists, it is clear that congregational leaders see music as a means by which people of different racial and ethnic backgrounds are attracted, negotiated, and merged into a dynamic unity. This book will have occasion to specify the degree to which leaders are successful in their "music projects" and the extent to which the use of music masks the operation of other social structures within congregational settings. Nevertheless, the view that music is being used to operate at the level of personal identity on the part of church attenders is unmistakable. Along with DeNora, I see the "structuring properties" of music are "understood as actualized in and through the practices of musical use, through the ways music was used and referred to by actors during their ongoing attempts to produce their social situations and themselves *as* selves."[39]

Consequently, this book highlights music's structuring powers. Music is an ordering device as it structures behavior in the here-and-now in both subtle and not-so-subtle ways. As a means of structuring social action, music allows opportunity for coordinated activity with other people. Indeed, music is a form of social control.[40]

While congregants and church leaders often accept the music in church as merely another aspect of sustained worship and community, DeNora's framework offers an opportunity to accentuate the subtle, yet powerful ways music operates as part of the social structure. She writes, "A thorough examination of these practices would have the potential to illuminate the (typically overlooked) aesthetic structures of social action, structures that undergo constant revision and renegotiation at the level of action." Thus congregations are particular settings in which music constitutes a specific social force. DeNora writes, "At a time when public spaces are increasingly being privatized, and when 'people management' principles from McDonald's and Disneyland are increasingly applied to shopping precincts [and congregations], sociologists need to focus much more closely on music's social role. Here, the concern with music as a social 'force'—and with the relation of music's production and deployment in specific circumstances—merges with a fundamental concern within sociology with the interface between the topography of material cultural environments, social action, power, and subjectivity."[41] In short, her work brings attention to the aesthetic dimension of social being. By appropriating her perspective, worship music provides an opportunity in this research to see how meanings come to be clustered in particularly socially located scenes.

Seeing music as socially produced reveals similarities to other settings. In reading the work of William G. Roy, I find a strong parallel between what is occurring in diverse congregations to the use of music during the People's Songs movement of the 1930s and 1940s as well as the civil rights movement in the 1950s and 1960s.[42] The Old Left self-consciously used what they thought of as racially inclusive music but paid little attention to the social context of music. Those who sang and those who listened engaged music in different ways yet created an inclusive and unifying dynamic. More than simply promoting a message, the music allowed a place for corporate action. Both Roy and I find that it is not the sound of "music" alone but social context that makes music powerful.

Overall, we are left with a set of critical questions: How are the structuring properties of worship music appropriated within multiracial congregations so as to have organizing effects on social and embodied action? And how does worship music work at the interactive level where diverse churches are sustained and reproduced over time? It will seem to many people initially counterintuitive, but this book reveals that multiracial churches do not achieve integration by diligently accommodating to supposedly distinct racial music styles, constructing assumed universal forms of worship, promoting highly intentional leadership for diversity, or raising racial awareness. Rather, successful multiracial churches produce places of interaction through their musical worship practices. Multiracial churches successfully diversify by stimulating unobtrusive pathways of interracial/interethnic interaction, and this book shows how layers of practical activity through structures of music and worship guided by notions of race routinely produce diversity.

A Look Ahead

This book challenges many common sense assumptions about music, worship, and racial dynamics. I urge readers to be patient in working through the arguments throughout this book. In talking about my preliminary findings over the past few years, I quickly find that people have very strong opinions on race and worship and can be put off by a "scholarly" reporting of research. Especially among those who make the study of worship their life work, I see how social scientists and students of Christian liturgy have an uneasy relationship. The questions and investigations of social scientists often clash with the programmatic aims of liturgists. There is a profound difference between a study that attempts to understand the nature of worship in a congregation and the idealized models based on a particular paradigm or preferred pattern of Christian worship.[43] By carefully observing a range of successfully multiracial churches and closely attending to leaders and attenders among them in my research, this study isolates the persistent dynamics of worship found among diverse churches. In the process, the study attempts to provide answers to questions most commonly asked by those interested in racial diversification and the potential for achieving it through music.

Most importantly, this book does not intend to privilege a point of view from any particular religious establishment, nor does it seek to understand worship practices from the prescribed or idealized practices of what "should" be practiced in any particular congregation. During my observations, I see how often pastors and writers on worship present prescriptive approaches that insist on a particular way of accomplishing worship through music rather than a thorough analysis of what is actually occurring in churches and the distinctive dynamics that different approaches have on the life of a congregation. In contrast, this study focuses on what racially-ethnically diverse congregations are doing regarding worship and music regardless of their ecclesial or denominational imperatives. Although I use the term "liturgy" in this book, by the use of this term I do not mean to imply that church services are all highly structured within established denominational practices often prescribed and explicitly written out. By "liturgy," I mean a structured way in which participants in a church service experience church; whether Reformed or Charismatic, all Christian churches have a liturgy that incorporates music.[44]

Every chapter represents an expanding portrait of the dynamics of worship and music uncovered within successfully diverse congregations. In this first chapter, I described the new imperative for racial and ethnic diversity in American churches and how worship music adds a significant complication to the demand for diversity. After introducing the core question guiding the study, I presented an initial orientation to approaching music and worship from a "practice-based" sociological perspective. Chapter 2 confronts pervasive, popular notions at the intersection of race and worship found in the "advice books" on multiracial worship and among the church leaders I interviewed. Both church advice books and church leaders attempt to fill the gap in knowledge. They argue essentially contradictory points: first, that racial-ethnic groups are radically distinct cultures that require racially-ethnically specific congregational music for worship; and second, that all people share a common core of humanity that resonates with certain, specific forms of music that transcend all racial-ethnic cultures and are effective for achieving a universal worship experience. The chapter shows both beliefs are flawed and their shortcomings create the need for a more adequate approach to multiracial worship.

Chapter 3 further confronts racialized notions of musical worship by revealing the pervasive assumption that the ideal multiracial worship is found among African Americans singing gospel music. Even among blacks, an African American singing gospel is the universal "icon" of true worship. The positive stigma of African Americans in worship is not only a persistent belief; it effectively structures the vision and programming of all multiracial churches—regardless of their likelihood of ever attracting any African Americans. The chapter forcefully cautions against racial essentialism and argues against accentuating and absolutizing supposed racial-ethnic distinctions—even seemingly complementary ones—that further crystallize notions of difference that extend rather than diminish racial divisions.

Chapter 4 builds on the last chapter by focusing on the experience of worship across racial and ethnic groups and shows how individual worship experiences fail to be distinguished by race. Instead, the chapter reveals worship to be an inherently social phenomenon by using the actual lived experience of worshipers to describe how attenders learn to worship by "letting go." Through worship, members of all racial-ethnic groups pursue an intensely private spiritual experience in a very public setting through "liturgical entrainment." The responsibility for creating that publicly stimulated private worship experience falls on worship leaders. Chapter 5 centers on the work of worship leaders, music directors, and church musicians who design liturgical processes in these multiracial churches. Moving from individual to organizational observations, leaders are caught in their roles, constantly negotiating between competing demands from the pastors they follow and the people they serve. The challenge of worship is consistently complicated by the demand for racial inclusion. Chapter 6 focuses on prominent concerns by church leaders: questions of musical style and leadership intentionality. Surprisingly, successfully multiracial churches vary widely in the musical styles used in services and the degree of intentionality for diversity present in the design of services. The focus on leadership intentionality typically discussed by "advice books" and church leaders is flawed; despite popular belief, a particular style, genre, or approach to music is not the secret to diversity.

Chapter 7 presents a key argument for the book by looking carefully at racial awareness and racial presence. Rather than focus on musical styles, the chapter argues for a focus on the structural practices of congregational worship. Specifically, all multiracial churches confront the challenge of achieving a racially diverse presence on the platform through "racialized ritual inclusion." Recruiting for visual diversity is a subtle, yet fundamental, imperative in all multiracial churches. Diversity is demanded from the platform, and the achievement of "conspicuous color" is an important goal frequently discussed by both scholars and church leaders. Chapter 8 culminates the book's overarching argument by demonstrating how interracial communities in American congregations are shaped through multiracial worship practices. Scholars and practitioners often "push" for diverse musical styles and visible diversity, but it is the structures of integration underlying the performance of worship music that actualize racial and ethnic integration. Essentially, music and worship create spaces of interracial/interethnic interaction as worship practices, both on and off the platform, effectively promote cross-racial bonding in successfully multiracial churches. The visual presence of diverse performers therefore indicates the covert presence of underlying practices inherent to congregational worship that lead to a sense of togetherness and community.

Finally, the conclusion restates the book's argument that the diversification of churches is not about racially accommodating distinct music styles or enacting simplistic notions of leadership intentionality, but rather about stimulating cross-racial interactions through musical worship practices. The chapter also provides further theoretical framing for examining worship processes in multiracial congregations and suggests that conspicuously diverse worship is becoming an institutionalized norm of legitimacy among "Diversity Congregations" in America.

PART I

Confronting Popular Notions of Race and Worship

2

Popular Beliefs about Worship in Multiracial Churches

This is a very racial country. People look at music very racially. Sometimes I do a black song first and then white, but no matter what we do both.

—TERELL, AFRICAN AMERICAN, music director

DEVOUT CHRISTIANS SHARE a conviction that worship has a transformational force and that this powerful force is able to accomplish racial unity. One popular Christian book, *The Heart of Racial Justice* by Brenda Salter McNeil and Rick Richardson, states that by being in the presence of "the God of all creation—the One who made all ethnic groups, tribes and nations and who pours out his presence wherever people are gathered together in his name—all the boundaries and distinctions that keep up separated from each other are worn down, and authentic community and reconciliation result."[1] This theological conviction is rooted in a core Christian practice that takes attention away from our imperfect humanity and its persistent problems toward a spiritual ideal that melts away mere earthly divisions.

Despite such conviction, church leaders quickly find that the ideal of worship that produces racial unity in all-too-earthly ministries is difficult to put into practice. Even when Christians confidently agree that unity in worship is the key to racial integration, they disagree on the exact nature of worship that actually produces such unity. As I read through all the books I could find on multiracial worship to see what they recommended, I found their confident assertions to be both complicated and contradictory. No wonder people are confused. The inevitable ambiguity drives the continued publication of even more books and the promotion of seminars to address the endless practical issues regarding the "how to" of multiracial worship.

After working through books and seminar notes on multiracial worship, I started working through my own data and sifting through my interviews to look for the informal theories held by church leaders and members on the connection between worship and music. Nearly every person offers at least tentative conjectures on the relationship between music and diversity. At the same time—and to my surprise—when I looked back through the interviews with the lead music directors and staff worship leaders in successfully multiracial churches, I found that most of them ultimately confess they have absolutely no idea how the worship music of their services connects with the racial diversity of their church. Those who are most responsible for the planning and execution of the musical portions of church services often have at best a vague notion of how music and race connect. Many simply assume that if people of different racial and ethnic backgrounds attend their church, then "they must like it." This is part of why worship leaders generally take a very pragmatic view of worship music as an element of their weekly ministries that must be faithfully planned and implemented.[2] My finding that most leaders lacked a comprehensive articulation for connecting worship and race was both comforting and disorienting. It became one of the key motivations for focusing less on musical style and more on worship practice.

But it is ironic that even when the musical leaders most responsible for the structuring of worship services express no particular set of beliefs, their congregations are full of pastoral associates, church staff members, musicians, lay volunteers, and regular church attenders who confidently assert a connection between the diversity of their church and the worship music of their church. In contrast to the "theoretically non-committal" worship leaders and music directors, the majority of the people who participate in planning and performing worship music—and the great majority of church members who regularly participate in multiracial church services—deeply believe worship is fundamental to achieving racial diversity. Uncovering the assumptions and complications of their normal, everyday talk about race and worship lays the base for understanding the importance of describing the actual cultural practices in their churches. Before looking into the cultural practice of congregational worship in successfully diverse congregations, it is important to review these dominant, "popular" approaches that connect race and worship as a means to eventually rise above the endless (and, frankly, largely unproductive) conversations on musical styles and genres.

Popular Theories on Achieving Ethno-Racial Diversity through Music

Integrating the ideas gathered from interviews about the relationship between worship music and racial diversity with the ideas found from my reading through "advice books" and articles promoting the use of music for racial and ethnic diversification, two competing "theories" of worship music emerge. They orient around two alternatives for understanding how certain sounds, rhythms, and "beats" connect racially diverse church members. First, there is a generalized belief in universal music that invokes the notion that music is a universal language. The belief that music is a universal language that communicates and draws all people equally is a prevalent, although mythological, belief. Studies from ethnomusicology summarized by sociologist Tia DeNora shows that however music is meaningful, its meaning is not derived from its structure as a "language" communicated and shared by people but rather from its particular use and corporate engagement through specific communities of people in concrete social activity.[3]

The second, and equally pervasive, notion is that all music is essentially racialized. Rather than focusing purely on music as sound as the belief in universal music assumes), the belief in racialized music points to certain patterns of song (rhythms, melodies, tonal ranges, etc.) that appeal to an ethno-racial group. Music is not "neutral" but rather connects with particular people. Particular styles or genres of music appeal to certain racial groups. In this perspective, people do not succumb to music based on its "hypnotic" appeal. Neither is it due to some inborn attraction to one style of music. Belief in racialized music understands music as an observable aspect of a social system. Music is believed to come from members of ethno-racial groups as the creators, or predominant influences, on their style of music, and members of that ethno-racial group are drawn to it. To understand music is to understand how music functions in the life of that ethno-racial group. Yet, even among those who hold to racialized conceptions of music there remains a quest to find music that carries universal appeal. Paul DiMaggio conducted a study that described "crossover music" that appealed across racial groups. For example, jazz is a genre of music that has been found to appeal to both blacks and whites, and therefore appears to transcend racial boundaries.[4] Among multiracial churches, leaders and attenders often believe that "gospel music" is racialized yet appeals to all audiences. Gospel is a prime example of racialized music with crossover appeal as it began to appear in secular settings while invoking an exotic mystique.[5]

Overall, when the various suggestions, formulations, and considerations within these two "theories" are placed alongside each other, the inconsistencies and contradictions become evident. What becomes even more problematic is that despite their contradictions, all "theories" seem to work. Church leaders who advocate these opposing theories regularly accomplish diversity in their multiracial congregations by using both of these approaches. Even so, while both "theories" seek to aid racial integration, in the end they may actually undermine well-intended attempts to overcome ethno-racial divisions as both encourage dangerous stereotypes that lead to a racial essentialism that exaggerates the racial divide.

The Quest for Universal Music—the "One Size Fits All" Theory

The first theory I call the *One Size Fits All Theory*. Those who promote this theory assume that certain specific types of music effectively transcend racial/ethnic differences. The One Size Fits All Theory is based on a foundational belief that music can be universal medium of communication and bonding. One white worship leader staked a claim on this belief, saying, "From my own personal a standpoint, I think it can be universal" even though he was frustrated in his attempts to find that specific musical form. Other leaders consciously commit to a musical genre with the assumption that this music is so basic that it touches all people. For example, Mosaic in Los Angeles commits to "Rock 'n' Roll," while the Oasis Christian Center only plays a blend of gospel, soul, and R&B styles.[6] In one interview at Oasis, a church musician said, "It's all about rhythm." He and other One Size Fits All theorists believe certain rhythms are universal to humanity and effectively tie into the deep resonance of shared human existence. It is as if the DNA of all people are similarly wired with respect to a particular type of music. Although there are some worship pastors that ascribe to this theory, it is especially popular among attenders of multiracial churches.

Despite its popularity, the One Size Fits All Theory is easily refuted. First, simple observation shows that multiracial churches manifest various musical patterns. No single dominating style or genre exists among them, and many different kinds of music can accomplish congregational diversity. While there are broad statistical patterns that may be asserted regarding the types of music that may be "average" among multiracial churches, these formulations describe music in a highly abstract manner drawn from survey data that masks the variety of musical forms present in the lived experience of these congregations.[7]

Another problem with the One Size Fits All Theory is the inevitable disagreement regarding what actually constitutes "universal" music. Whether the music is described as a rhythm, style, or genre (e.g., classic hymns, contemporary praise music, or R&B-Funk-Soul Music), I found through my reading and interviews that the particular form of "universal" music being promoted is different for each person. When the creed "music is a universal language" is followed, the style of music considered universal is not, in itself, universally shared. Still, this is largely unproblematic among adherents; those who express these ideas rarely experience the variety of music found in other multiracial worship services. And of course the regular presence of racial and ethnic diversity in their own churches consistently confirms their views. "Sure, it works," they say. "We see it happening here every week!"

As for myself, I confess that I began this study with the assumptions of the One Size Fits All Theory. I was sorely tempted throughout my research to find a way to describe a universal form of music that is acceptable and important to the existence of multiracial churches. Yet, I found none. Ethnomusicologists as well as missionaries also strived to find musical universality among world cultures but have also been disappointed. S.T. Kimbrough, Jr. summarizes the findings of ethnomusicologists, saying, "It is clear that there is no universal song per se that speaks to all human beings everywhere, and hence, no unequivocal international language..."[8] Despite the abandonment of universal music among ethnomusicologists, the idea of music as a universal language remained a common framework among legions of Christian missionaries who took Western Christian music and translated "words" without questioning the appropriateness or foreignness of the musical rhythms themselves for centuries.[9] Missionaries eventually abandoned this standpoint to shift toward working alongside indigenous musicians and to develop new musical forms that express the Christian faith. In the study of music, the search for the "holy grail" of musical forms that surpass culture ultimately failed.

In sum, sociologists, ethnomusicologists, and missionaries all conclude that there are no universals in music. Summarizing decades of research, C. Michael Hawn writes, "Perhaps it is advisable to speak of music as a language or experience founded on universal acoustical laws but given sonic presence (occurrence) in myriad cultural dialects."[10] In other words, the physics determining the sounds of notes on a guitar or keyboard are "universal," but the significance of those notes in how they are heard is not. In the realm of human experience, people ascribe meaning to the same musical sounds in different ways. It becomes impossible to pose any form of shared musical experience.

Authenticity, Musical Specificity, and Christian Hospitality—the "Musical Buffet" Theory

We can be confident that no common musical form provides the explanation for the binding of people into common fellowship. Many have come to recognize this and now seek to build commonality through music on a different basis. They believe that the manner of playing music represents native cultures in fundamental ways. Representation and connection to ancestral music will allow a dignified, mutual recognition of indigenous cultures to create bonds of unity. All this boils down to issues of musical authenticity. Particular groups connect with particular forms of music that can be traced by language, history, and geography. This notion leads to a reorientation in how the connection between race and music is understood.

The second popular "theory" connecting worship and race emphasizes musical authenticity and is almost entirely opposite from the One Size Fits All Theory. I call the second theory the *Musical Buffet Theory*. A Hispanic associate pastor expressed it well, comparing the music of his church with the standard fare offered in other churches, saying, "I love that gospel flair, I love hearing those Latin rhythms thrown in there. I love it when the bass goes off and gives me a little funk. It's just such a variety. It's the difference between ordering a dinner plate and going to a buffet." The Musical Buffet Theory is the most prominent and the most mentioned by church leaders who express any "theory" at all. Indeed, while most attenders "in the pews" think of music as a "universal language," this other idea of ethnically targeted musical plurality is often considered by church leaders and lay leaders as a more sophisticated "next step" in the development of musical consciousness.[11]

This approach comes with an array of racialized assumptions regarding the connection between music and racial-ethnic identity. In general, people tend to associate rap and hip-hop with blacks; techno and trance with Asians; pop and alternative with whites; and Tejano music, salsa, and merengue with Hispanics. Those who subscribe to the Musical Buffet Theory, then, call on and enact these stereotypes and see implementing different kinds of music into worship. Stylistic change happens from song to song. There exists a racial tinge about how people worship. The Musical Buffet Theory asserts that attenders bring cultural expectations into church worship. Carol Doran and Thomas H. Troeger calls these worship expectations "liturgical homelands."[12] The Musical Buffet Theory assumes that different forms of music resonate with different ethnic and racial groups. A sincere effort is made by worship leaders to include songs that "relate" to various races/ethnicities. Kathy Black similarly emphasizes "Culturally-Conscious Worship."[13] The congregation as a whole is encouraged to learn songs that are unfamiliar to them and absorb words and rhythms sampled from across the cultural spectrum. These leaders believe that in order to diversify a congregation, the music of the congregation must acknowledge and include the music of various races/ethnicities, particularly through the sacred music of worship. A white worship pastor described the ideal, saying the music "would translate into the things that they get up and dance to. The things that they respond to, the things that make you cry. The things that make them laugh. The things that hit them emotionally. That's how it should be happening. That's where I want us to go."

Music is said to "touch the heart" and is a way of "speaking their heart language." The incorporation of musical diversity includes diversity of language. Particularly among mainline music directors concerned with expanding hymnody (through inclusion of new music in hymnals), "global music" introduces words and rhythms beyond that of Anglo Europeans dominant in mainstream American Christianity. An African American music director said, "I guess letting them be a part of certain things where they sing a song in Spanish or put the words up in Spanish or a verse or two, at least you are including them. They feel included, and that's the trick." A Latina member at another church said about her worship leader, "He'll do something in Spanish, like last Sunday, they played salsa music. They'll just say a little phrase and then they'll go back to English. There's this one song you start out in English and then it goes to Spanish, but it's just four sentences and then back to English. If it were salsa—like my old church, that was like real salsa. It's not the same, but it's ok." Many congregations have started regularly singing Spanish choruses in their services—even if no Hispanics attend.

The Musical Buffet Theory is popular among Christian writers of contemporary worship music and many Christian leaders.[14] Sociologist George Yancey's influential book *One Body, One Spirit: Principles of Successful Multiracial Churches* offers key Musical Buffet principles for church leaders. From his observations, Yancey asserts that multiracial churches that emerge through intentional leadership skills use a greater variety of choirs and congregational music styles. "When a church limits its style of worship to only one racial culture it is sending out signals about who is supposed to be comfortable at its service." Yancey calls this "inclusive worship," writing, "It is extremely important that the worship styles of multiracial churches are inclusive in nature. What I mean by an inclusive worship style is a worship style that includes the cultural elements of more than one racial group. Inclusive worship means that the congregation does not limit itself to a worship style that is identified with only one racial culture." The variety of sacred music is important because it communicates a welcoming attitude to attenders. Yancey continues, "How we worship can be an important way to symbolize acceptance. An inclusive worship style communicates to visitors of different races that they and their culture are respected. Therefore, it is vitally important to include worship style elements from the racial groups that a ministry hopes to reach."[15]

Yancey writes, "Churches that desire to become multiracial or to maintain a racially integrated congregation tend to look for ways to incorporate different racial cultures into their worship." He provides an illustration: "For example, in one of the multiracial churches in our sample most of the leadership and congregation was Hispanic, yet the worship music was led by an African American. His presence brought in elements of a black gospel style that was combined with contemporary Christian praise and worship. This gave the church a multiracial style of worship. As a result of this worship style, the church had an atmosphere of acceptance toward non-Hispanics—despite the fact that all four of its paid clergy were Hispanic." Other churches he observed "rotated the racial nature of their worship style" by week. The focus would be on one racial group one Sunday, and then switched to another the next week. A core component of inclusive worship is this rotation (i.e., turn-taking) of the racial nature of the worship music. Rotating the racial orientation of music style promotes appreciation of other styles, yet requires sacrifice of preferences among members. A particular type of music may draw in certain visitors for whom the music is familiar, but at the same time turn away visitors uncomfortable with an unfamiliar style. Nevertheless, within a single service churches with inclusive worship "honor the racial culture of several different groups within the span of fifteen to twenty minutes."[16]

For Yancey and others, churches are encouraged to avoid an Anglo-centered hegemony—what Brenda Eatman Aghahowa calls "liturgical imperialism"—and to try appreciating and accentuating a broad range of musical subcultures in America.[17] For example, in a discussion on "authentic African American worship," Nancy Rosenberger Faus states, "All congregations need to sing such heart-wrenching songs, slowly, rhythmically, passionately, in *a capella* voices or accompanied by strong, pulsating piano and/or organ arrangements."[18] Robb Redman is another writer on contemporary worship who asserts, "Music is a vital feature of African American life as a whole, and it often reaches fullest expression for blacks in worship."[19] Faus also describes the music of Hispanics, saying, "If the North American church wants to reach and fully welcome Hispanics into the church, it is challenged (possibly even compelled before too many years) to include worship litanies and hymns in Spanish." Anticipating the reticence of church leaders, Faus encourages church leaders to incorporate what may be an unknown tongue:

> Command of the language is not necessary at all in order to sing. Even a bumbling attempt at pronunciation of an unfamiliar language shows a willingness to step into the culture and language of another person because of Christian concern and love. A congregation might begin learning a Spanish hymn text slowly, with a soloist or quartet first singing it, then the congregation. An exciting hymn to try is "Cantemos al Senor," which repeats the opening phrase on each verse and ends with "Aleluya!" At least, such an attempt shows a willingness to try another language.[20]

With these and other writers, the musical orientation of ethno-racial groups is clear. African Americans are passionate and participatory; they have freedom of musical expression with moving and dancing. Hispanics are passionate and communal; they are upbeat, social, relational, and "quite tactile, with lots of touching, hugging, and holding hands, including the men."[21] The choice of songs matters, but the style with which it is played matters even more so. (It is interesting to note that Asians, Native Americans, and other prominent ethnic groups are not characterized in these writings at all. See next section below.)

Church leaders are paying attention to these suggestions. A white worship administrator of a multiracial megachurch is typical among those making ethnically based musical diversity a priority. "I'm interested in ethnically going to a diverse spot musically for the sake of those that are not here at this point." Through our conversation I found that this worship administrator had no musical training at all, yet this does not keep her from giving firm direction in the construction of the weekly worship program. "Although I'm not a music person, per se and a lot of the selection and how it's put together comes from our worship leaders, we sit down as a team to plan these services and frequently I'm saying, 'Let's do something with a little more of a Latin feel.' " For this staff member, the shape of worship music should ideally reflect the ethnic populations not already present in the congregation in the hope of drawing them into the church. When I asked her how this translated into actual music, she said, "Our Hispanic population likes the Hispanic music. And our black population, when we have a gospel group that comes in, you can look around the congregation and you've got several black people on their feet in the middle of the service—when everybody else isn't. Do you know? They are up. Because they are just connecting."

Worship leaders who ascribe to the Musical Buffet approach specifically talk about "flavoring" the music with different ethnic approaches. One white worship leader said, "Definitely. We'll do old hymns and stuff like 'Amazing Grace,' which would be considered a pretty traditional song, and spice it up—make it sound more gospelly, or like 'Leaning on the Everlasting Arms' or something... So, yeah, I definitely try to incorporate a chord here and there to try to spice things up." James, a white worship pastor, talked about adding "different styles of music and adding whoever could bring whatever to the plate, so to speak." The metaphor of adding "spice" to flavor the "plate" of music is a prominent theme indicating an attempt by church leaders to racialize the musical space in ways that create stereotypic ethnic signals to appeal to members of different racial-ethnic groups. This is distinguished from playing completely different styles of music. Another worship leader described, "I find the musical flavor that each one has good in it."[22]

Recognizing the Complexity of Connecting Race and Worship Music

The Musical Buffet Theory assumes church leaders can definitively isolate distinctive musical spaces between the racial and ethnic groups. Overall, church leaders holding this "theory" take a bureaucratized approach to music and culture by boxing identities into categories in order to know which "worship procedure" is most relevant to them. This approach to worship music is influenced by a form of musicology that combines music, community, and identity. It looks at music patronage and the role of cultural institutions that support musical activity among groups, sees musical transmission as occurring intergenerationally, examines how music articulates and challenges social constructs (like gender and race), emphasizes the importance of on-the-ground observation and fieldwork, and incorporates advocacy efforts on behalf of marginalized and exploited peoples.[23]

If aesthetic preferences are learned from one's culture, one can conclude that "race-as-culture" will inevitably impact one's musical preferences. For example, a study by R. Serge Denisoff and Mark H. Levine analyzed musical preferences of college students at California State University in Los Angeles and found among these diverse young people that race determined the boundaries of their aesthetic taste.[24] In another study of popular music, George H. Lewis asserts that cultural and social structures like ethnic and racial backgrounds impact personal taste.[25] In yet another study, Karl F. Schuessler concludes that "if sociological theory postulates that human behavior is learned in culture, it follows, therefore, that aesthetic preferences are learned in culture."[26] So, aesthetic tastes like music may indeed be influenced by one's ethnic or racial background.

But, those who believe in the Musical Buffet Theory neglect broader cultural and social structures. The Musical Buffet Theory misses the nuance of socio-cultural dynamics because it assumes that even fully acculturated races and ethnicities are radically distinct in their responses to music. For them, response to music is not culturally learned but rather something that is *deeply rooted* in the essence of persons from a shared racial/ethnic group. The primitivist-essentialist assumptions embedded in these beliefs betray a type of anthropology of race that assumes individuals maintain deep affective ties to ancestral culture through early formative years regardless of their later circumstances, acculturation, or attitude.

Looking at the connection between race and music in both my reading of the advice literature and my interviews, what I find troubling is the extent to which Musical Buffet "theorists" consistently exaggerate the supposed differences between racial groups. The differences are asserted to such an extent that people of different races are said to be emotionally alienated from connecting with the music of different racial groups. It begins with simple statements like "Hispanics like conga drums," "Blacks like gospel," or "Whites like acoustic guitar." Yet, these seemingly innocent statements culminate to insurmountable chasms of musical response.

Pedrito Maynard-Reid's influential book titled *Diverse Worship: African-American, Caribbean, and Hispanic Perspectives* is one of the most comprehensive statements regarding the ideal worship in multiracial churches and is highly endorsed by prominent Christian leaders including theologian Justo L. Gonzalez, the late seminary professor Robert Webber, and *Christianity Today* executive editor David Neff.[27] The book is presented as a survey of three "cultures" of worship: African American, Caribbean, and Hispanic. Maynard-Reid catalogs the different styles of worship that are most appropriate for these different ethno-racial groups and describes multiethnic worship by describing three "cultural contexts" for worship. At the core of Maynard-Reid's book is the idea that indigenous groups exhibit modes of worship, and church leaders need to sophisticate themselves regarding these modes in order to accommodate them in their worship services. That the groups discussed are highly selective (Blacks, Hispanics, and Afrocentric Latinos from "the Caribbean") and limited geographically to the United States, Canada, Mexico, and the Caribbean is freely noted. The point of the book is that God is worshiped in a variety of ways, and the distinction between these ways is ethnically based. Moreover, a necessary aspect of Christian discipleship today is to learn to get out of one's "comfort zone" to acknowledge and perhaps even learn how to engage God in ways that are unfamiliar.[28]

Maynard-Reid states that the "worship patterns" within each culture are "not monolithic"—"Each culture includes a diverse spectrum," he writes—yet, he emphasizes the need to cultivate "worship patterns that utilize indigenous cultural elements and attempt to incorporate them into traditional, orthodox Christian worship to produce a wholistic [*sic*] and meaningful worship experience." What Maynard-Reid means by "traditional, orthodox Christian worship" is not defined, although I assume it means some conglomerate of Euro-American worship practices as the audience for books like this one is almost always targeted to Caucasian Christians. The promotion of musical diversity is an attempt to educate and enrich the worship of Anglo-centered churches by actively incorporating the worship practices of other ethnic groups. Despite a brief discussion on the "dynamic, fluid, and open" nature of culture, Maynard-Reid's book typifies worship and makes it both static and concrete to the average reader. The theoretical strategy of this book is to isolate ideal types and "sensitize" white church leaders.[29]

What distinguishes African American, Caribbean, and Hispanic worship? For Maynard-Reid, African American worship is "experiential," "a community event," and "celebrative." For African Americans, church is more "wholistic" emphasizing "connectedness and interrelatedness." Maynard-Reid asserts that music is "the most permanent characteristic of black heritage" as it expresses both social and spiritual struggles that work within themes of liberation. Music is "a vehicle that permits blacks to move from frustration of inarticulate emotion to adequately satisfying expression." "Melody, rhythm, and improvisation" is emphasized. The call-response structure emphasizes community. The gospel emphasis is on the present, introspection, and optimism. According to Maynard-Reid, "Liberation is experienced in worship, and the fruit is joy and ecstasy. Worshipers cannot keep silent. Throughout the service exclamations break out: 'Thank you, Jesus!' 'Praise the Lord!' 'Hallelujah!' 'Amen!' These are charismatic proclamations of the goodness of God and the gladness worshipers feel in their souls."[30]

In contrast, Caribbean worship music is marked by syncopation, rhythm, antiphonal style, repetition, and simple harmony. Musical instruments are said to invoke "rhythmic response." Maynard-Reid laments that Carribean worship more often reflects a "Euro-American ethos" than an indigenous one. He writes, "Too often we are wedded to the rusty old organ that has no appeal to the soul of the islander. How much more alive would the worship experience be if the steel pan and the raggae rhythms in themselves were not seen as sensual, sacrilegious, and carnal but as elements that can awaken the spiritual chords of the soul." He goes on to say, "Churches and communities that have successfully incorporated music with African elements are the ones that have made Christ central in all their musical expressions."[31]

And Hispanic worship? Maynard-Reid describes Hispanic worship as a "liturgical fiesta" done in conjunction with sacred time and space in relation to the sacred event. "It is therefore just as festive as the birthday party or graduation celebration in the dominant culture." Worship is done "with the fullest emotion and the liveliest celebrative acts." Similar to African Americans, music among Hispanic Christians expresses both struggle and hope.[32] Referring to Eldin Villafañe, he describes a "musical élan" as "a particular quality, a 'gift' from the African heritage" in that it "expresses and impresses all religious experience with emotional depth of transcendence, joy, and liberation."[33] The music recaptures rich heritage and history while expressing "their inner and total self." Hispanics are turning away from Gregorian chants and classical European music because it lacks *sentimeinto* which means "the 'feel,' the 'passion' which only authentic cultural expression can bring."[34] Instead, Hispanics sing *coritos*, short songs of praise coming form Pentecostalism.[35] Among my own interviews, a white female music director said, "Oh man, you go to a Hispanic congregation and it is lively, alive, and growing, and they are singing a lot of songs that have a tremendous beat to it." When I asked an African American female worship leader what attracts Hispanics or draws them musically, she said, "More passionate songs, because they are a passionate group."

The irony is that for Maynard-Reid and other Christians, worship music is intended to melt away differences at the same time that playing music that "honors" particular (and stereotyped) cultural backgrounds explicitly reinforces distinctions. The notion of indigenous worship practices is highly abstracted and idealized. For unity between these groups to occur within a church service, each must be willing to musically "wait their turn" while music of other groups is played and sung. This polite turn-taking is seen as a necessary act of civility required for people to experience a sense of unity; although within this framework, where the unity of all people comes from through music is not possible to truly say.

In practice, the creation of Buffet-style turn-taking becomes nearly impossible. One prime difficulty is that diversity within any racial or ethnic group is inescapable. Maynard-Reid is saddened by the difficulty of creating a systematic representation of each culture of worship "due to the enormous diversity that exists." In defining Hispanic worship, for example, he admits that "part of the problem is the difficulty in identifying or defining this cultural group of people" and ends up focusing on Hispanics in Mexico, the United States, and the Caribbean region. In the face of such difficulties, Maynard-Reid insists on calling these three types "cultures" and proceeds through the text to treat them as having static boundaries. Later, in discussing African American worship, he states that "underneath this variety, however, there lies a commonality that makes the worship of this American subculture unique."[36]

More than the back-and-forth tension between isolating cultural styles and admitting the "diversity" within them, this book and others neglect many ethno-racial groups, especially Asian Americans. In my own research for this book, about one-third of the congregations I studied had a significant presence of Asian Americans, yet I was struck at how the Christian literature available never characterizes worship music for Asians. I did, however, seek opinions on "Asian worship" from church leaders.[37] Some interviews accentuated a musical uncertainty regarding Asians. After asking Jack, Asian, about his descriptions of the different musical styles that resonate with different groups, he neglected to mention Asians. So, I asked him:

GERARDO: OK, what's the Asian style? Do you have an answer?

JACK: I wouldn't have an answer to that. I wouldn't have an answer. And actually, that's a great question. That's interesting. But no, I wouldn't have an answer, honestly. Other than what you hear on like, I don't know, on Kung Fu movies or whatever [laughs].

Others expressed intriguing opinions about Asians enjoying white American styles. Kristina, an Asian American in a pan-Asian church, said, "I kind of think there is an Asian American worship style... Okay. You know, when you go to a church that has contemporary music that is predominantly white, they will get a lot of these electric guitar players but are more influenced by like Rock 'n' Roll? It's more like—It is kind of like modern—It's like Passion.[38] Do you know, like that kind of music? Or it could be more mellow and subdued." Kirstina also said, "It's hard to say what it is. Some people disagree with me."

Tim, a white worship leader who interacts with Asians in his ministry said, "My experience is that they love American culture and that they're really interested in American culture. From what I've seen, that's what my experience has been. They are very drawn to American music like Rock 'n' Roll and jazz." But Tim was not confident in his opinions. When I pressed him later about Asians and music, he said, "I don't know about the Oriental. It would be interesting to see the results of your study on the Oriental." He looked off to the side and thought a moment before turning back to me again and said, "From my experience doing missionary tours in Tokyo and Okinawa, Taiwan, and Hong Kong, they seem enamored with American music in general, in my experience. It's just really interesting to see what they are really interested in. Again, kind of like it's a more supped-up version of pop culture in the U.S., and it's adapted a little bit to their style." While "American music" is adapted to "their style," the Asian "style" was never defined by Tim.

An interview with an Asian worship leader in a dominantly Asian congregation also expressed that Asians and whites have similar musical affinities. Daniel said, "It seems like we don't have our own distinctive style because we're so heavily influenced by the styles that already exist here in the states, mostly the Caucasian styles." An Asian member of a worship team with majority Asian attenders said, "I guess the best way is to describe it in a secular sense would be like Top 40 Pop kind of stuff." In yet another church, a white worship leader suggested that "the Asians listen to pop music on the radio."

What accounts for the musical affinity between Asians and whites? Allen, an Asian American, expressed it as an indication of power dynamics between racial groups in American society. He speculated that Asian musical preferences actively accommodate to white-dominant culture in an attempt to avoid stigma and seek prestige within the majority culture:

ALLEN: Let's just be real here. You move to America, you're not going to try to be like African Americans. You're going to try to be like the white man, so they connect to his culture, the type of music. . . .

GERARDO: Because why?

ALLEN: Because their parents come here, and they want to have a future for their kids. They're like "Hey, I want you to learn the English language, and I want you to go to these schools." You look at the school system, college, these people are engulfed in the white culture. You see when an Asian woman brings home a white man, that is more acceptable than her bringing home a black man. It's more accepted, so therefore they connect more to that kind of music than they would to African American music.

I found that many members of multiracial churches believe that Asians and whites have a similar affinity to music because Asians have chosen specifically to acculturate toward white-dominant culture. The acculturation toward white cultural tastes is assumed to help them to be successful in American society as a whole. They believe Asians have not moved toward black styles of music because they understand that there's a power dynamic behind their musical preference. When I restated Allen's beliefs in these terms, I asked him if that is what he believed. "Yeah," he said. "And you're convinced of that?" Allen immediately said, "Totally convinced."[39]

Reciprocity and Countering Western Hegemony through "Global Song"

Maynard-Reid in his book admits to the difficulty of combining multiple styles in single services, but he and other writers never provide directions on how to do it. Despite the stated difficulty of blending, people remain optimistic in insisting that worship is the "primary activity" of multiethnic churches. Robb Redman asserts, "Worship creates community and outreach, not the other way around; it is the core ministry of the church out of which all others flow." For Redman, musical style is not universal, but the experience of worship is. And corporate worship—however it is achieved—is the means by which unity is achieved. "Without a compelling awareness in worship of the presence of the God who draws all nations to himself, there is not enough motivation in a religious philosophy of multiculturalism to form a lasting and meaningful multiethnic Christian community."[40] The assumption is that at some point in time during the sacred assembly the shared worship between diverse groups will elicit enough appreciation among each other that certain songs come to bring them together. A particular unity is born out of exposure to other cultures and the caring community of interaction within a multiracial framework.

The intense belief in shared unity out of exposure to different cultural music styles is particularly expressed in liturgical writings on "global song." S. T. Kimbrough confidently affirmed that "there is one way for Christians to be in community and to emulate unity and oneness to the world—share and celebrate in one another's song!" According to Kimbrough, "Global song offers much enrichment for the contemporary and future liturgies of the church and provides a vital linkage among peoples of diverse ethnic, cultural, linguistic, and denominational backgrounds."[41] The intent of bringing global music to the local congregation is clear: to promote unity of the worldwide church. And the effort has gained support from a wide range of denominations. Sigvald Tveit argues that "influential countries have dominated and controlled others in ways that have to be characterized as suppression and cultural imperialism." Tviet asserts that the use of folk music can help to challenge the oppressive and hierarchical arrangement of aesthetics among national cultures, saying, "These influences are that they take on the color of the local culture to create a synthesis of the foreign and the known, the global and the local."[42]

Also advocating the use of global song, Andrew Donaldson writes, "God is doing something new among us. Congregations who normally speak one language are learning to sing with the sounds, rhythms, and body movements of another culture. They are experiencing other views of the world and of God through other people's song." Donaldson, a Presbyterian music director and hymn writer, states that a core reason for the emphasis on global singing is the principle of reciprocity: "[O]ur sisters and brothers in Mozambique (and many other countries besides) have been singing from our hymn books for generations... It's time we sang from theirs." It emphasizes unity. "Singing songs from the world over is one way that we recognize the Body of Christ is one with many parts." Another principle is one of hospitality: "Singing their songs as well as our own is a constant reminder to welcome others. It is a way of practicing hospitality." Yet another reason is the belief that music conveys similar spiritual experiences. "As we sing another person's song, we share another's experience of God." The most important aspect of this experience for the Anglo world is learning vulnerability and loss of privilege. "As we learn another person's sounds, we place ourselves at a disadvantage; we're playing by their rules. We are also accepting the possibility of standing with them, seeing God through their eyes, experiencing justice or injustice as they—and not we—define and experience it.... In short, we become like children." Through worship, the experience of global song brings unity. "In the process, we break down the dividing wall of 'they' and 'we,' (or, at the very least, confess that it exists) so that we can work together in the realm of God."[43]

The typical advice for bringing "global music" into a congregation is to obtain translations and paraphrases of lyrics, introduce less difficult songs, and incorporate indigenous-language-speaking people as much as possible. "While we hope that original languages will be sung by many peoples, we are aware that something becomes a part of hymnic repertory because it touches the hearts and minds of people in a special way."[44] A romanticized notion of singing together is often attached to the tone of writings among those who have a profound passion for hymns. Overall, mainline churches tend to accentuate global diversity in the universal church wherever it is found while evangelical and charismatic churches tend to accentuate local diversity in areas more immediately surrounding their local churches.

While encouraging global music, Kimbrough also articulates its limitations: Not all forms of music are available and accessible; languages have sounds (tones and syllabifications) uniquely their own which cannot be readily reproduced by congregational singers (Romanized transliteration in English hymnals is problematic); rhythms can be extremely complex, making them difficult to transcribe and reproduce; arrangements and harmonizations are problematic; and the emphasis on playing-singing the music can obscure the importance of the "faith journey" content represented in the piece as a whole. Kimbrough insists that since music is vital in almost every culture, the importance of music alone makes it a "global song. And it is in this sense that it is a universal language. Hence, when [specific forms of music are] shared from culture to culture, it provides a vital inner link between the deepest, innermost reaches of human identity."[45]

Overall, the writers on global song manifest a high level of musical training and sophistication. One of the most prominent advocates for global song is seminary professor C. Michael Hawn, who sternly criticizes introducing music from other cultures as a type of "ethnotourism."[46] Instead, the careful selection of music from other nations collapses into what he often labels "global music," which would promote understanding between cultures while simultaneously forging a further development of ecumenicism among (mostly) mainline denominations. Hawn is concerned that our standard musical practices are exclusionary and that musical resources developed in other parts of the world become cultivated into our own contexts, "reaching beyond our provincial experience to others different than ourselves..." For example, Hawn acknowledges within Latin America that there are various Spanish-language traditions at the same time that he reveals a deep contextuality to the music of Latin hymn writer Pablo Sosa. In the end, Hawn writes, "Cross-cultural liturgical experiences are one way of appreciating the distinctiveness and beauty of an inherited tradition, and to see those areas of exclusion that are also by nature part of the baggage of any provincial view."[47]

The advocacy of global song in the work of C. Michael Hawn reveals an interesting twist to the One Size Fits All Theory. Although Hawn does not attempt to impose a single universal form of music on churches, Hawn persuasively argues for the use of "polyrhythmic" music in a "pluriform" liturgy. He draws on the work of Paul Bradshaw to argue that the worship of the early Christian church incorporated various practices that produced a "pluriformity."[48] Liturgical plurality would acknowledge and even encourage the diversity not only of music but also of rites and rituals as a public manifestation of the global unity of Christian churches.

In practice, the argument for global music by Hawn and others encourages a conscious attempt to minimize westernized Christian music, especially those influenced by market-driven, "pop music" styles. Hawn boldly states that popular music in North America "may undermine or contradict the gospel" and place churches "in danger of cultural captivity."[49] His argument is similar to the claim frequently made that "world music" breaks down ethno-racial barriers.[50] Assessments like this create a harsh environment for contemporary worship music in North America in favor of the popular music of other peoples; indeed, the "popular music" of Africa, Asia, and Latin America is to be preferred over the "popular music" of North America. Churches in the United States should eagerly embrace the popular culture of foreign nations but carefully and consistently resist their own.

Rejecting Racial Essentialism in Music

Congregations that care about diversity and worship would do well to remember that racism was inherent to early musicology. Racist biology in the early twentieth century attempted to relate basic intervallic structure in music, and the scales that formed around it were matched with measurements of skull shape in an attempt to catalog global patterns based on racial groups.[51] More modern ideas regarding connections between social groups and musical characteristics emerged in the 1970s with debates on the racial origins of music focused on African Americans. These debates led to assertions about music based on discourses on race, power, and identity.[52] Many ethnomusicologists still search for "the authentic" by mixing anthropology and musicology.[53] Scholars like Arjun Appadurai stimulated studies connecting identity, ethnicity, community, and music, and several publishing efforts like *The Garland Encyclopedia of World Music* manifest the tendency to connect music with race and ethnicity using specific social and cultural contexts, issues of musical identity (class, race, and gender), and geography to frame its musical stories and emphasize the interactive nature of musical cultures with the variety of ways music is experienced in a pluralistic society.[54]

Yet, Kay Kaufman Shelemay warns that the geographic approach used by ethnomusicologists both distances and exoticizes musical practices.[55] While Anne K. Rasmussen lists regions of music in her own work (Latin musics, the musics of Northern, Southern, Eastern, and Scandinavian European communities, Asian [East, South, and Southeast] musics, and the Eastern and European and Middle Eastern/Mediterraneian musical presence in the United States), she is quick to say,

> Any serious investigation of these large, geographically defined groups, however, reveals myriad and complex distinctions. For example, we can ascribe genres like mariachi and conjunto to people of Mexican heritage.... The music of Puerto Rican and Cubans in the United States—from Machito, to Tito Puente, to Gloria Estefan—is an entirely different Latin scene involving various spaces, races, histories, and politics, each with its own set of musical biographies, repertoires, and contexts for performance. When taken into consideration, the details and complexities of the Latin musical landscape in America render our mainstreaming mission an act of dilution and, perhaps, delusion. Mainstreaming the musical tributaries of Mexicans, Central Americans, Cubans, and Puerto Ricans (and this list does not even touch upon South America and the Caribbean) into the larger river of American Latin musics becomes an act of generalization that would be inexcusable in the discipline of musicology.[56]

Her discomfort with this type of musical cataloging is palpable.

Rasmussen is entirely correct in saying, "If the first danger of mainstreaming is simplification, a second is that it tempts homogenization." She reflects on a study by Timothy Taylor on the commercial use of world music to sell cultural elites expensive commodities like Audi, Chrysler, and Delta. "For me, Taylor's article is a real wake-up call. The moneyed elite is moved to consume (plane tickets, cars, whatever) by music that transports them to an 'exoticised elsewhere,' a place far-away, spiritual, primitive, mystic. Their first-world, English-only elitist perspective is indulged. They are not challenged to investigate the spaces where these musics are made. They are not troubled with the notion that such spaces exist, not in an exotic elsewhere but within our own great nation. They are encouraged to listen and to consume without ever being asked to 'understand what they hear.'"[57]

To put the noblest motivations on the trend to incorporate music targeted to specific ethnic-racial groups in American churches, many congregational advocates for distinct musical styles are also committed to the protection of indigenous and exploited peoples. At times the Musical Buffet theorists argue for the obligation to protect and continue distinct cultural identities through worship music. Cultural identities are to remain distinct with differences highlighted rather than absorbed into a single, overarching style.[58] For example, Robb Redman is not alone in stating, "Some African American and Hispanic leaders would affirm the goal of an inclusive worshiping fellowship but also warn against loss of cultural identity in attempting to blend their liturgical and musical styles in a melting-pot approach to worship."[59]

While we can commend the sensitivity to cultural differences that Musical Buffett "theorists" of worship bring to the discussion, the difficulty of the Buffet Theory is that there simply is no monolithic musical tradition within any racial or ethnic group. Manuel Vásquez rightly criticizes essentialism found even in the scholarly literature which views racial-ethnic groups, like Hispanic and Anglo cultures, "as static wholes opposed in an ahistorical, quasi-manichean fashion."[60] Even C. Michael Hawn insightfully writes, "When approaching liturgical plurality from an understanding of musical meaning, one soon realizes that there is no universally meaningful musical experience."[61] Profound differences in musical experience are especially notable in the contemporary Black Church, an entity many people unknowingly assume to be monolithic.[62] James Abbington, professor of music and worship at Candler School of Theology at Emory University and an expert on African American worship, insightfully uses the term "multicultural" to refer to the differences of musical tastes and styles *within* the Black Church. The conflict between "hip-hop" for younger blacks and "anthems" for older blacks is one interesting generational dynamic similar to the conflict between "Rock 'n' Roll" for younger whites and "classic hymns" for older whites. It is vital that we come to understand that not all members of a particular race/ethnic group share the same musical tastes or heritage.

Incorporating the Musical "Other" in Congregational Practice

The argument for incorporating "global music" and "global song" is a bold effort to de-center what is perceived to be Anglo-dominated musical forms to embrace the music of non-Western, non-white peoples. It is also an attempt to push against the encroachment of contemporary Christian music that reduces musical harmonies and imposes pop-culture elements into the liturgy of the service. Yet, because the incorporation of Christian music in other languages from other countries is usually beyond the skills and resources of most local congregations, most churches opt for another musical strategy.

Rather than embrace the complexity and nuance of global song as advocated by Hawn, Kimbrough, and others, my observations indicate that American churches polarize and essentialize music to represent a few stereotypical notions. The next chapter will show how the American church has adopted black gospel music as the ideal music for diversification. It is perceived to be non-Western in origin, and it is most certainly non-white in its historic orientation. Of all the styles, black musical styles, especially gospel music, are the most prevalent in discussion and the most pervasive in practice.

After describing the notion of African Americans singing gospel, this book moves away from attempting to create categories from a handful of different races/ethnicities and, instead, reveals concrete dynamics within churches that govern the connection between worship music and the ethnic and racial diversity found in multiracial churches. Rather than attempting to enact supposed differences in order to overcome them, attention to interactional and organizational dynamics provide a more nuanced and more accurate appreciation for the accomplishment of racial integration.

3

African Americans as the Icon of "True Worship"

I just wish I could be black.

—WHITE WORSHIP PASTOR OF A MULTIRACIAL CHURCH

OF ALL MY interviews, one especially stands out. At an outdoor café on Los Angeles's Westside, a Caucasian worship leader and I met to talk about his congregation. We drank coffee as he talked about his desire for racial diversity in his church and the type of music he worked into each Sunday service. Then, in the middle of our conversation, he suddenly blurted out, "I just wish I could be black!"

I was struck. Although it was not the first time I had heard a white person express admiration for black music performers and styles, this blunt yet seemingly natural statement stuck out as one of the most significant I had heard in all of my interviews. This leader's abrupt remark crystallized observations that had been building on racialized perceptions of worship over the previous months. Although I heard many different comments about different racial and ethnic groups throughout my research, statements about African Americans were by far the most common and consistent. Over and over again, nonblacks especially expressed a profound belief in the ability of African Americans to attain a deep, emotional, and, for many, inspiring worship through sacred music. African Americans themselves also agreed that they had a racially specific connection to worship. It was this one interview in sunny Southern California that led me to uncovering a profoundly shared belief about African Americans, a belief that emerged as a striking similarity across all people and all churches.

African Americans as Superior, "Soulful" Worshipers

The experience of "true worship" is consistently viewed as one of the distinctive markers of the Black Church experience. Moreover, people of all backgrounds believe gospel music is really for blacks because gospel allows blacks to experience a more full worship experience. As one worship pastor told me, "It makes for a lot more deep response." Even in a church that did not have African American attenders, one musician said that to attract blacks, "it would make sense if we did a gospel kind of thing once in a while." However, gospel music in multiracial churches rarely carries the qualities that fully characterize traditional gospel music, nor does it contain the same weight of "ideology" that Mellonee Burnim identifies in gospel music performed within the African American church.[1] In other words, the mere incorporation of gospel music does not create a "Black Church" experience. Jackie, a black female choir member in her early 50s, said, "I've never really seen our church as having the black church music experience, I've never felt that. We sing black church music, but it's not the gospel experience."

The image of blacks in worship found among members of multiracial churches is universally associated with a spiritualized ideal. The overarching belief of the best kind of worship orients around a universally held idealized image of blacks singing gospel. For example, a white female church member said, "I love black gospel music—like when Whoopi Goldberg did it in the movie *Sister Act*." Another white female church member in another congregation said, "They all [meaning blacks] really know how to sing." Blacks singing gospel are iconic because of the belief that music is inherent to the religious life of African Americans. Anthony Pinn writes, "Regardless of where one goes, the particular denomination does not matter, music is a central component of black worship."[2] Pedrito Maynard-Reid writes on African American worship, "It is impossible to 'have church' without good music. In the African American community, music is to worship as breathing is to life."[3] One woman said, "When I think 'gospel,' I think of the 'old gospel.' I think of how strong they must have been in their worship, and it just comes across—it's very deep." Blacks sing gospel, "real hard-core gospel" as one black member described it. At times, conversations about the experience of personal worship would take people back to an experience in a black church like when a white female worship leader said, "I've always enjoyed occasions to visit a black church. I mean, who worships better than that?"

The clear assumption in these and many other conversations is a shared orientation regarding the power and superiority of "black worship." Gospel music is perceived to be an independent stream of music that most preserves, captures, and characterizes the black experience. And playing gospel music (or "negro spirituals") in church is seen as an affirmation of the dignity and value of black Christians. In addition, the presence of gospel music in a multiracial congregation constitutes much more than an attempt to appeal to African Americans as potential attenders. African Americans are uniquely suited in the singing of gospel to achieve the pinnacle of sacred adoration. African Americans are universally believed to experience authentic worship more profoundly than any other racial-ethnic group. And while it may seem such notions of race exist only within the minds of "white people," my research finds the assumption is equally shared among African Americans as well. A black male church member told me, "If you want to see the most energetic types of worship you may want to go see black people worship at an all black church... That is the best type of worship." The ideal of multiracial worship is an African American singing gospel music.

African Americans occupy a unique place in the moral economy of multiracial congregations. Like the canary in the coal mine, the assumption across America is that if there are few African Americans in a congregation, then the congregation's culture is racially "toxic" against blacks. If congregational leaders are going to be serious at addressing the racial issues, they will seek ways to alter their culture in a way that welcomes and accommodates more African Americans into their midst. George Yancey notes the unique challenge of incorporating blacks into mixed congregations, citing residential segregation, less interracial marriages, and the difficulty of gaining acceptance in mainstream society. He reports that the most common racial configuration of multiracial churches combines whites with either Hispanics or Asians. He states, "African Americans are more difficult to attract into multiracial congregations than other racial groups."[4] For Yancey and others who advocate diversification, the priority is integrating African Americans into non-black congregations.

Gospel music is generally understood to be the music required to successfully bring African Americans into a congregation. The introduction of gospel music into a congregation is a form of instrumentalism as the music is intended to achieve a particular effect. Even though there is widespread appreciation for gospel music, gospel is believed to be most enjoyed by blacks. "Gospel is a very African American thing," one Asian musician said. A white choir member said, "The African American spirituals we sing intentionally acknowledge the African American members of the church." A black female church member said, "I'd say black people do mostly enjoy gospel music." Another black female and member of her choir referred to the more diverse of two Sunday morning services and said, "That service is for the African Americans predominantly, and the music is different. More gospel."

A black male church attender said, "Black music has a force all its own." On a superficial level, everyone seems to believe African Americans worship "differently." An Asian male church member said, "African Americans, they do worship a little differently. They'll go off on a tangent and they'll drag the song a little bit longer. They'll 'Praise the Lord' or 'Amen.'" A black musician said, "Black people are doing the same contemporary music that white churches are doing; they're just doing it differently... with a black beat. They change it up a little bit." He quickly added, "I shouldn't say 'black beat,' but something that is a little more rhythmic, and black churches tend to be more rhythmically complex—that sounds so racist!" An Asian female church member said, "Black culture is a different music. If you ask black people, the contemporary music here has nothing to do with black music. It's extremely different." And a black female church member simply said, "African American worship is totally different."

Such vague descriptions were frequent, and eventually I began to ask respondents to clarify the perceived character of "black worship." A white male church member said, "They are not afraid to show their praise or afraid to say 'Amen' or 'Praise God' or a 'Yes, Lord' or raise their hands or say 'Alleluia,' it just comes naturally." A white female church member told me, "Black people are very spiritual. They are more spiritual than we are...." Another white female choir member said, "They [blacks] seem closer to God." Similar comments were surprisingly frequent. When I prompted another church member, a Middle Eastern female, to further characterize African American worship, she paused before confidently saying, "More of a *soul* kind of feeling or a *black* feeling to it. That's it." Many used the word "soul" as a key descriptor. A white worship leader told how he much he admired black worship and quickly added how he "just loves the soulfulness of it." Indeed, I found it consistent that "soul" always equals "black."

C. Eric Lincoln writes, "Soul is an ethnic concept, a product and a creator of black culture. It is the art, the music, the religion, and the style of black people." He notes, "Whatever else it is, soul is the essence of the black experience—the distillate of that whole body of events and occurrences, primary and derivative, which went into the shaping of reality as black people live it and understand it. It is the connective thread that runs through the totality of the black experience, weaving it together, making it intelligible, and giving it meaning." Soul is inherent to the black experience because of the existential conditions of their lives. Again Lincoln writes, "Soul is a kind of cultural élan vital developed through the experience of living and performing constantly on the margins of human society, under conditions of physical and psychological stress beyond the boundaries of ordinary human endurance. It is a quality and an art developed in the matrix of the African-American experience."[5] Musicians and attenders, regardless of racial or ethnic background, all affirm Lincoln's assertions. Blacks have unique access to God through their "soulfulness" in singing gospel, and this makes worship for blacks a unique arena of envy and privilege in the United States.

African Americans by virtue of skin color—even before people hear them sing—become imbued with authority on worship and connection to God in multiracial churches. Indeed, I found that the fewer the African Americans in a multiracial church, the more they are emphasized by members, as each African American attending becomes imbued with authority on music and worship. One twenty-year-old white member in a church with a small percentage of blacks remarked on African Americans who had visited his church, saying, "They were a black couple, they have a lot of rhythm and stuff, and they were going to town. Everybody got into it because they watched them." In another church, a black woman attender told me how she was aware of others watching her as she worshiped. The attention prompted this woman to believe she was a model to others in helping them learn how to worship. These "stand-out" African Americans are not only watched but also consistently recruited by church leaders to sing in the church choir, serve on worship committees, and play even simple instruments like tambourines regardless, even in spite of, a lack of musical experience or training.

"Black People Suffer a Lot": The "Gift" of Gospel

Connecting African Americans' "gift" for singing "gospel music" to their "suffering" is what unlocked for me the underlying logic of why African Americans are thought to have a deep connection to God through worship. Blacks do not need to have proven experience, credentials, or training because "God has gifted them" musically. African Americans are superior worshipers with a "natural" or "soulful" connection to excellent worship. One male church member said, "This may be prejudice on my own part, but I believe that black folks are very gifted musically and that God has given them gifts like no one else has—their expression of worship through the Spirit and what God has given them...." The "gifting" of music for African Americans makes musical training unnecessary.

A white male church member said, "They have a beauty and a freedom about their worship.... They've got rhythm, and I call it a gift because it seems to be poured out liberally on them. It's not that others can't and don't have it, but by and large it's poured out liberally on them." He went on to say, "If we can figure out what it is that God has given those black folks and we could recreate it, we could make millions. But honestly there is just a gift that... comes out of pain, the roots of the gospel music, the pain and suffering brings forth a depth of character." A white male church member said, "I think its part of our character or the building of character to suffer. And black people suffer a lot."

While I was initially struck that white church members connected African American's musical gifting with suffering, it became clear that blacks also held the same belief. Both blacks and whites (and Asians and Latinos as well) connect the music of African Americans with their suffering through slavery. A black female worship leader said, "Slavery is where a lot of our songs come from, I'm sure you know."[6] A white male church member said, "Their music tells their life history from slavery to now and the freedom they got being able to express themselves through music, so it's part of them, they lived it, the hardship."

Comments on the "living" of the hardship of slavery are interesting because both blacks and whites relate the suffering of blacks to the superior quality of their worship—even though no one they have heard sing has ever actually been a slave. Instead, they assert a historic continuity between blacks today and their ancestors. In one church, a white male choir member said, "When the Jordans sang a Negro spiritual, those songs, *they sang it exactly like you would imagine the slaves were singing it....*" Here and elsewhere, members idealize the sound of slaves singing. For example, in a different church, another white male choir member said, "The Franklins could sing gospel, black gospel, soul. Whatever the African slaves sang, that's what they would sing." Moreover, the belief in "whatever the African slaves sang," this idealized image of what true black worship is, impinges on notions of racial authenticity in singing gospel music.

Black music is consistently associated with the harshness of the world. Specifically, the force of African American musical expression is believed to come from their personal and collective experience of suffering and racial oppression. Sociologist and activist W. E. B. DuBois believed that music gave him the unique entry point to understanding the African American experience, writing, "I have stepped within the Veil, raising it that you may view faintly its deeper recesses—the meaning of its religion, the passion of its human sorrow, and the struggle of its greater souls."[7] Joseph B. Bethea writes, "Worship in the African-American community is unique because it was conceived within a peculiar experience. It is an experience with roots in the African continent with its primal worldview, but also an experience growing out of 'a long and bitter night of slavery, segregation, discrimination, oppression, deprivation, exclusion, alienation, and rejection in this country.'"[8] Samuel Floyd writes, "The power of black music is based on the assumption that African musical traits and cultural practices not only survived but played a major role in the development and elaboration of African American music." The music is "expressive of cultural memory," and black-music making becomes "the translation of the memory into sound and the sound into memory."[9] Gospel music, then, exists within a broader set of beliefs that define African Americans as a people.

Accounting for the Iconic Status of Black Worship

The iconic status of black worship is intimately connected with the development of gospel music as an expression of "black culture." Black gospel music has a unique and powerful history.[10] Although strictly speaking, gospel music emerged half a century after Emancipation and the end of the Civil War, gospel music is always considered a collective response to blacks' oppressed status and experience. The medium aesthetically expresses the trials and yearnings of a distinctive group bearing under similar social constraints. Joyce Marie Jackson writes, "There is no doubt that African American gospel music will continue to exist as a changing expression of cultural identity. It remains one of the most genuine forms of the communities' expression of values and aesthetics, and has remained the least encumbered by Euro-American influence."[11]

Jackson astutely advises researchers to pay close attention to "cultural, societal, and historical processes that influenced the development of gospel music rather than to consider musical structures alone."[12] It is more than the sound of gospel music, but the social context of real people that is needed to understand music. Gospel is a symbol of black life that summarizes history and aesthetics in a single whole. In his lyrical book *The Souls of Black Folk,* W. E. B. DuBois describes what he considered the utter beauty of African American musical worship, "that plaintive rhythmic melody, with its touching minor cadences," and pronounced this "the most original and beautiful expression of human life and longing yet born on American soil." DuBois reinforced the notion that only blacks could sing gospel; other churches may have attempted to mimic this music but simply could not. Instead, he considered "the mass of 'gospel' hymns which has swept through American churches" to be "debased imitations of Negro melodies made by ears that caught the jingle but not the music, the body but not the soul, of the Jubilee songs."[13] African American religious music was uniquely, and solely, the province of African Americans.

Well before the development of gospel music, blacks and whites were considered to have religiously distinct natures. The racially essentialist separation between black and white religious orientations is rooted in nineteenth-century race theory, which emphasized that all sorts of traits and temperaments are inherited biologically along racial lines.[14] Scholars and church leaders of the mid-nineteenth and early twentieth centuries made a clear distinction and separation between the "religion" of blacks and whites, supported by strenuous arguments and vigorous "research" efforts. In 1853, Arthur de Gonineau published his thousand-page tome[15] and argued that black and white races have different, although complementary, traits, which are best actualized in the vibrant mixture of urban metropolitan centers. While Gonineau unquestionably sees whites as superior, they are "insufficient in and off themselves and need the contributions of other races for the development of civilization."[16] He argues that "Africans contribute positively to the mixture of races in prosperous metropolitan centers by offering Dionysian gifts such as passion, dance, music, rhythm, lightheartedness, and sensuality. Whites, for their part, contribute energy, action, perseverance, rationality, and technical aptitude: the Apollonian gifts."[17] Blacks were characterized by their emotionalism while whites were known for their intellectualism. In 1903, Kelly Miller, dean of Howard University, stated that blacks possessed a "deeply religious nature" and with "emotional and spiritual susceptibilities."[18] For Miller, blacks and whites each possessed virtues that the others lacked. From whites, blacks might gain a higher standard of "concrete morality" enabling them to have more "rational modes" of worship and "orderly habits of life."[19] From blacks, whites could learn meekness, humility, and forgiveness.

The naïve opposition between black and white religion had dangerous implications. Howard Odum was among many who were deeply critical of black religion. For Odum and others, religion for blacks was primarily "pleasurable excitement" and failed to properly restrain the primitive emotionalism among blacks.[20] By 1910, Odum claimed that the "function of the negro church is to give expression and satisfaction to religious emotions," not "to direct moral conduct."[21] As Odum described it, "Black religion lacks practical application or moral content" and possessed a "scarcity of thoughtfulness and will-power."[22] Their religion did not elevate their moral standing but rather debased it.

By the 1920s, black emotionalism and spontaneity were seen as authentic expressions of primal human urges and a necessary corrective to white urban culture. The notion of a "racial complementarity" advocated that the emotionality of black religion was an asset for the enrichment of American culture. For example, in a 1925 essay, Albert Barnes transformed belief in blacks' fundamental emotionalism from a threat to civilization to its antidote by virtue of the black race's large emotional endowment, sensitivity to nature, excellent oratory, sublime music, child-like spontaneity, infinite patience, fine humor, and what Barnes labeled a "peculiar depth of religious life."[23] For Barnes and others, worship manifests the "essence of the Negro soul."[24] Through their lyricism and poetry, black music allows for a deep religious expression of the inner Negro being. Scholars and church leaders soon became so impressed with the quality of African American worship that they believed whites could not "compete with the Negro in spiritual endowment."[25] In the next decade, the understanding of black worship was accepted as a positive religious force and superior to whites' worship. Theologian Dietrich Bonheoffer while a student at Union Seminary attended a black congregation in Harlem and wrote a letter home in 1930 contrasting his experiences with white congregations, saying, "I'm increasingly discovering greater religious power and originality in Negroes."[26]

Overall, there came a historical shift between the Emancipation and the Depression from perceiving African Americans as an "uncivilized" people who could not fit into mainstream American society to becoming a highly regarded people for the quality of their worship.[27] The introduction of world music in the classroom in the early 1900s included African American music, which contributed to the acceptance of gospel music as a valid cultural form of music.[28] High society could no longer argue that blacks were not capable of sophisticated creativity and skill. John Davis is among the musicologists who acknowledge the cultural prominence and uniqueness of gospel music by claiming, "Of course, the American Negro's great contributions to the world of music have been his spirituals and his gospel songs, the former truly without parallel in the field of religious music and poetry."[29] Soon, the emotionality of black religion would be channeled into conceptions of gospel music. By the mid-twentieth century, gospel would become known as the African American style of worship and portrayed as the epitome of "true" spiritual worship.

Black Gospel Music for White Audiences

Gospel music's great popularity among whites led to its being considered quintessentially "black Christian music" even when gospel was controversial among many segments of the Black Church.[30] Gospel music incorporated the sound and rhythms of secular blues and "boogie woogie" and thereby scandalized many members of the Black Church.[31] Conservative African American Christians saw gospel singers as more "worldly" than spiritual. New black Christian songwriters, especially Thomas Andrew Dorsey, blended jazz, blues, and ragtime with explicitly Christian messages. Dorsey is credited with catalyzing the union of blues and spirituals to create the most popular and characteristic gospel music of the early twentieth century, calling it "good news in bad times."[32] Gospel music developed as a sanctified form of the blues, which was considered earthly and of the devil. Gospel as developed by Dorsey greatly appealed to non-blacks, largely due to the popularity of Dorsey, who is often recognized as the "father of gospel music."[33]

Although conservative black churches initially objected to this new music, its outstanding popularity led to its being accepted as a legitimate vehicle for worship. With the advent of gospel music in the 1930s came a proliferation of choirs that integrated themselves within the Black Church.[34] Hettie Jones writes, "By the forties gospel music had become an institution in black communities... Gospel music was a national affair, but a national Negro affair."[35] During the Harlem Renaissance, whites patronized African Americans and the market for music and performances soared. Gospel music became accepted and admired by non-blacks in a secular setting in the form of popular music through radio and concert performances. For example, despite prevalent racist structures in the South, the Fisk Jubilee Singers is one of the more prominent black groups that performed for white audiences for profit.[36] It was not until later that this deeply religious music was associated with the African American church as a form of worship. So while gospel music originated in its modern form in the early twentieth century, it did not achieve widespread recognition in African American churches until around 1940.

In the 1950s, gospel music gained greater popularity when both Mahalia Jackson ("Move on up a Little Higher") and the Ward Singers ("Surely, God Is Able") sold a monumental one million records, joining the ranks of mainstream American music artists.[37] On a more modest scale, gospel musicians began traveling and performing concerts, often charging admission fees and successfully transforming gospel into a commercial venture. Concerts and recordings helped gospel music reach a wider, multiracial audience. In the late 1960s, the hit "Oh Happy Day" recorded by Edwin Hawkin's Singers in 1969 was included on "Top 40" lists, which further broadened the diversity of listeners to an even larger multiracial audience. As gospel music developed, writers and musical commentators continued to assert the distinctiveness of black musicality. The Frenchman Olivier Despax characterized African Americans, saying, "Negro musicians have a unique character: a spirit of their own, one which the whites lack, a kind of ferocity of rhythm, a violence which they call 'swing.' They also have a great deal of sensitivity, but a brutal sensitivity, absolutely not the sensitivity of whites."[38]

The 1960s and 1970s brought new forms of gospel that incorporated electronic instruments, including synthesizers, bass guitars, and drums. Andre Crouch of the Church of God in Christ was a prominent innovator merging gospel with the "funk" sound of George Clinton. Eventually, Kirk Franklin incorporated current secular musical trends and worked a gospel message using contemporary idioms and slang. Franklin and his musical entourage also played to the audience and wore fashionable clothing. Further, Franklin collaborated with secular rap stars like L.L. Cool J and R. Kelly. "Their sound and embrace of popular culture appeal to young people and have resulted in a forced rethinking of what a Christian and 'looks like' and what the proper ways to worship are."[39]

As gospel was performed for secular audiences, it included "metaphors and musical embellishments" that would not be suitable for a church service. Nevertheless, with immense popularity and acceptance by whites generally and younger blacks specifically, gospel music entered back into the institution of the Black Church. Pinn writes that gospel music was developed first in the Baptist Church and refined in the Pentecostal Church with a mix of R&B influence before finally becoming "the defining expression of musical devotion to God. . . ."[40] Thus, "with the passage of time gospel music received near universal acceptance in most quarters of the Black Church."[41] According to Franklin Frazier, "Some of the so-called advanced Negro churches resented these gospel singers and refused permit them to sing within their churches. They've gradually become more tolerant let down the bars as the gospel singers acquired status acceptance within the white world."[42]

Gospel music took root equally among whites and blacks. Secular music industry leaders began recording popular music for its financial potential among whites, and pastoral leaders used gospel "as a tool for evangelizing communities" among blacks. Pinn writes, "Many churches in fact experienced growth based on the popularity of their choirs. Hence, excellent choir directors were in as much demand as charismatic preachers, and most churches now make it their business to nurture at least one choir with an understanding that there is a direct relationship between good music and full pews."[43] Gospel choirs were evangelistic and church-growth tools. Gospel music was "baptized" and accepted as truly sacred.[44] C. Eric Lincoln and Lawrence H. Mamiya found that almost all black churches (97%) approved the use of some form of gospel music, and also incorporated an average of about three choirs per church. It is become a stable, anticipated, and expected component of Black Church services.[45]

Black Authenticity Established by Singing "Like Black Folks"

A consistent theme that emerges from both the history of gospel music and the interviews from my own research is a sustained belief in authentic black worship. The distinction of music "for" blacks consistently creates a distinction between black musical performers and white listeners. A black female choir member said, "For the white folks, they are very structured, for the black folks, the African Americans, I'm sure they have a good time when we clap and sing. We don't need a lot, but there are times that we do it. The whites of course just sit and enjoy what is going on." Whites are quieter and more often seen as audiences, while blacks are exuberant and more often seen as performers. Distinctions like these foster beliefs in other essential differences between whites and blacks.

Most importantly, because blacks are the only group to have experienced slavery in the United States, they are believed to have a deep connection to suffering and therefore a deeper connection to the mercy and grace of God in comparison with other groups. Mahalia Jackson is quoted as saying the singing and worship through music "has always been a way in which the Negro has often renewed his strength," and again, "through the songs they've expressed years of suppressed hopes, suffering and even joy and love."[46] African Americans become the only people who can authentically actualize a deeply affective, "soulful" worship experience.

So gospel music not only involves who most enjoys gospel but also who can authentically sing gospel. One Latina worship leader told me about long-time church member "Mrs. Montgomery" who sang gospel like they did in "the old black-style churches like in the South." Although "gospel music" is considered to be the "best" music to accomplish diversity, the only racial-ethnic group that can properly sing gospel music is African American. A white male church member said, "You have to accept a man [referring to blacks] and assume part of their worship outdoes ours and it's mainly in the music." One must be "black" to sing "gospel"—this is fundamental even for non-black church musicians who enjoy singing gospel or actively participate in a gospel choir. A white female church attender said, "If you are going to have the gospelish style, if you are not black, you don't feel that you can pull it off." An Asian female member who sings in the "gospel choir" of her church said, "I wouldn't say our gospel choir is fully gospel though. We don't really have the *soul* of a gospel choir." (Note again the use of "soul" as equal to "Black.")

One of the most interesting conversations I had about African Americans and gospel music occurred with Sheryl, a black choir member. We were talking about her experience of worship where she made a careful distinction between "gospel" music and "Vineyard" music, a distinction that came up several times in other interviews as well. The Vineyard Church is a charismatic congregational movement that originated under Pastor John Wimber in Anaheim, California, and emphasized ecstatic worship through contemporary Christian music. The production and distribution of more soft-rock, simple lyric, and affectionate-to-God original music helped redefine popular religious music among evangelical Christians.

Sheryl told me with wide-eyed surprise that she "actually worshiped" when Vineyard music was played in her church:

GERARDO: It's interesting that you say you experience full worship with a Vineyard song when black gospel was so important to you.

SHERYL: Yeah I'm like, wow, I like this song. And in fact, I've even felt guilty about it, like I'm betraying my race...

Sheryl was actively negotiating her racial identity in relation to the music with which she "worshiped." For Sheryl and others, "Vineyard" music is often used as a euphemism for "white" music, so Sheryl indicated that her allowing herself to worship with white music made her feel as if she was betraying her African American heritage.

When I asked Sheryl to clarify her surprise, she explained, "It's very engrained in me since I was a little girl that I identify myself as African American, so I sing like an African American would sing. I don't stand still when I sing, I rock a certain way. So that's who I am. I'm African American, therefore, I worship like an African American..." She begins to describe the interaction between identity and activity, the performative aspect of worship, that makes her form of worship a racial marker. She describes the social expectations that govern the form of worship, saying, "You have to put feeling into your songs, you can't sing flat. If you're a singer, and if you're singing to a white congregation, you sing what they expect to hear."[47]

Sheryl's self-awareness regarding her own performance of worship is instructive. As an African American, worship music becomes a cue for the performance of a form of worship behavior that is guided and governed by other church-going blacks: "If you're at a black church you will sing differently because we expect it to be powerful and strong and with feeling. Drag it out and go up and down. It can't be flat or you aren't giving us what we expect." Her description of "what *they* expect" and then "what *we* expect" makes explicit the expectation of how African Americans worship in particular ways. Sheryl agrees that African Americans are specially gifted and have a special bent for worship and that "what makes it true would be to just look at the historical dynamics of the African American. A lot of the style of worship and there are a lot of things that are connected with the motherland and Africa that have come down traditionally that never will be taken away and that we teach our children."

The performance of black worship becomes an element of socialization among blacks from a young age. Sheryl told me about training children to sing, saying, "Even when we teach our kids songs, I say, 'I'm going to teach you the words,' and then I'll say, 'Now that you know the words, *sing it like black folks*.'" She quickly added, "It may be a stereotype from your perspective, but from our perspective, it's our culture." Eric Porter writes that styles of music associated with African Americans are "commonly seen as a product of emotion or instinct rather than as self-conscious activity."[48] Sheryl provides an up-front acknowledgement that African Americans indeed fall into stereotypical behaviors with respect to worship, yet it is due not to their nature or a simplistic genealogy of culture but to a pervasive expectation of a style of worship inherent to the performance of their identity as African Americans. They personalize the icon of black worship not as a negative racial stigma but as a form of positive racial privilege. When she says, "sing it like black folks," she moves us from seeing worship as inherent to African Americans due to either biology or shared history of suffering but rather occurring as a disciplined form of behavior subject to overarching normative expectations for what authentic worship looks like for all black people.

Occasionally in my interviews, there is a subtle recognition that being able to "do gospel" requires socialization. An African American choir member spoke about a previous black worship leader, saying, "She would play the more black gospel, black spiritual, she could actually play that better than our minister of music now, because she has that history and experience and that flavor." And another African American church member said, "Obviously stereotypically, black people are supposed to have a lot of rhythm and things like that, but I think that's because you grow up going to a place that develops that rhythm. I think it's just training." So while gospel is "learned," it is still believed to be "inherent" to the African American experience.

Authenticity means that singing gospel music "like black people do" becomes an inherent part of black religious identity. It is characterized by what one black member described as "a lot of motion in their worship, swaying, and clapping and shaking your head." It is critical to note that ethnic identity is not based on physiology but cultural belief as ethnic identities consist of internalized meanings that are associated with an ethnic group.[49] Expressive worship is central to black identity. And this expectation appears to be accentuated in racially mixed church settings.

Ethnomusicologist Jacqueline Cogdell DjeDje writes, "It is the advocates of gospel that have maintained an identity that is distinctly black and in many ways is closely akin to traditional African culture."[50] Another black ethnomusicologist studying gospel music, Mellonee Burnim points out her shared ethnic identity and its ready connection to her ability to perform gospel music. "My ethnic identity cannot, however, be separated from my ability to perform in the black gospel tradition." She saw a fusion of her "cultural background" and her "musical talents." Her performance at the church "resulted in my becoming a source of *racial pride*."[51] Burnim argues that gospel music is, "far from being a mere musical genre, but rather it exists as a complex of ideology, aesthetic, and behavior."[52] Similarly, Pearl Williams-Jones is among many who claim gospel music "retains the most noticeable African-derived aesthetic features of all" aspects of black American culture. Gospel music performance and practice provides ongoing opportunity to incarnate "a clearly defined black identity growing out of the black experience," which Williams-Jones states "is indicative of the indomitability of the African ethos."[53]

The singing of gospel allows not only the performance of racial identity but a particular preservation of history and ancestry tied to African American identity. Williams-Jones writes, "Cultural ties of the ancestral lineage have been preserved in various forms within the enclave of the black gospel church and its music—black gospel." She argues that "Black gospel music, a synthesis of West African and Afro-American music, dance, poetry and drama, is a body of urban contemporary black religious music of rural folk origins which is a celebration of the Christian experience of salvation and hope. It is at the same time a declaration of black selfhood which is expressed through the very personal medium of music." In the end, "Gospel has distilled the aesthetic essence of the black arts into a unified whole. It is a colorful kaleidoscope of black oratory, poetry, drama and dance. One has only to experience a gospel 'happening' in its cultural setting to hear black poetry in the colorful oratory of the black gospel preacher, or to see the drama of an emotion-packed performance of a black gospel choir interacting with its gospel audience, and the resulting shout of the holy dance. It is indeed a culmination of the black aesthetic experience."[54]

For Williams-Jones, gospel is a source of African American self-identity that should be preserved. Gospel, then, is "a performer's art and a method of delivering lyrics which is as demanding in vocal skills and technique as any feat in Western performance practice. Learning or acquiring the art takes time, practice, and dedication. The performing process is so intuitive as to be almost unteachable. The greatest gospel artists are usually those who were born nearest the source of the tradition."[55] (Note how she stresses that singing gospel is "almost unteachable.") Williams-Jones asserts, "It is to be desired and anticipated that gospel music will not abandon its significant and singular role as the dominant force in the preservation of black cultural identity." Moreover, "It is imperative that black gospel maintain its strong self-identity and continue as the positively crystallizing element in the emerging black aesthetic."[56]

The idea of authenticity, regardless of its variety, shapes social norms in the belief of tradition.[57] Among scholars, gospel music contains what Joyce Marie Jackson calls a "continuity of consciousness" that "flows through various aspects of African American culture, and this continuity is evident in gospel music." She writes, "Since the church is the most conservative institution in the African American community, it is logical to assume that ritual services, including the mode of worship and style and function of music, would be preserved there in their truest form." Moreover, Jackson asserts that African American gospel music "remains one of the most genuine forms of the community's expression of values and aesthetics, and has remained the least encumbered by Euro-American influence."[58] DjeDje states, "Because of its roots and development in black culture, the gospel-music tradition is now recognized as *a symbol of black identity*."[59] Thus, gospel music becomes a powerful symbol for black racial identity, even among blacks who do not know or sing gospel.[60] For Molefi Kete Asante, the music of the traditional Black Church emerges out of African roots and is "truly an African expression" and "may be the essence of our Africanity."[61] This is an essentialist argument about the unique nature of Africans as a people, an essential aspect of the racial nature that persists even in the Diaspora.[62]

Whites came to assume that gospel music was sacred music because of the lyrics. White audiences were listening to the words and appreciating the rhythm; moreover, the popularity of gospel music among whites created unique connection between the Black Church and mainstream white culture.[63] Frazier writes, "They sing their gospel songs which are a blend of sacred and sacred music, not only Negro churches but addressed to the white world as well which is beginning to sing them too."[64] There is a centrality to seeing the original "Negro spirituals" as a profoundly affective experience, both ecstatically emotive and serenely emotional. The religious spectacle of blacks in worship is intertwined with the rise of "gospotainment" in which black worship is displayed for non-black consumption.

Sociologist David Grazian's analysis of the belief in racialized musical talents among African Americans in today's Chicago blues scene is relevant to what is occurring in multiracial congregations. The famous blues scene in Chicago is dependent on black performers who fulfill an urban fantasy of diversity. Grazian writes, "For slumming whites, these black-and-tans promised the call of the wild, a chance to experience the so-called primitiveness of black culture and its blessed gifts."[65] White tourists experience the exoticness of settings and the accentuation of black performers as fundamental. What Grazian observes in the Chicago blues scene is true in the "congregational diversity scene." There is a deep belief in a racially based musical authenticity that presumes only African Americans can achieve a particular style of music. Not only is that style of music distinctive, it is actually held to be the supreme form of music for worship. Just as authentic blues music can best be played by African American performers, authentic musical worship is best achieved by African Americans. This belief influences recruitment for worship leaders and musicians as part of the effort to diversify a church.[66]

Black Gospel Music as a Strategy for Diversity

The history, variety, and ambiguity of "black music" is utterly lost on church leaders and attenders today who radically simplify the style of music to fulfill an imperative of what "should" be included in their church services. In conversations among church leaders, gospel music is perceived to be a unique vehicle for accomplishing racial integration in churches. For example, when I asked a worship leader, "Do you feel that you are doing anything in the service which would particularly attract African Americans musically?" She replied, "Musically, yeah. By incorporating a little more gospel songs." The use of gospel music is a powerful, shared musical orientation adopted by worship leaders because of several overlapping, yet complementary, beliefs that reinforce the importance of gospel music for addressing the problem of diversity.

Overall, bringing black gospel music into the service is a strategy to create a liturgy that boldly proclaims "*We welcome blacks here.*" Church leaders believe the black-white divide is the most fundamental, defining obstacle to overcoming racial divisions, so "something" must be done. Among blacks, gospel music has become a primary symbol of black identity. Non-blacks accept the use of gospel music in liturgy as it is deeply entwined with the Christian tradition in its expressive, passionate sentiments of grace, salvation, and calling to God. Also, gospel music is seen as a form of "black culture" that is willingly assimilated by other racial-ethnic groups (similar to the assimilation of hip-hop music beyond black audiences today). Adapting to gospel as a genre of sacred music is also perceived to be an "easy" liturgical shift among church leaders compared to radically altering the European traditions embedded in white-dominant churches.

Many pastors have moved toward adopting black gospel as a style and attempt to hire African American worship leaders for that purpose.[67] Yet, African American churches are facing their own "worship wars" on the styles of music that are acceptable for worship.[68] Even within black Baptist churches, there is an astounding variety of worship styles. We should not be too quick to isolate one form of music as "black worship music." People commonly believe that certain linguistic and cultural practices are traditional. But, as Linda Wong writes, "No one has a problem accepting these traditions until some researcher comes along and presents evidence debunking them as myth."[69] James Abbington, Associate Professor of Church Music and Worship at Emory University, calls worship in the Black Church "multicultural." The *African American Heritage Hymnal* is attempting to encode the sacred music tradition of the Black Church. Denominations are publishing hymnals for their African American churches beginning with the North American Baptist Church, then the Episcopal Church, then the United Methodist Church, then the Church of God in Christ, which published its first hymnal, *Yes Lord*. There is even a hip-hop hymnal.[70] A study conducted by Brenda Eatman Aghahowa, a staff associate of a black church, focused on the contrasting styles and attempts at "ecumenicism" in two black churches whose styles she distinguishes as Charismatic versus Reserved. One congregation is Pentecostal while the other is liberal mainline, and not surprisingly, one style of worship is characterized as "ecstatic" while the other is described as "formal." The book was ground-breaking in its attempt to generate religious understanding between worship communities.[71]

Black Attenders versus Black Performers: The Irony of Black Performance

The notion of black authenticity in worship, especially in singing gospel music, therefore deeply influences the criteria for religious musical selection for churches seeking greater diversity. In other words, universal assumptions about black worship and gospel music provoke liturgical questions of selectivity (musical choices) and authenticity (who performs). At the same time, these assumptions raise contradictory pressures regarding when such "authentically black worship" is performed.

African Americans are expected to act "black" in some cases, but in others they are expected to hold back. For example, what happens among African American members of multiracial churches when they are only a few members in the congregation? Some find modeling how to worship is a key reason for them remaining, like an African American woman who said, "Seeing my identity as ambassador helps me stay as a black person, the only black person, in this church." Her participation as a racially or ethnically distinctive "worshiper" gives her as a black member a distinctive role. In contrast, Steven, a white pastor, stated that in his church African Americans "sense" their style of worship does not belong. He said, "We've recently had some African Americans that visited our fellowship, and they are far more into an African American experience in terms of body movement during the service, hand movement, but that is not reinforced. As they became aware of what was going on. . . ." Steven suddenly shifted into the point of view of these African American visitors, saying "as you are aware of what's going on around you, you suddenly realize that no one is moving to the music the same way. Suddenly you begin to feel the pressure, even though no one is literally saying sit down and not to move." Steven was both direct and sad in telling me this story. It clearly pained him to know this happens in his church. "So at that point they either acclimate to the group or they leave. Because we clearly don't have that style of music."

The irony of black worship performance is that when African Americans are on the platform, they are encouraged to "sing like black folks," but when they are in the pews they are encouraged to fit in.[72] Damien, an African American staff member of a church where African Americans constituted a very small percentage, said when you "go to a predominantly African American church, they're going to be dancing and clapping." When I asked if African Americans are more expressive in his own congregation, he answered, "Yes and no. They understand that we're outnumbered in a way. They don't want to do anything that brings attention to themselves, or that distracts other people from worship. So maybe they suppress a little bit." In talking about suppression, Damien provides a further complication to the performance of African American worship. In some settings, expressiveness is expected, while in others it is suppressed. In his church, African American worship attenders are intended to keep calmer and quieter; nevertheless, when I observed an African American participate up front with the band on the platform during services, the energy—the enthralled buoyancy and "soulfulness" of worship—was clearly evident.

There are, therefore, contradictory expectations for African Americans in diverse congregations; if they are to stay as worship attenders in the pews they are to "suppress a little bit," yet when they are on the platform as worship performers they are simultaneously encouraged to let it out in a much more expressive style. A white worship leader was among many who told me about creating special occasions for the performance of black gospel. He told me, "We brought in this African American guy, and we did this *old* gospel song—I mean, *he took us to church*, you know, just how you would expect." The largely unacknowledged contradiction of expectations between black worship attenders and black worship performers adds a nuanced understanding of African American worship as reported in Korie Edwards' fascinating case study of an interracial congregation.[73] Edwards asserts that blacks in interracial congregations must suppress black styles of worship in order to adapt into a white-dominant environment. Such suppression is clearly evident not only in Steven's and Damien's congregations but others as well. Again, suppression is evident in the pews, while accentuation of "singing like black folks" is the expectation for African Americans when they are worshiping up front.

The distinction in worship activity between black attenders and black performers was again brought out in an interview with Julie, an Asian worship leader. She told me about Cherise, who "for the longest time was the only African American we had in our church." Julie told Cherise's story as celebrating the successful incorporation of an African American onto the worship team. Yet, the story also served to emphasize the subtle, contradictory dynamics of black worship performance:

> Cherise was never part of the worship band or anything like that. But then Brandon [our current black worship leader] comes, she starts getting in there, and he is doing gospel piano, and she is up there with her mom, and they are rocking, and she whipped off an e-mail going, "Glory! Finally! Not only do I love this community but actually now,

> I was in tears, and I was moving, and my hands were up, and I was clapping because, right on. That moved my spirit. And I really felt released to worship." And now we have more African Americans here at our church.

Cherise's enthusiasm for feeling "released to worship" indicates she had felt "suppressed" before coming onto the platform. The platform expectation of actually worshiping with the "gospel piano," full of expressive action of "tears," "hands up," and "clapping," not only helped Cherise feel happiness and gratitude as she was "released to worship," but also was viewed by church leaders as the event that "released" the congregation to attract more African Americans.

In Steven's, Damien's, Julie's, and in other congregations, blacks are clearly encouraged to vividly express their "distinctive culture of worship" as a means to promote a value for diversity. Even though there is a belief by non-blacks that African Americans "have a beauty and a freedom about their worship and their personalities too" (as one white attender expressed it), clearly the key distinction of whether this "beauty and freedom" is welcomed is whether blacks are expected to melt into a diverse crowd (as mere attenders) or whether they are expected to contribute their own "flavor" of worship (as worship performers).[74]

Not Being "Too Black": Black Gospel Music in Non-Black Churches

I found it interesting when the lead pastor from a white-dominant church avoided using the word "gospel" to describe the music in his services. The church had a significant proportion of black members, yet he explicitly avoided the word "gospel" due to the stigma of "gospel" being associated with "black." For me as an observer, the presence of a mostly black choir, led by an African American, and incorporating the prominent use of an authentic Hammond organ, indicated that the service featured a *gospel* choir. But the pastor quickly corrected me, saying, "It's not a gospel choir. We particularly stay away from that word 'gospel.' We don't want to give people the impression that we are trying to turn that service into a gospel, black-oriented, music-style service."

While the use of a gospel choir both attracted and incorporated blacks into the service, the pastor was careful to not make the music seem "too black."

He told me that he had wanted to include more gospel music in the services but was discouraged by other leaders. "When I first came here, I thought there would be a lot of the stereotypical types of black music, and I tried to do a few things to make that happen." The lay leadership of the church put the brakes on his initiatives. "Some of the church councilmen said we are trying to get away from that because we don't want to be known as a black church that has black music and black preaching." The lead pastor said, "What we really tried to work hard for is a balance. We didn't want people to walk out of here saying the service is this style or that style. The whole key is diversity. The diverse service has its own unique identity but it can't be characterized by one particular style of music. It cannot because if we did that I think some people might get the wrong impression." This pastor tries to avoid labeling the music as racialized for blacks so that other groups, especially whites and Latinos, would not be deterred from attending the service. "When it's in a diverse setting like our church where we want to keep our integrated image very much in the forefront, we have that kind of music sometimes but we don't have it on a regular basis because of a stereotype."[75]

Overall, the beliefs oriented around African Americans and gospel music can be troublesome for cultivating unity. While one pastor avoids the stigma of marking the worship music as "black," another even more problematic issue surrounds the use of gospel music in all of these churches. Seeking to honor differences while overcoming them is inherent to the project of congregational diversity, yet music is deeply and inextricably inherent to the communal practice of religion. Specifically, when church leaders mix the belief of black superiority of worship, the need for gospel music to be included in musical liturgy, and the requirement of black authenticity in the performance of gospel music, music becomes the basis for radical separation on the basis of race.

All combined, the beliefs surrounding black gospel music has the potential of creating conditions for separation and difference rather than unity and togetherness. This indicates an inextricable tension. In short, if only blacks can truly perform gospel music (e.g., *they have soul*), incorporating gospel music creates a tension between "black performers" and non-black audiences. The universal assumptions regarding the nature of black worship radically separates experiences between racial-ethnic groups, makes racial groups absolute, and reinforces the dynamic of "black performers" for non-black audiences. Therefore, insisting on gospel music inadvertently exaggerates, rather than ameliorates, one of the fundamental sources of racial divisions in America—beliefs of racial essentialism.

However, my research contributes yet another twist. While beliefs of racial authenticity and performance promote profound assumptions of racial difference, these same beliefs simultaneously drive the imperative to include people of diverse racial and ethnic backgrounds into worship ministry structures. Beliefs of difference lead to recruitment and involvement on the basis of difference. Before describing these structures of involvement, the next three chapters will examine whether worship experiences differ by race, the distinctive role of worship leaders, and the variety of approaches to constructing worship services.

PART II

Worship Experience and Music Selection in Multiracial Churches

4

The Naïve Experience of Worship in Multiracial Churches

> Gerardo: How would you say your racial and ethnic heritage affects your worship experience?
>
> Keith: That's a great question [laughs]. I don't—that's a good question. That's—wait, how—? Could you say that question again?
>
> —KEITH, ASIAN AMERICAN, worship pastor

I HURRY THROUGH the parking lot and make it into the auditorium of yet another racially diverse congregation right before the start of the service. It's nice to shift from the cold weather outside to the warmth of the building inside. People are draping coats and jackets over the seats; a woman next to me sets down her purse while a man looks to his left and right before focusing their attention to the front. The band is already on stage. A drummer, two guitarists, and three vocalists at microphones are adjusting electrical cords and shuffling papers. When the tallest guitarist looks to the others with a knowing nod, the lights go down. The people around me are shuffling in their seats as the lead guitarist says into the microphone, "Good morning, everyone, let's all stand together." He brings his hand down to the strings of his instrument, says a quiet "one-two-three" count, and starts the first song of the morning. Worship is officially started.

I look and see waves of people stand up out of their seats and face the platform. People's mouths start to move as the crowd gets in sync with the program. Soon, the tempo encourages people around me to sway, singing words displayed on screens, and a syncopation emerges. The ambiguous crowd now shares a unity in being guided through this corporate Sunday gathering. Over the next twenty minutes, we pass through a succession of songs, a togetherness evident in the ebb and flow from song to song, until the lead pastor comes to the platform to start his morning sermon.

Visits like this at churches small and large, traditional and contemporary, consistently focused my attention on the corporate aspect of worship. Yet, I came away with a persistent question regarding the true level of "togetherness" occurring in services. Through interviews I knew that the diverse attenders of multiracial churches came from widely different ancestral backgrounds, complicated by their differences in generational ties to their countries of origin and their varieties of ethnic-specific religious upbringing. The question of similarity was provoked as to whether the attenders with me were similar in the responses to the services they attended. In short, in this and in other churches I consistently observed diverse attenders in a multiracial service share a common worship setting, but do they share a common worship experience? And how is music related to this experience?

The question of worship experience is difficult to grasp and the difficulty is complicated by the inherent contradiction of beliefs held by people regarding the power of music in the face of race.[1] Presumed racial distinctions are essentialized such that supposed differences affect the actual experience of worship. Blacks and Hispanics are passionate; whites and Asians are calmer and quieter. Blacks and Hispanics require louder, deeply rhythmic music while whites and Asians favor smooth melodies and moments of quiet.[2] In other words, the assumed differences between races are believed to have real implications for how racial and ethnic groups experience worship. The puzzle of racial differences is confusing considering that the goal of worship is to bring together people into a corporate worship experience. The analysis and description of worship dynamics presents particular challenges for social scientists because social science does not attempt to describe "spiritual dynamics" directly. Nevertheless, careful analysis of people's description of their routine worship experiences reveals interesting patterns.

Everything surrounding the attempt to understand and cultivate worship in Protestant congregations centers on individuals communing with their God. Members almost always reflected on their worship experiences with tears in their eyes, visibly moved in recalling deep, satisfying moments of joy, rapture, and exaltation. The profound catharsis regularly experienced by worshipers affirms to them a profound sense of the miraculous power they see embedded in the very act of worship. Worship is a time of experiencing healing, reconciliation, and spiritual community through the collective focus of a diverse people on a single God. Through their experiences, they see the power of worship as including the capacity to create bonds of unity and togetherness despite racial conflicts and ethnic divisions.

Tia DeNora notes that Western culture considers music to be powerful emotional force that connects intimate subjectivity of individuals to broader social structures.[3] However, the force of music is also believed to be impervious to empirical research. John Rahn called it the "gap between structure and feeling."[4] How are we to understand the "human-music interaction"? For the purposes of this study, it became important to attempt such an analysis. I seek to understand how the musical experience of worship affects people of different racial and ethnic groups. Is there a difference between people on the basis of race? This consistent question pursued with regularity and intensity yielded a unique data set on worshipers and their worship. To what extent are there similarities or differences in the experience of worship among people from various racial and ethnic backgrounds? More importantly, do members of different racial and ethnic groups experience worship music differently?

Music and Worship Brought Together in the Practice of Congregational Life

Many church leaders are quick to point out that "music" and "worship" are not synonymous terms. Indeed, worship encompasses far more than the use of music in liturgy. Worship includes prayer and preaching, an alternation between noise and silence, and many include connecting with others and "fellowshipping" as part of worship. Even more, although music is a routine aspect of congregational worship in all the congregations I studied, certainly the phenomena of music is not circumscribed by the effort or goal of worship alone. Nevertheless, among all the people I spoke to in these churches, music is an essential—and treasured—aspect of congregational worship. Dora, a white choir member, said, "The first singing is when it's worshiping for me... As soon as you start the song." Elizabeth, a white lay leader said, "For me, it's an intangible experience that I have when I hear the music." Stacey, an African American woman and a member of her choir, said, "Music does something to me that nothing else can do." Gina, a white choir member, said, "I definitely feel something spiritual when there's music." For Samuel, a Jewish man who converted to a more Pentecostal-style faith, said, "You get a good feeling like the presence of God and you really get into it, and it's a certain song that really touches you, you really get into it." Carol, a white member, said, "During that time when music's playing, for me that's the most worshipful."

Music is consistently associated with worship. In Protestant congregations, music as a customary, even necessary, activity required when participating in services. Music, then, is embedded in the overall activities of being part of a congregation. Music is not "part of" the culture of a church or "embedded within" the culture of the church but is a practice that constitutes any congregational community. Yet music rates low in comparison with other factors in the decision to join or leave a church including sermons, pastoral personality, children's programs, church location, theological tradition, and, most importantly, a feeling of warmth and belonging. These other considerations are far more important. For some, music may seem significant at first, but most members say music becomes less important the longer they stay at the church. In some cases, music may be a factor in member's choice in joining or leaving a church only to the extent that the music symbolically represents an overall orientation for a church. The music of the church can "announce" the nature and orientation of the church such that in a religious marketplace of congregations, music can serve as a marker of overall congregational style for church consumers.

Church leaders may feel the necessity to appeal to people's interest in leisure music, but this is simply not supported in my interviews with members. There is research that argues that with musical taste "birds of the same feather flock together" and that niches are confined by specific socio-demographic and socio-geographical locations such that music preferences are based upon "niche centers."[5] However, I find church worship music does not at all correlate with the music most people listen to outside of church or to what they grew up hearing.

In talking about music, members consistently separated the music of worship from music in other arenas of their lives. Many, like Judy, an Asian member of her church, distinguished between music that is *for worship* and music that is *for entertainment*. Judy told me she mostly listens to jazz music, and when I asked if she heard anything similar in church, she said, "Rarely." Yet, it did not bother her that the music she listened to outside of church was not found in church. "When I listen to jazz, I'm not worshiping. I'm just like being entertained. Because that's for entertainment. I'm not coming to the church to be entertained." In particular, the performance and consumption of worship music accentuates an experience that is separate from everyday life and special because it is qualitatively different than everyday life. Worshipers' sense of time, space, and motion is distinguished from the sense of an ordinary flow of time. The importance of the setting, in contrast with the "music," is evident in that even people who are the most moved by the worship in their church do not listen to such music outside of the congregation. In talking about Christian music on the radio, Kristina said, "I'm not really that into it." Sue, who attends a church with mostly contemporary Christian music, said, "No. I don't really enjoy Christian music all that much."

Members simply accept the music of their church as it is. Hearing worshipers talk about how they learned to worship in their church moved me to pay less attention to the dynamics of race as accounting for inherent differences to the response to worship music and more to the dynamics of anticipation and socialization among members of particular churches. Overall, if a member chooses to remain in a church, they accommodate themselves to the overall worship style of the congregation because members do not expect the genres of worship music to mirror the music they listen to for leisure. Even more, when some members tell me they switched their leisure music tastes toward the music they heard at church, it was consistently connected to their desire to become more spiritually devoted believers. In short, a conscious decision to avoid listening to non-sacred, or "non-Christian," music is associated with an attempt to purify and sanctify their world and the influences on their life. Their musical tastes are not a problem if the music they typically consume is not seen as "evil" or a bad moral influence; the perception of moral influence is key.

Most congregants do not have extensive exposure to different styles of music in worship. Practical considerations of time and travel limits are some of the reasons that members have little experience with worship music in other congregations, and this tends to constrain their perception of the range of choices available in sacred music. Yet some individuals find that learning to worship in their current church involves reconsideration of previous church experiences. For example, some African Americans who previously attended ecstatic worship services found that they needed to relearn how to worship in a quieter setting. Charles, an African American member of a black-white mainline church, said, "When I came, I learned to appreciate the quietness of the service. When I first came here I noticed how silent it was, you couldn't get an Amen or a hand clap. But I found that there is a certain spirituality in silence." Similarly, Trey, a white musician, reflected on the range of styles he now hears in his congregation, saying, "I did learn to like gospel and funk and jazz... And when I realized it, I thought, 'Wow! That's really weird.' Because I never grew up on this stuff or anything. But I've learned to really like and appreciate it." He added, "Honestly, before I had no idea. I really didn't know about like gospel or funk or all that. But right now that's where I consider a lot of my heart. It's stuff I can really attach to."

For the great majority of congregants, music does not emerge as an important factor in people's decision of why they come to a particular church as people do not join a church mainly for the worship music. Casual observation challenges this conclusion, and there are people who insist that music matters a lot. However, based on the interviews conducted for this research I find people telling me that the music would have to be radically different and either grating or offensive for them to leave. One respondent likened the music of the church to a "bonus." Conversely, the music does not appear to be the thing that keeps attenders coming. Perhaps people find the music of their church familiar as I frequently heard members saying the music of their church was "just like the church I come from." Nevertheless, because respondents so often tell me how they come to "learn" the music, I conclude that music alone does not attract or keep members over time. Instead, it appears most people come because of family or friends and stay because they are involved. Because music is so embedded within the activity of participating in the congregations, what happens in the worship music is simply perceived to be a basic aspect of what happens in their church. In addition, music provides places of interaction and involvement. Accounting for how music creates spaces of involvement is fundamental for creating diversity.[6]

Does the salience of music differ among people of different races/ethnicities? Assumptions about race and worship lead us to expect differences, but analysis of actual worship in multiracial churches brings me to accentuate their profound similarities. I see little reason to believe there are differences between racial and ethnic groups when talking to them about their actual worship experiences. As an interviewer, if I do not invoke the expectation that one's race or ethnicity *should* affect worship, members rarely articulate racial or ethnic distinctions in their experiences. My results are interesting and, to me, surprising. If interviews with church leaders and members are to be believed, worship experiences should be different according to one's race or ethnicity. I would expect that there are individuals of different ethnic and racial groups that would systematically feel excluded from a deep worship experience because of racially or ethnically specific expectations of what is required to experience "authentic" worship. Instead, my observations and interviews show little if any exclusion and continually reveal deep similarities of worship among people of various ancestral backgrounds.

The Work of Worship

Despite pervasive beliefs about racial-ethnic differences, worship experiences are not distinguished by one's racial or ethnic affiliation. In looking through my interviews, I found that members of all racial-ethnic groups regardless of ancestral backgrounds describe worship as the pursuit of an intensely private spiritual experience through participation in the very public setting of church services. Rather than being guided by expectations of racial or ethnic differences, my interviews and observations lead me to conclude overall that individuals "learn" to worship in their churches. Attenders rarely blame worship leaders for failing to have a full worship experience. All members of the multiracial churches that I studied describe similar experiences of "worship" in their congregations and reveal a process of learning how to worship, especially if they have no experience or a markedly different previous experience with church. The focus on learning is an aspect of seeing worship as a personal responsibility. Consistently, worship is seen as something people must accomplish on their own.

Even more, church members from all racial and ethnic backgrounds experience a series of stages in learning how to worship. As Wendy, an Asian member of the choir, described her experience of worship, she said, "It's kind of a progression." The experience of worship for all congregational members takes the form of a progression of "learning" to worship over time. Members describe a process, a type of socialization for entering into a worship experience.

At first, members arrive to their congregations as guests or newcomers and experience worship as "outsiders." A Hispanic member said, "When I used to come to church way back I used to think, gosh they sing a lot... like they sing too much. But now you get used to it, and you get into it and now its like, they don't sing enough." For all church attenders, the goal of worship is to release one's self-consciousness, what I describe as the experience of "letting go." The process of "letting go" is evident throughout my interviews regardless of the liturgical style of the churches that they attended. Eventually, members take on a congregational identity. As members learn to worship, the experience of worship becomes intimately intertwined with their perceived connection to the congregation as a whole. So, worship is always an inherently social process both in the manner by which a person becomes engaged in worship as well as the connection between one's person and the congregation as a whole. Once this progression is taken in one church, the same progression to achieve worship in other, future congregations appears to come more readily.

Worship for church members is a "task," something that is to be accomplished in a fairly efficient manner (within a few minutes), so the use of music to focus is highly intentional.[7] The experience of worship begins with a time of personal reorientation of attention. Lauren, an Asian American member, said, "A full worship experience [is when] I would be open to God, and it doesn't really matter what is going on up front as long as I'm focused on Him." In this reorientation, music serves as a device for moving away from one's own concerns to the corporate event that is now taking place. Simeon, a black worshiper, said, "You come in and the music is already playing. They'll start playing a song for people.... You don't really sit down, you are up clapping. It really gets your adrenalin up and going. You are having fun." Mike, a white member, said, "The first couple of songs get you pumping, but then the next two songs are meditative. One gets you going, the moving of the spirit so to speak, and the other one is the spirit moving inside you, it's more internal rather than clapping your hands. Because the first couple songs are movers and you clap your hands."

The process of focusing can take some time. Kenny, an Asian American, said "It takes me a while—probably the first song just to kind of—I probably won't find myself singing." For some, the work is centered on focusing on the words of the songs. Seth, a white member, said, "I tend to be more of a lyrics guy. A lot of times I'm not necessarily singing. More internal singing. Just really dwelling on the words themselves." The aspects of music that help to achieve worship can involve more than just the sound or "groove" of the music. In lieu of musical style or acoustic rhythm, members describe that the words of songs have greater impact. People who are new to the music style of a particular church or who are hearing "worship music" for the first time as part of their growing commitment to Christianity pay attention to other signals and cues for inscribing meaning to their experience in the services. Especially among recent immigrants, worshipers pay special attention to the words of the songs as they are written or projected. Conscious attention to words results in their taking in those meanings more deliberately and allowing themselves to immerse more completely into the setting as a whole.

For others, the work of focus encompasses all aspects of the service. Andy, an Asian American member, said, "It's a mix of reflecting on where I am right now but also where I want to go, and so it's very emotional for me. I feel very drained afterwards." Achieving focus takes work, so much so that many describe the work of worship as starting *before* the service begins. Chris said,

> Obviously my heart has to be in the right spot. And for my heart to be in the right spot in any service, I have to feel at home there... And so you know, to be perfectly honest, the thoughts we all go through in worship experiences, "Who's looking at me?" "Am I out of place?" "What is the cultural mark here?" I mean that kind of a feeling in any new place. There was a little bit of uncomfortableness. For me now being at this church, to have a full worship experience is knowing that this is where I belong, this is my home, I am loved here, I am accepted.

Learning to worship has much to do with moving away from simply focusing on music and words to opening oneself to experiencing the broader social happenings in the room. Ilene, an Asian member, talked about her first true experience of worship in her church, saying, "That day I cried and I really think that that day I got the Spirit and I got that connection with God and I think from that day on I really started to worship like other people...." Ilene said, "At the beginning I said it was the words that touched me the most, then comes the music. But I guess sometimes the whole environment. Sometimes when you arrive at service and as soon as you step in you can really feel the Spirit, it's already there because everybody is enjoying so much and they sing and their full hearts, so as soon as you enter in you already feel it."

DeNora describes a process of "getting into focus" that combines music and mental concentration.[8] Music helps people to produce the kind of focus they need to carry out mental work. The capacity for music to allow for "focus" resonates with church members as they describe the process of worship. The sense of allowing a type of release of the self in worship was briefly described in my book *Hollywood Faith*. At Oasis Christian Center, worshipers abandon themselves to a participation in the divine and experience empowerment. Danielle described "learning" to worship, saying, "The first time I actually got into praise and worship and the first time I ever raised my hands, it was kind of like a submission. The first time I just kind of like submitted my heart to God. That was a huge step." She said, "I felt compelled to just kind of raise my hand and let go, I felt self-conscious at first but it was just I closed my eyes and decided, you know what, Pastor always talks about how the praise and worship time is your time to be with God and to worship as a church but also as a very private moment for yourself. So, I decided not to think about anybody that was around me." Friends who had introduced her to church had become familiar and safe. "I felt a level of comfort with them. So I felt safe around them to kind of let go. And it was just a feeling of letting go. It was the first step of me believing that I was in God's hands. And there is a way that I have to communicate that back to him. And it was just a really great feeling."[9]

The use of repetition and familiar music for worship follows the conditions DeNora describes as important for music to accentuate the capacity concentration. She writes that her respondents "engaged in self-conditioning" with the use of "familiar, focus-producing music with concentration such that, when the music was replayed, they were able to induce concentration." She continues, "Music was used here to reproduce an aesthetic environment of 'working' and to circumscribe within that environment 'where the mind can go.' One literally stays tuned, through such practices, to a mode of concentrated focus, to the mental task at hand."[10] DeNora also connects the experience of worship and the body, describing it as a body-culture interaction through temporal body practices.

"Musical entrainment" involves the body as it unfolds in relation to musical elements and involves social role and action styles.[11] Essentially, entrainment involves syncing body and processes in relation to music. For entrainment to occur, a routinization of the body with the environment depends on a level of awareness of anticipation for what will happen next. DeNora writes, "Aesthetic materials here may be seen as akin to what Robert Witkin once referred to as 'holding forms.'[12] They provide motifs that precede, and serve as a reference point for, lines of conduct over time." She adds, "Holding forms thus provide a touchstone to which actors may return as they engage in expressive activity. They are resources against which future agency takes shape."[13]

Some people further engage the setting and social contagion of worship by placing themselves into the most immersive opportunity for worship in the service. Kenny, an Asian member, said, "I try to sit as close to the front part of the church as possible." The importance of the social environment for worship is most recognized by choir members and members of worship teams. Sue said, "When you are in the choir, I think you are more connected to it, so there is a greater sense of synergy. If people are worshiping, then you feel it and it helps us to worship God too." For musicians and singers, they are fulfilled in being able to completely immerse themselves in the service.

However it is achieved, worship begins with focus aided by music, which then allows for a fuller engagement with the happenings of the service as a whole. June, a white lay leader, describes when she worships, "I would say that I'm focused, when I come with distractions I am able to put them aside. I am really thinking about what the words are saying and expecting the Holy Spirit to apply that to me and maybe change my heart before we get to the teaching."

Again, she said, "I think just focusing. Focusing not on what the team looks like or even how they're playing or what they're playing and being able to take off my leadership hat and not get distracted by things that are going on and thinking about the worship song itself." Music is critical to the process for Amanda: "Music is very soothing in itself. So no matter what has happened before I entered that door, it's a calming thing for me and sort of calms my spirit and gets me ready to worship. I can sort of examine my heart and why I'm being so hard and not willing to let go of whatever it is. I bring it to God in that moment and let it go so that I'm free to worship."

Distraction as the Enemy of Personal Worship

Worship is delicate work and can easily be displaced by more mundane concerns. Members are consistent in saying that "distraction" is the main enemy of achieving a full worship experience. Linda, a white member, said she achieves worship "if I'm not self-conscious, and if I can just, I don't care about who is around me, or whatever, but I want to just be in my worship time. I really try to I guess just focus on what God wants to say to me through his worship." Focus is critical. "I try to tune everybody else out." Seth, a white member, defined worship as "being in communion with Christ and not really much focused on what's going on around me or who is around me or even necessarily the style of music or type of song."

Across my interviews, members consistently fight against distraction. For example, what distracts Steve, Hispanic member, is "too much talking. Up front, sometimes the person would be talking so much, it was like, 'Okay, let's get with it.'" When I asked Chris what keeps him from having a full worship experience, he talked about his occasional responsibilities up on the platform, saying, "If I'm doing announcements and thinking about what I'm going to do during announcements, that inhibits me because of my role." Chris also mentioned children sitting in the room. "Kids can be distracting as well." Kristina, an Asian choir member, said her worship is compromised when "I am feeling disconnected for some reason from what's happening in the moment, thinking about something else, or maybe even being critical of the surroundings or the band." Judy, an Asian member of another church, said, "When I don't get a good worship experience, it's usually because I'm just distracted—it's too noisy, it's overpowering. I'm so like, 'Ugh.' And when I do get a good experience, it's because I feel like I can participate and it's music where I can sing and keep up with ... I feel like I can totally participate and it kind of just sets up this mood, like you can really feel like the Holy Spirit is there and not being distracted."[14]

Even for musicians, the challenge to focus on music is difficult. Judy said, "When I say 'distracted,' it's usually the music." Trey, a white man who recently joined the worship team, said, "Sometimes I would be too absorbed in the technical things or getting the right notes or getting the right rhythm and keeping time." He said, "When I'm playing the song or something, I'll be concentrating on the song. I'll be like, 'All right, the chorus is up now. I've got to play this.' It's still new to me. I was never really able to let go and just worship." Michelle, a white member of her choir, said, "Most of the time, receiving and being a part of the congregation is actually better for me. I just want to be on the receiving end, to be a part of the congregation, not have to remember any parts, be able to sing, close my eyes, not think and to do that."

The freedom from distraction is part of what makes quieter, more contemplative services seem more worshipful, even for members who had been more used to "loud" and "celebratory" worship in previous churches. As Chuck, an African American member, said, "Sometimes I would find myself here by myself and just sit in the sanctuary and appreciate the quietness. I think it made me closer to God. You know you come to church and hear all that loud noise, but also to actually reflect and think about things." The quietness of the sanctuary and the service allows for focus. Similarly, I found it interesting that for many respondents the most worshipful moment of a service is frequently a quieter moment, when the volume is lower, the instruments stop, and the singing is *a capella*. People define it as a more contemplative moment. Carol, a white member, said, "There's a period of time where you're able to be by yourself, not by yourself but there's time [when] it's more of a reflective period." Even in churches that have ecstatic worship, it is when the music comes down, a point of quieter focus or even when the music will stop and there are only words—that is the moment when they feel they are most connected with God. Especially in these reflective moments, as Trey said, the process is one of getting to a point of letting go, "You've got to let go and just worship."

"Letting Go"

After achieving focus, all congregants spoke about achieving a "connection." Kristina, an Asian American, comments, "There is a sense of being connected to God or a sense of focus, being able to focus on God and on his quality, his goodness, being able to like emotionally connect..." Sharon, African

American, said, "Connecting. I feel like [I'm] connected, I feel like I'm connecting. It's [pauses], yeah it's like making a connection, and I feel like I'm opening up and connecting." A "connection" happens when you can "surrender" or give yourself over to a complete focus on God through music. Connection does not happen if there are "distractions"—which seem to imply things one cannot control, or involves instrumental tasks that cannot be avoided like playing music correctly or music components being "too loud" or technical problems with sound equipment. Common distractions can be both external (e.g., poor music quality, disruptions around their seat, "showy" performances on the platform) and internal (e.g., stress, personal worries, being late due to leadership commitments, responsibility for music and/or service, relational disputes like having an "argument with kids or spouse"). Particular emphasis is placed on the internal distractions consisting of "burdens and worries," which are emotional weights or concerns, especially relational ones that are consuming or occupy one's thoughts.

Kenny, an Asian American member, spoke about transitioning from volunteering with children in Sunday School to participating in worship, saying, "I find myself quieting myself, trying to prepare myself to come into God's presence and the whole worship experience. So I find myself needing time to stop from worrying about how Sunday School went or what we talked about or my conversations with parents and just focusing now on concentrating on my worship experience." When I asked Kenny his process, he said, "Most of the time I stay seated, close my eyes, and sit either silent or say a prayer to God and ask Him to open my heart. I prepare myself." Full worship is achieved when there is an absence of distraction. "When I'm worshiping, it's like I can't tell anyone's in the room or anyone is around. I'm so—if I have my eyes closed and so focused on just offering praises to God. As far as what I'm experiencing what's going on whether it's from a video clip or the sermon, it's like I'm not letting the distractions or things that I've got on my plate affect me during that time. Just totally focused and present." Walt, an African American musician, said, "A couple of minutes before we start, I always have personal prayer time, and just sort of leave everything that's outside of the church outside of the church."

In congregants' minds, external distractions are difficult and almost impossible to ignore, but internal "worries" are up to the individual who just needs to "let go" and not let those things intrude. Worship involves focusing on the immediate setting and forgetting everything else. Some describe it as getting into "the zone." In overcoming distraction and achieving focus, music provides the means for people to move inside themselves and "let go." Damion said, "I had to learn how to worship and the way I had to learn how to worship is to just let go, to let go. To let go and let God." An attitude of surrender is implicit to worship. "Any time that you're aware of people around you, then I honestly feel that you're not praising God the way that God wants you to praise him." Damion broke down the process, saying, "The music would touch my soul. If it touched me, then it moved me. So at that point, the music touched you, and it got you emotional, and when it got you there, then that was the point that you let go."

Church becomes an important place to allow for the process of "letting go," which means "letting go of my problems and everything else." Worship is "letting go and you don't care." What is most important is "Learning to just let go." Individuals willingly, voluntarily, and with anticipation yield themselves to the elements of worship for the duration of the service in order to experience God. They abandon themselves to participation in the divine as structured by the church services. The key, then, to good worship is to lose self-consciousness and concern that other people are in the room. In all the congregations studied for this project, this experience of "letting go" is transracial.[15]

The process of "letting go" is a process of releasing inhibitions and allowing a fuller emoting of the self in public. Betty, a white woman, defined worship, saying, "I like where you can express your feelings of the Lord." The experience is social, but still personal. Betty said, "It's just your personal, own worship of Jesus. That's why you are there." Steve, a Hispanic, said, "It takes me where I hear the music, but I'm not really concentrating on who's giving the music. That's when I am totally focused on the Lord through the words. To me that's worship. When it takes me away from paying attention to who is delivering it. I'm one-on-one with the Lord."

DeNora writes how "music is used to seal off an environment, and to regularize that environment by predetermining the types of sonic stimuli it will contain. Music is thus a device with which to configure a space such that it affords some activities—concentration—more than others." Consistent with this framework, members describe the music as central to achieving focus. DeNora continues, "Music affords concentration because it structures the sonic environment, because it dispels random or idiosyncratic stimuli, aesthetic or otherwise. It places in the foreground sounds that respondents associate with mental work, sounds that are familiar and that recede to the background. With the addition of music, an environment comes to be configured for mental work."[16] In this sense, any space (a sanctuary, a warehouse, a coffeehouse, a nightclub) can be configured for worship. Despite beliefs to the contrary about the importance of architecture, the addition of worship music in a space can make it a place for the "mental work" of worship. Worship music does not need to relate to "regular" music people listened to in the car or at home because it creates a particular kind of focus. The music is associated with the focus of cultivating a particular attitudinal and affective state.

Amanda, a white member, described when she's "really worshiping," saying, "When I'm really worshiping, I'm not focused on anything else around me. I'm not even focused on who is up front and what they are doing or who is leading worship or anything. I just zone in on the words of the song and really taking in the full meaning of the song and what I'm saying or what I'm singing." Michelle, a white choir member, said, "I feel more free when I am on the stage [with the choir] to move or to raise my hands, that type of thing, than when I am in the congregation because the congregation is more subdued. So that's a different aspect as well that I face. I feel more free on the stage than I do off the stage, which is strange."

Freedom is characteristic of letting go in worship. John, a white member of another congregation, said the experience of worship "is a sense of freedom. I think there is something about worship in my mind and my heart, but I worship God with my body and with my hands. I can dance if I want to. There is a sense of freedom." One woman from a charismatic church still felt that the church was "too structured," saying that her own private worship is fuller because she does not always feel comfortable worshiping freely in the church service. "Yeah, it is because I don't dance in church, you are more or less going along with what is happening what everyone else is doing...." Yet she insisted that being in a corporate service is "better," saying, "because there are other people there. It's exciting. People are praying for each other, it's an exciting thing to see how God is moving in one service so many different ways with so many different people. That's exhilarating, really neat. Better than being by myself."

Timothy Nelson emphasizes giving up of control as characteristic of emotional worship. Individuals willingly, voluntarily, and with anticipation yield themselves to the elements of worship for the duration of the service in order to experience God and by doing so enhance the performance of those on the platform, increasing their own intensity, which further accentuates the corporate experience in a circular fashion, leaders to worshipers, and worshipers back to leaders.[17] Through participating in a corporate orientation to the sacred, the reconstruction of identity happens in the abandonment of self to worship. Corporate worship recalls a process of identity construction to a transcendent divinity, which also constitutes a process of dynamic bonding among worshipers through the shared experience of empowerment.

Barbara, a white worshiper, described being "submerged in the Lord,"

> I am completely submerged in the Lord. You could just feel him moving, you could feel him talking to you. It's not even what's being sung, it's just worship, it's just praise. You speaking to the Lord and the Lord talking to you, it's just feeling the presence of the lord, how do you explain it. There's a magnitude of the presence of God that is just beyond any words and that is what I feel and what I like to feel. If I just close my eyes and think about those words and sing it to the Lord. If I make it more prayer, and I just close myself off and I just invite the Lord to speak to me and minister to me and I invite him to do that and I tell him that I want everything that he has for me.

When speaking about experiencing "freedom," worshipers mean a freedom to express themselves more emotionally in public.

It's ironic. While worship occurs most intensely in a public setting, these believers continually reflect on their needing to get to a point when they could express their private spiritual affectivity in public worship. Paula, a white member, said, "I felt freer. People were, just the music was, I don't even know how to say it…It was so in unison and so amazing because we were repenting and really coming before God as a congregation." When I asked if she was able to experience this same feeling of worship alone, she said, "Not quite the same. You need to have a group that you are connected with on a soul, spirit level, which is what this was, it lasted for such a short time and I don't think that is something that happens very often in life. I think it's rare."

Letting go occurs in a community in which members allow themselves to be vulnerable. Kimberly, an African American woman who is a member of the choir, said, "I'm feeling the presence of God, I'm feeling very vulnerable, that one-on-one relationship with God. When I'm singing, I'm really letting God know that I'm with Him. There are some songs that really bring in the Holy Spirit and speak to me and there's no on else there, it's just me and God." However, there can be a racial aspect to the process of "letting go." Racial aspects of "letting go" came up in my discussion with Kimberly. She said, "I think that I had [my] guard up, so when I let my guard down yeah. Just because of the history and dynamics of the African Americans and white people, you just have your guard up. You let it down once you feel trust and get to know people. I had a good experience once I really opened up and allowed myself to be ministered to and let the Spirit work." Kimberly's is one of only two interviews in which members describe racial tensions affecting the process of letting go; among all others, racial or ethnic tensions did not appear to affect their practice of worship.

A Diverse Community of Worshipers

In my interviews, I found that when members commit to a congregation, they come to accept the music as part of that congregation. One member said, "That music is Grace and Grace is that music." In learning to worship, members find themselves connected to the broader congregational identity of the church—regardless of genre or style of music in the church. There comes a simultaneous connection between the experience of "God" and the experience of the godly community. Rueben, a Hispanic member, said he felt like he worshiped fully in church because "everybody is singing," doing the same thing together. The two (presence of God's Spirit and being in the presence of spiritual people) are continually intertwined in discussions with worshipers.

Interviews frequently combine experiencing God with experiencing the worshiping community. Chris said, "Yeah, I mean the songs that we do sing and we move into full worship experiences where you just feel like, "That was God. We just felt the presence of God." Those kind of special Sundays usually come because that spirit, that tone was able to be released in whatever the song was. I mean, it works because of the people who are up there, because of what they have been through, because of their authenticity, because you know their stories, because of their brokenness and I think that all plays into it." The intertwining of God and community is also reflected in the experience of John, a white member of a black-white church, said, "I just feel the presence of God... just seeing the choir up there alive, worshiping and rejoicing." Alice, a Hispanic member, said in worship, "Everyone is singing, it's just wonderful, you can just feel the Holy Spirit there." Lottie, a female Asian staff member, said "[You] get that feeling that really as we worship that we feel the Spirit amongst us." The worship music is viewed as being in sync with the identity of the congregation as a whole.

Private worship is different from corporate worship, yet there is a distinct advantage to being gathered. Lauren, an Asian American, said, "I think God created us to be with other people, so to worship God, to love God, as a community is an experience that you need to have the full picture of who God is." She said, "I am reminded that this is what Heaven is going to be like, and—its going to be awesome—its being a part of his people, in the word he always talks about his people, so if you're by yourself you aren't getting the full picture." A public setting of the congregation gathered is necessary to experience the fullness of a private worship experience. Nadine, a Middle Eastern member, said, "You have the private worship, the intimacy and stuff, [but] for me when you step into corporate, it's that plus the ability to be led by the Spirit." Andy, an Asian, said in worship he achieves a profound sense of self-reflection before God, "just very cleansing and like being aware of stuff in my life that I haven't been paying attention to lately. But it's weird because it is an isolated feeling but at the same time I don't think I could have it if I was by myself."

In sum, worship music is a practice that constitutes the congregation as a community. Kimberly said, "The world is so hard out here, you can go into a worship service and we immediately worship, and we greet each other, and we sing together." Worship, relational interaction, and a feeling of community are embedded within each other. Andy also said that sensing others are worshiping gets him in the same mode, "Because there's a sense of community. Knowing that what I'm feeling and what I'm being convicted by isn't just me." In all the congregations, a mingling of individual worship with corporate togetherness came up frequently in my discussions with church members. Simeon said,

> It's like when you are there and worshiping, sometimes you'll wake up in the morning and you just don't want to wake up and you might come to church tired, and you are in there worshiping and you aren't really as much into [it]. You're still clapping and singing but you aren't really into it that much? It becomes a contagious effect in that you see other people around you worshiping and you see the joy in their faces when they worship and it starts to take over you. And that extra energy that you have makes you happy. You are up and clapping and having fun and worshiping the Lord and it's contagious.

The experience of great, personal depth of worship with a flowing, corporate togetherness of spirit is a constant thread throughout my conversations with church members. David, a white member of this black-white church, talked about how the music is powerful for ushering him into a worship experience. "It's really deep," he said, "I mean why do they sound the bugle and play powerful music when men were on the battlefield in the days of old? It galvanizes you in some way." He began describing his experience during the worship, saying, "I can tune out whatever is going on around me." Then he quickly added, "A more accurate description of what I feel here is that I am able to harmonize with the other believers in spirit." He said, "Together we submit and worship God, and I feel that harmony here in our service. That is very fulfilling and satisfying to me."

David's worship is an individual experience, but it is one that is accomplished in concert with others. And when I asked David what most helps him have that full worship experience, he didn't point to himself. He pointed to church leaders. "I believe it starts with the ministry," he said.

> [It's starts with] those people in charge, that they have the mind of the spirit and that they are in tune and in sync with what God has for the people at that service. And it flows right on through the musicians and the congregation and how well they receive it. You could have the ministry on the mark and geared up with God and everybody is not distracted with anything else and in tune with God.... So when there's harmony from the pulpit right on down to the last pew, that's when it is satisfying.

David, like many others, believes the experience of worship is infectiously spread from pulpit to pew, a socio-spiritual virus that catalyzes a contagious expansion of connection to the sacred.

The experience of worship is described in similar ways by worshipers in very different church contexts and goes beyond a supposed distinction between black and white worship styles, and even beyond evangelical and mainline liturgical forms. Juanita, a Latina woman, said, "I'll probably start crying because I'm so touched and so moved and its so wonderful and so beautiful, it's like wow... it's beautiful. Everybody worshiping together." Tears well up in her eyes as Juanita starts crying as she recalls the memory of worship. "Everyone is singing; it's just wonderful, you can just feel the Holy Spirit there." Her personal experience occurs amid the corporate gathering. An Asian woman said, "I am experiencing something that's beyond just like being in a room full of other people. Like experiencing the presence of God." A white choir member said, "Whatever is going on inside I guess, I look to see what people are doing. I sense them worshiping too. Even like the people around me, I can feel as they are praising God...." So much that happens in church-service worship suggests a deep level of similarity of a corporately initiated experience. Ashley, a white member of her worship team, said, "It's really cool to hear your voice and hear everybody's voices come together and sing songs to the same person or being." Mike, an African American musician, described his ultimate worship experience as, "The experience of where everybody comes together, where it seems like everybody's on the same page, and you've just had this phenomenal experience. Everyone in the room is just lit up, and you're on a cloud."

Overall, it is togetherness that stands out as worshipers recount their experiences. The experience of full worship can be personally overwhelming, but it is not strictly personal. It is based on seeing oneself as fully immersed in worship as the others around one. Doug, a white member, said his most treasured moments come when they "sing the Lord's Prayer together." Another example comes from Mike, a white member of his choir, who said,

> We've developed this ritual that's been fun. At the end of service we sing "This Little Light of Mine." That's always really enjoyable for us, I don't know why, we always break out and do silly things. Just to be able to bellow it out; it seems like people's spirits are really opening up when people sing like that. Everybody seems to really enjoy that for whatever reason. It's a lot of life that comes out of that song. One member does this thing where she does this hop step back and forth. My wife really enjoys that and everybody's clapping in the congregation. When we finish there's this big kinda "whoop" and our music director sometimes will bang out some really neat version of that on the piano. It's fun when you finish, everybody cheers. Touchdown! So maybe that for me is the most worshipful time.

Music and the Social Structure of Worship Experiences—Regardless of Ethnicity or Race

Listening to people narrate their naïve experience of worship consistently reveals the inherent social nature of worship. What initially appears to be spontaneous, very individualistic behavior turns out to be highly structured. The experience of worship requires the corporate setting of a church gathering to stimulate the conditions for individual worship to occur. So while every person learns to worship individually, they can only accomplish worship corporately. The following chapters show that the importance of race and ethnicity is not found in differing experiences of worship, but rather in the manner in which race relationships and notions of race pervade the planning and performance of worship services.[18] Rather than being a racially specific mechanism, music is a more nuanced phenomena that socially structures the individual experiences in church services regardless of racial or ethnic heritage.

Understanding how music works in the individual worship experience allows us to see why members do not expect music in a congregation to reflect their private aesthetic tastes or specific racial or ethnic preferences. My conversations and interviews indicate that members of churches seek out a worship experience and learn to worship from whatever music is present in a service. Rather than be bothered that the music of the church does not represent the music they hear in their cars or homes, the priority for them at church is "worship." Daniel, an African American in a dominantly Asian congregation, said he mostly listens to hip-hop music; nevertheless, "I'm still able to worship, I'm still able to recognize God and I'm still able to get into it, but if you're talking about personal preference then that's a little bit different." He and others are willing to set aside their personal preferences.

For our purposes, DeNora's work contributes an illuminating theoretical framework. DeNora writes that music can "afford a variety of resources for the constitution of human agency, the being, feeling, moving and doing of social life." DeNora finds that "music is an accomplice in attaining, enhancing and maintaining desired states of feeling and bodily energy (such as relaxation); it is a vehicle they use to move out of dispreferred states (such as stress or fatigue). It is a resource for modulating and structuring the parameters of aesthetic agency—feeling, motivation, desire, comportment, action style, energy." In understanding how music "works," DeNora writes, "Music is an active ingredient in the organization of self, the shifting of mood, energy level, conduct style, mode of attention and engagement with the world. In none of these examples, however, does music simply act upon individuals, like a stimulus. Rather, music's 'effects' come from the ways in which individuals orient to it, how they interpret it and how they place it within their personal musical maps, within the semiotic web of music and extra-musical associations."[19]

Describing "aesthetic agency," DeNora points out that "music is used as a catalyst that can shift reluctant actors into 'necessary' modes of agency, into modes of agency they perceive to be 'demanded' by particular circumstances." In the same way, worship as a particular mode of aesthetic agency demanded by participation in liturgy of services and music is utilized in order to shift participants within that particular circumstance. Although DeNora talks about this as a "musical strategy" for "getting ready to go to work" or "getting moving with household chores," the core process is similar to that of "getting ready to worship" or "getting into worship" or "into the Spirit." She goes on to say that "the creaturely ability to locate and anticipate environmental features engenders a kind of corporeal or embodied security, by which I mean the 'fitting in' or attunement with environmental patterns, fostered by a being's embodied awareness of the materials and properties that characterize his or her environment." The notion of "embodied security" allows for a person to "let go," as there is certainty about what's coming next. Musical patterns allow opportunities for a "synchronous connection with an environment." In other words, regularity and anticipation equals security.[20]

The notion of aesthetic reflexivity emphasizes that the vagaries and ambiguities of the self in modern life require people to use mechanisms to adjust or maintain the self despite "incongruities" and "clashes" between values and imperatives of different social spheres. While there are consumer markets that exist to help people maintain their religious selves,[21] individuals possess the capacity to self-segregate the meaning and purpose of music for their lives in different settings. In a word, music provides an aesthetic means for the management of the self in different settings in which individuals find themselves in modern society. Paula, a white member, said, "Even at home in my private quiet times, music definitely helps me. I will put on head phones and sometimes just pray with music the whole time. But it definitely brings me to a place where I am more able to, I think, connect, just closing my eyes and trying to focus...."

Recall above how musical entrainment involves syncing one's body in relation to music. Entrainment requires a routinization of both the body with the environment and depends on anticipation for what will happen next. The process described here might be conceptualized as *liturgical entrainment*. Through the process of liturgical entrainment, appropriating worship music becomes an inherent part of an individual's management of their religious self that includes a choice to enter into a musical sphere and participate in a communal experience of God. The choice to enter a church with a particular kind of music becomes a type of musical consumption that reflects the self. And what appears to drive these choices is less the corporate imperatives of the congregation (what we do together as part of our mission) and more part of personal aesthetic choices that reflect one's identity (what I do to actualize my own religious involvement). DeNora indicates that music is appropriated as a resource for the constitution of one's own self. Moreover, music can be used as part of a "self-regulatory strategies and socio-cultural practices for the construction and maintenance of mood, memory, and identity."[22] Worship music becomes an inherent part of maintaining one's identity as a Christian believer.

Both Arlie Hochschild and Timothy Nelson's discussions of "emotional work" describe how organizational circumstances can compel individuals "to configure themselves as certain kinds of agents, characterized and internalizing certain modalities of feeling."[23] DeNora continues by saying that people connect "musical works, styles, and materials on the one hand and modes of agency on the other, such that music is used, prospectively, to sketch aspired and partially imagined or felt states." She writes that music is considered part of the care of the self by thinking about how the music of a particular setting that might "work" for them.[24] The process of liturgical entrainment then is a transracial process that allows for a configuration of the religious self through liturgy.

"Latching" is another insightful term for understanding liturgical entrainment introduced by DeNora that represents the ability to get individuals to "latch on to music" or "get into" the affordances produced by musical entrainment. This points out that worshipers are not passive recipients of the music but are "active sense-makers trying to use or appropriate music, agents who try their best to work with available materials, who are engaged in human-music interaction." What's more, the "ability to shift and respond to semiotic cues is part and parcel of socialization into any institution, where one takes on organizationally sponsored feeling and action modes."[25] Miriam, an Asian member, said, "I'm experiencing the people up there... Rather than just being focused on God—It's less prayerful between me and God and more of a whole church worshiping together and I'm appreciating the musicians up there and their skill and all." Wendy, an Asian member of her choir, said, "With the musicians up front, I can actually see people in the sanctuary worshiping God. And that's so the whole focus." Jocelyn, a white member, said, "I also focus on the worship team, and if I see that they're worshiping too, then that helps me to get in that mode."

What happens on the platform during church services points to the most important person involved in the process of liturgical entrainment—the worship leader. As Andy, an Asian American member said, "It always starts with the leader." Understanding the role of the worship leader in structuring corporate worship is pursued in the next chapter.

5

The Challenge of Leading Multiracial Worship

> Our pastor is not a musician at all. He's not an aspiring musician either. He doesn't sing, he doesn't even really listen to music for pleasure even, and so he really relies on me for that.
>
> —STEPHEN, AFRICAN AMERICAN, worship leader

STEPHEN IS AN African American musician hired to his first pastorate as a worship minister. He had no previous experience in diverse congregations (coming from all black churches), yet his race and musical training seemed to give him the qualifications to serve as the music minister in a large, white-Hispanic-black church. His ability to conduct worship services was important, but the emphasis on being hired was not just on his musical skill but on the promise that he would further stimulate the diversity of the congregation. Hiring a musically sophisticated African American worship leader was, therefore, strategic for the goals of his congregation.

Behind Stephen's staff position lies an important assumption: Stephen's pastor believes music is a key component for stimulating diversity, specifically the music resulting from hiring a black pastor who will incorporate a number of ethno-racial musical genres into the worship services.[1] "My pastor really sees the priority of different styles." Attempting to fulfill his task, Stephen told me, "I will bring things to him, and I'll say I was thinking about this or that song." Ironically, Stephen spoke about the utter lack of musical sophistication of his pastor, saying, "Our pastor is not a musician at all. He's not an aspiring musician either. He doesn't sing, he doesn't even really listen to music for pleasure even, and so he really relies on me for that."

Worship Leaders Carry the Burden of Diversity

Stephen's story accentuates a consistent finding throughout my research, namely that worship leaders, music directors, and church musicians who design liturgical processes bear much of the weight for the perceived corrections and visionary expectations for diversification. Worship leaders are to use their structural position of power in the congregation to actualize a shift in the demographic composition of the congregation. Yet, carrying out the mandates of their pastors and the (often capricious) desires of congregants in the way each believe they should be accomplished for the work of the church becomes an impossible task. First, even the best trained musicians do not have the versatility to switch musical styles quickly, repeatedly, and with variety, in addition to being able to recruit, lead, and conduct less-trained volunteers, who are often expected to come from various ancestral backgrounds and play multiple musical genres. Second, worship leaders are not prepared for issues of diversity. Indeed, the common solution of hiring a black worship leader (like hiring Stephen) sidesteps more serious considerations of how to truly accomplish racial diversity. In short, although worship experiences are not distinguished by race, the challenge of leading worship by both lay volunteers and full-time professionals is consistently complicated by race as they implement ill-conceived diversity efforts with little support, no training, and often only obligatory enthusiasm.

Music ministers are central to the study of music and worship because they become nexus points within diverse congregations by virtue of their role. Not only do they occupy a structural position of being responsible for worship, but also they are expected to be "experts" in all aspects of music and worship in their congregations. Yet, several of the leaders I talked to felt ill-prepared for the roles. Mark said, "I've had to learn a lot...I think a lot of worship leaders don't have training from either going to seminary, or things like that." Whether music ministers truly understand issues of music, worship, and diversity or not, they are expected to be experts on their interrelationship, and much of the discussion about worship and music in achieving diversity revolves around buttressing the expertise of these leaders.

The rise of seminars, conferences, and books on multiracial worship geared toward worship leaders signals an ambitious attempt to build a comprehensive "expert system" on music and diversity, a repository of technical knowledge that can be used by worship leaders in a wide range of actual contexts. The assumed decontextualization of processes of diversity is inherent to this process. According to Malcolm Waters, "An expert system gives guarantees about what to expect across all contexts."[2] In the context of globalization, an expert system is intended to provide a means of accomplishing things without regard for context. Music ministers, therefore, are expected to understand such issues regardless of specific context and to be able to achieve significant diversity even in spite of context. With the proliferation of "experts" on worship and diversity, we are seeing a radical institutionalization of a form of knowledge that overly determines the proper look of diversification and how it is to be achieved, creating a narrow form of legitimacy for diversification that is accepted and even seen as proper.

The Demand for "More Color" in Music and Musicians

Worship leaders constantly negotiate between the competing demands of the pastors they follow and the desires of the members they serve. For these leaders—many of whom are volunteers giving only a few hours a week—the goal of "quality worship" is first and foremost. Yet, stories from worship leaders reveal how the continual challenge to stimulate engaging worship experiences that "lead people to God" and "prepare hearers for the Word" is consistently complicated by the added imperative for racial inclusion.

After serving in several churches, Brian arrived at Celebration Community Church, a fairly new church currently meeting in a high school gym. Brian is a laid-back, generally happy person who takes his responsibilities for three services every Sunday in stride. He loves music and spends much of his time reviewing new music, meeting with members of his worship team, and preparing song sheets, instruments, and orders of service for the upcoming weekend services. His priority every week as a worship pastor is to make worship "engaging," where people "seem to be touched by what's going on. It's not just what's happening onstage. It's just a community kind of thing. People are actually physically involved, and they're actually singing, they're not just listening."

Brian was hired because of his past experience with what he called "multiethnic churches," including "mostly Anglo multiethnic or mostly Asian or more African-American churches that were multiethnic." His pastor expects Brian to use his "expertise" to build on the level of diversity the congregation had already achieved. Yet despite Brian's extensive experience, he was befuddled during our conversation in trying to define or describe what "diverse worship" means. He knew what it wasn't—it couldn't be "manufactured." He said, "I've been in situations where we tried to manufacture multiethnic worship. 'Let's do a Latin song, let's do a black gospel, or let's do this.' And then you're doing things that are outside of who you were musically." He found such attempts to be ridiculous. Brian finally said, "I don't know what multiethnic worship would be like. Churches will become multiethnic, but I don't know at the point where the music changes. I don't really know."

Jodi is another worship leader who was hired with a "mandate." I asked how the mandate was phrased. Her pastor told her, "You're going to change everything about worship, and you are going to do it as fast as possible." He told her she was "to come in and change the worship culture of our church," adding, "I believe God wants us to be a multicultural church and that means that we have to break out of our mold of what is most comfortable for our congregation to reach out and to worship God in other ways." Jodi described her task as bringing "a more expansive view of worship," a vague desire that translates into racialized notions of what qualifies as diverse worship. Essentially, Jodi was hired with the understanding that worship music is a tool—"it's an incredible tool that God uses"—to stimulate diversity more efficiently, specifically by incorporating a broader range of racial-ethnic styles in the services. Yet, Jodi's pastor was not quite clear on what "qualified" as diverse music and left her to make all the decisions. In the process of being hired, her pastor told her, "I'm not going to get into your business in music at all. Because that's your thing. I have no expertise there."

What emerges from Stephen's, Brian's, and Jodi's stories is that the production of worship in diverse congregations is not the result of the individual talent of the worship leader; rather, music directors and worship leaders are caught within an organizational system in which a variety of desires and demands are pressed upon them. Yes, these worship leaders have a value for diversity, like Jodi who said, "I came to this church because it had the vision of being multicultural." And the sense of working together in God's ministry can be exhilarating, as Jodi said of her pastor, "We have been an amazing partnership, an incredible blessing." Even so, Jodi, Brian, Stephen, and all other worship leaders I interviewed are accountable to the demands and perceptions of their lead pastors. As a result, just as members of the congregation place their own demands on worship leaders to facilitate a "good worship experience," the lead pastors of the congregation also place their own authoritative demands on the work of worship leaders.

Racially and Ethnically Targeted Music

Early on in my interviews, I was confused when a music director said of his lead pastor, "He never tells me what to do musically." Up until that point in our conversation, it was obvious that the congregation's head pastor had definite desires about music in the services, specifically the expectation that services exhibit "non-Anglo" styles and sensibilities by being more "black" or "Latin." In talking about his reactions to musical worship, this music director said, "Pastor will say if he likes it or not." In these few words lies the source of the anxiety faced by worship pastors told to stimulate diversity through worship. Worship leaders are given broad, "visionary" imperatives without specific direction of how to fulfill them. Since lead pastors cannot expect the attendance of a congregation to further diversify overnight, the weight of evaluation comes in assessing the "sound" of the music. Mandated diversity through music coupled with unclear standards of assessment leaves worship pastors scrambling to clearly demonstrate diverse musical styles *in a way that their lead pastors will recognize as legitimately diverse*.

Music directors and worship leaders commonly report how the imperative for racial and ethnic diversity comes directly from their lead pastor. Vincent said, "Pastor brought me on with the intention of really changing the style of worship at this church." The difficulty lies in the ambiguity of the demand itself. It seems that lead pastors carry an intuitive sense of what qualifies for them as success. One lead pastor told me directly, "I really believe that the way we are doing the music has a huge potential to help diversity they congregation." In about one-quarter of the congregations, this demand on the part of head pastors translated into particularly strong opinions about style of music. Most often the demand for diversity by pastors encourage their worship leaders to invoke stereotypical styles that will satisfy their "bosses" that initiatives for diversity are being faithfully implemented—regardless of their eventual outcome.

The expectation of racially and ethnically targeted music is explicit in many of my interviews with worship leaders. For example, Jodi believed she was successful in fulfilling her pastor's mandate because of the prevalence of recognizable, ethnic-based musical rhythms that can be heard in the worship services:

> Music is hugely instrumental in actually changing a worship culture at a church. That's primarily the biggest instrument of changing the culture because it's so much easier to identify, like, "Oh, that's Latino music. That's got a little Bossa Nova; that's got a little bit of salsa. That sound is African American because I can hear the little R&B gospel thing. Oh, that's the white church. I can hear a little bit of high church in there. I can hear a little bit of pop." Or "I can hear a little bit of jazz

> in there." Or whatever it may be. So, the ability to identify music by cultures is infused into our culture.

Following through on pastors' mandates, congregational leaders like Jodi fall into the acoustic trap of equating diversity in a congregation with the ability to distinguish presumably ethnic-based musical styles in a worship service.

Of course, not every worship leader agrees that introducing musically distinctive genres is the key to diversification. Some worship leaders saw the attempt to intentionally "color" the service through music as "insulting" to the people church leaders are trying to reach. Brian said, "I've been in that situation before where we're trying to reach a certain target [of race and ethnicity], and we try to become something, and I think it's insulting to people. And it doesn't work very well because you do less, the quality is really bad, and you're playing karaoke that you can't really play or trying to play styles you can't. It is insulting." Jeremy, a white worship leader, believed diversity should not be forced through music but rather that music should emerge naturally from type of people already in the congregation, saying, "It really should be the diversity in the church that affects the music." He told me about a congregation that was "very Caucasian" that decided to shift their music and "get some different people up front that are different races" as a catalyst diversify the church. "I don't think that it really did it," he concluded.

While the demand for specific ethnic-racial styles is not universal to the orientation of worship leaders, there is a universal expectation that worship leaders produce sounds that would both accentuate racial-ethnic diversity as well as inspire more diverse racial-ethnic attendance. Even within their lead pastor's oversight of worship, these music ministers will translate those demands into terms that make sense in their own experience. When Vincent was brought on staff, his pastor wanted music that connected to African Americans. But, rather than isolate the imperative into a racialized dynamic, Vincent interpreted the demand into a broader understanding of worship as a whole, saying, "Pastor wanted something 'soulful'—not referring to a genre but referring to connection with the soul. That has been my experience of worship, knowing that there have been times where, you know, God has met us right where we are. And the sense of Spirit was so heavy. In my mind, I try to let that be my paradigm of worship and just have a very real and deep worship time."

In conversations between Vincent and his pastor, "soulful" is the term his pastor used to describe the worship he wanted. Despite Vincent's reinterpretation of his pastor's words, I knew through interviews that by "soulful," he meant that it would have connections to African American gospel and R&B styles. His pastor wanted racially tinged music. However, Vincent quickly reframed the discussion for himself to gain a footing on what kind of worship he could do. He did not know how to do African American styles of music and had little desire to even attempt it. So instead, Vincent contextualized a racially specific demand (as "soul" always means "black")[3] into his understanding of meaningful worship that met his own personal standards. Worship leaders, then, emphasize the quality of the music; the lead pastor emphasize the connection and retention of people into the congregation as a recruiting and evangelizing mechanism.

The Core Task for Worship Leaders

The distinctive role of the worship leader in the multiracial church is universally acknowledged and variously defined as "leader," "chief worshiper," "enlivener," and "pastor," all labels which are intended to elevate the spiritual formation of a congregation through musical worship. Jeremy, a white worship leader, described his role saying, "There's a responsibility to be 'on,' to lead, to give people direction, and to direct people towards God, and to be a place of engagement and model some of that stuff." Whether as full-time personnel or as part-time volunteers, the music minister is solely responsible for programming, personnel, and placement of various elements in their (often multiple) weekly services, including recruiting, preparing, and conducting the liturgy. Their primary role is to design and manage the liturgy in services in the attempt to stimulate every person's connection to God. Because there is an ongoing attempt to interweave the music and liturgy of the service with the lead pastor's messages (and often their administration of elements of communion), there is a careful back-and-forth weaving between the intent of the head pastor's messages and the worship leader's management of the "flow" of the service. Some music ministers describe this in terms of "preparing people's hearts," meaning the emotional preparation of listeners so that the pastor's talks can have the maximum spiritual impact.

Patricia, an African American music leader in her congregation, said she understands how music takes an important place before sermons. "One of the reasons that the music always comes before the message is because if the music is good or decent, it sort of puts you in a receptive mood." The prominent placement of music before message is true for all congregations, even in the most "high church" congregations which orient more toward the church calendar (observing "Lent," "Pentecost") or follow liturgical reading schedules. Even in these more "liturgical" congregations, music ministers attempt to bring cohesive themes in music that mesh well with the intended thrust of the pastor's message. All of the churches ideally know something about the pastor's message for each service, and try to connect with the theme. But most do not fulfill this ideal situation as pastors most often develop their messages (or "finish it up") the week prior to services, and the need for planning, rehearsal, and preparation for services does not allow for a coordinated response to their pastor's message. Mark is one of several music directors who said, "What usually happens, even though he'll send the sermon passage that he's speaking on and the title, a lot of times it has *nothing* to do with what he's talking about. You know what I mean? It's just a title that's thrown out there, and so even though you might plan to find something that might fit with that, you're like, "Man, this song would have been a *great* closing song" or whatever." Often, the need to print the bulletin beforehand (hymn numbers, lyrics, placement in service) drives the deadline for deciding music.

Considering the process of decision making by worship leaders is important because ultimately it is the worship leader or music director who decides how the worship is structured, the music incorporated, and the style (pitch, volume, rhythm) in which it plays. While maintaining and even expanding the racial and ethnic diversity of their congregation is a priority, for all of the music ministers I interviewed, *diversity is always secondary* to the goal of cultivating a worship experience through music. Mona, an African American music director, said, "I do try to incorporate some of everything in the worship set. I try to put a gospel song in there, a contemporary song, a hymn. Yeah. But I can't honestly say that I try to think about the diversity—I just think about the songs and what I hope and pray that will draw people closer to God." Stephen said, "My first goal, I want to see people being engaged, that they had a sense of connecting with God." Ken said, "The first reason for worship is to bring us in the presence of God." A choir director flatly declared, "I would almost [rather] sacrifice the diversity than sacrifice people's experience in worship."

Too Busy to Worship

The worship leaders I spoke with have expansive notions of worship and bring their own standards for "proper worship" into their congregation. They are uniformly far more articulate about "worship" than they are about "diversity." Worship leaders are the most articulate and the most reflective on the place, function, and design of worship music. For Mona, not only does every song represent opportunity to worship, but also "in between those songs, I'm encouraging them to worship. I'm encouraging them to pray. I'm encouraging them to call out to God." Kathy said, "Something that we are concerned about is that we engage people so that they come to worship to worship, not that they see as the music part of the service—The ministry of being able to meet God in a musical place, to engage intellectually, to have prayer, to get the whole experience." Daniel simply stated, "We sing to God." Vincent said, "It's not the time of singing. You know, it's—worship is your personal expression of your relationship with the Lord." Kathy indicated her desire for her church, saying, "All I really want the music to do is be real and have it express a true relationship with God." Mark said, "I try to find songs that really reflect God, either His character, or as a responsive song, who God is and what He's done for us, and we respond with praise." Ted said, "My only goal as a worship leader is to focus people on God." John said, "The music is always about God."

No worship leaders see themselves as merely performers. "It's not about performance," several told me. And all of them stress that they are not about playing weekly "concerts" or playing music for passive listeners. Musicians distinguish between playing for worship services and playing music outside the congregation. Will, a white musician, said, "If I'm playing a show or playing for somebody in just any old club or whatever, then you can't connect with the audience. When you're worshiping with the church, you know that these people's hearts are more or less tuned the same way yours is. So that is something that is different about it for me, knowing that everybody there is at least endeavoring to lift their hearts up to God and knowing that what I'm doing is contributing to that and pushing in that direction." And yet, the arrangement of sanctuaries and auditoriums, the placement of leaders and their instruments, and the general prominence of their activity in the space of 90 to 100 minutes position music ministers in up-front, high-profile, and highly conspicuous places. The structural placement of worship leaders put them in central positions to guide and direct the congregation.

Consistently, leaders and attenders both agree that worship is dependent on the sincerity of those leading worship. The performative aspect of worship involves leaders who are actively guiding the complexities of the service while maintaining a purity, an earnestness, that communicates sincerity and authenticity to the congregation. As Andy, an Asian member, said, "It always starts with the leader, just like with anything else, not just talent-wise but a lot of times you can sense the sincerity, if they're into it, it's very evident, and it all trickles down into...everything from the way they're up there active and moving, to the words they're saying. The bottom line is how sincere are they when they're up there."

Worship leaders understand that "authenticity" is critical to the cultivation of worship in the people they lead. Worship leaders are to be "free" but not spontaneous, and "prepared" but not polished. It's a simple formula: doing music that is a "performance" or "showy" is bad, while being "expressive" or "authentic" is good. The formula is simple, but the attempt to strike that balance demands a high level of personal awareness and self-monitoring. Singing or playing in a "performance" mode that is "showy" and accentuates musical skill is to be avoided. Worship leaders who "indulge" in such actions (too many solos, long stretches of guitar licks or piano chords, or overly ecstatic swinging or jumping on the platform) provoke criticism both from members and from their head pastors. And volunteers who indulge onstage for the sake of performance will also be chastised and sometimes kept from being asked to play or sing on platform. Maintaining the delicate line between performance and authenticity is part of the hidden expertise of worship leaders in all the congregations I observed. While "performance" is ubiquitous to all performances (as it is inherent to the conduct of congregational services that skilled and prepared use of music is expected), it is nevertheless believed that "performance" does not accomplish anything in terms of proper worship. Worship is to be seen as a relationship between humans and God.

Worship leaders are usually successful in being perceived as sincere worshipers. They are special people who routinely accomplish worship. Wendy described leaders and other vocalists in her church: "Theresa, when you hear her praying, you can just see that she is talking to her Father. [Voice breaking, very emotional]. And when Joe—he has a favorite hymn, "The Old Rugged Cross," and when he sings it, it's just very—You can feel his heart. Well, you know where his focus is. And Sam is more of the older—not older, he is still young—he has a different worship style but it brings you before God again. He is just very soft and meditative and just helps you to focus on God. It's a whole different style." Overall, the perception of worship leaders and their fellow church musicians is that they are free and uninhibited. Foster, an African American member, said, "When the musicians are out there and it seems like the musicians have caught the flow, they are just up there worshiping God. They are diehard musicians, and when they catch the spirit, they are gone, they are off." They are consistently perceived to be, in a sense, the best worshipers in the building.

Although attenders usually consider anyone on the platform to be the most worship-full, in my interviews with worship leaders and church musicians I found the reality is quite different. Jane, a white former worship leader, said, "Of course, I'm not always a 100% being able to worship at the same time as I'm leading." Vincent said, "I would like to say all the time I do, but that's just not true." When I asked Jodi if she experienced worship when she's leading, she said, "No. Not usually. Because I'm implementing everything. I'm sort of the director [of a] production. There are moments when I'm completely lost in worship and completely oblivious. It's just that I'm also aware that I'm also making sure that each of the elements are ready to go and things are happening." Brian said, "There are times when I'm able to worship when I've spread a song out or do something where it [is] something that doesn't have any technical stuff going on or whatever, but most of the time I'm not able to really engage." Brian continued,

> I'm the producer, the programmer, the whatever, and even bigger churches where I've had a staff that helps, I'm still the bottom line guy, and I've got my set list on the floor with what's going on, and I'm thinking of what's next and even in the middle of the song thinking what's next.... Partly because of my job, and the responsibilities and also partly because I'm just a really high detail person. It's hard to cut it from my brain because I know I'm responsible for these thousand people or hundreds or however many are there and then all the people onstage to make this train go down the track and not derail. It's a sacrifice that I make. I'm leading them to worship, but I'm probably worshiping less than everyone else in the room. Just because of my role.

Jeremy, a white worship leader, described his experience up front, saying, "Definitely a lot more going on in my mind and spirit when I'm up front leading... I'm aware of leading the band and what's going on and giving them cues and where we are in the song and the transitions that are coming and the transitions we just did. Also trying to be aware of what's going on in the room to get a sense of what's going on and not have to feel like I have to stick with the format of the songs." Kristy, an Asian choir director, said, "It's distracting with so much going on and some of the arrangements are really complicated, and I have to sing and play—It's hard for me to concentrate." Francis explained the difficulty of experiencing worship, saying, "Because I work all the time, I'm lining up the next piece of music while the prayer's going out, I'm always working ahead, so that I can instantly start... So my moments [of worship] are one-thirtieth of a second moments when I'm suddenly touched. But moments of real worship are very few and far between for me." Paul, an

African American who assists in planning services, said, "I produce two weeks out of a month and so usually I'm working on a Sunday morning trying to provide that experience for others. And that's something I sacrifice in my service too, so that others can come to Christ and experience that worship."

Gabe, an Asian member of the worship team, explained the two-sided aspect of being responsible for worship, "Entering it is a lot easier, but getting distracted is a lot easier too." Steven, black member of the worship team, said, "Obviously my job entails a bit of distraction." The focus on worship in some ways allows a more ready access to an experience, yet the responsibility for worship simultaneously leads to quick distractions as soon as something appears to derail the experience. Gabe said, "I'll be singing, but if something is off or anything, I'm like 'What's going on?' I'm not even thinking about the worship." He said, "Because I am on the programming team, I'm on staff, it's easy to be critical about what's going on." Michelle, a white choir member, said about her worship experience: "It's probably better when I'm not leading. Because we learn a lot of parts. We have to remember what verse is coming before which verse and sometimes we have to do solo type stuff or we have parts, especially on Vincent's team. Like we could have six parts going with a group of like eight or ten of us. So there's a lot to remember. So sometimes that takes away from the worship experiencing because I'm focusing so hard, remembering what I'm supposed to be doing."

Being conscientious to sing or play properly gets in the way of releasing oneself into worship. In other words, the process of "letting go" is more difficult when one has responsibility for helping lead worship on the platform.[4] Larry said, "Personally, I've got my mind on a thousand other things. . . . If I'm still dotting I's and crossing T's, it's hard to be calm and disengage." Jonas usually plays the drums but said he experiences worship far more when he is working on the sound board at the back of the auditorium. "I guess when I'm on the board, I can allow myself to be really involved in the worship because I don't really have to worry about so much. So I know everything is fine, and it's just kind of a sense of relief and I can just really get into it. I don't think so much about the music, I can just naturally feel it and be able to play along. I guess the thing is I'm not as—I don't have to worry about chords or notes. That way I can really concentrate on the worship." Others also distinguished from when they operate as "a worshiper instead of a worship leader," and when they get a break from leading, as Bob said, "I'm free of other responsibilities, so that's probably why it's a fuller worship experience." Mona summarized, "Leading seems to be whole different experience than [being] down in the pews and just worship[ing]."

In short, with respect to the experience of worship leaders: the person most responsible for worship is the person least likely to experience worship in the service. Yet since their responsibility involves being good worshipers themselves, their personal standards of excellence make them highly self-conscious when up front. Mona said, "I never want to be up there and not be fully into worship. That's one thing I never want to do... because that is so fake. That is such a fakeness. I have to be fully into what I'm doing. I can't lead somebody else into worship if I'm not into worship myself. How can I?" Monique, a Hispanic worship leader, said, "It's great accountability for me to be down on my face before God before I get up there. I am really listening and having to tune myself to God and [be] sensitive to what He is doing within the congregation, really paying attention to what's going on and leading accordingly." Monique believes this attentiveness accentuates her worship, "Just really listening, *really* listening, and really trying to pay attention and really focusing on what we are doing." These few were exceptions; for nearly all other worship leaders, the attentiveness to leading is a distraction from personal worship.

The demand for being in full worship leads to unintended anxieties. Wendy, an Asian choir member, was thoughtful in saying, "Of course, I still have my personal anxieties. You know, I don't want to be a distraction." Kathy, a white worship leader, said, "Obviously it is much more personal when I'm not up, because I can sort of go off in my own zone and I don't have to play by the rules." Mark, a black choir director, said leading the choir was a distraction. "I am concerned about who's going to show up, are we going to have a choir, do I pick music that they can sing, are people going to feel what I hope they feel with this music, etc...." Melissa, a white member of the worship team, said, "If I had to pick something that would hinder [my worship], it's when there's a clear mistake or I mess up on the words or something that sets me back to reality a little bit, but that's not to say that I would be any less worshipful." Daniel considered his playing in the band, saying, "If I've practiced enough and feel comfortable, then I'm not so conscious [or] worried about playing the right cords, coming in on the right beat or wondering 'Am I going to mess up in front of all these people?' "

The challenge of "distraction" is different from merely being self-conscious about self and surroundings (as reported by congregants in chapter 4) but rather that worship leaders must have an organizational consciousness. Joseph, a white pastor, said, "There ar e moments when you're totally involved, but then a lot of times you are suddenly disengaged because you're worried about what is going on around you." One worship leader called it a "theater mentality." Their responsibilities continually propel them to pay attention to dynamics outside of themselves rather than solely focusing on their own internal emotional connection to the sacred. And this must be done while maintaining the personal integrity of a person who is truly worshiping God as they are leading others in worship. Among some worship leaders, the difficulty of experiencing worship is so great that they attend services at other churches in order to experience worship.

Three Phases of Every Worship Service

Worship leaders are responsible for guiding the overall flow of the service. Amidst the variety of musical styles and liturgical approaches in the multiracial churches I observed, I found a deep similarity in the underlying structure of multiracial worship services designed by worship leaders. The point is that worship music "does not just act on the body. Its effects are the result of a lot of work oriented to fitting musical material to movement style."[5] As a corporate activity, worship is social and organized. The overall structure of the worship services sustains a deep connection to the bodily coordination between music and activity. From the beginning of every service's initial "call to worship," worship leaders are bringing people into a proper orientation for worship. Congregational leaders work with those assembled to bring people in sync with each other to orchestrate a communal experience of worship.

In congregations, music is an important mechanism for bringing people a sense of togetherness because it is done all together. They are responsible for the "liturgy" of the service. The term itself is surprisingly difficult to define, but for the purposes of this study, "liturgy" will be used to mean the structured ordering of a worship service in any congregation. The roots of liturgy date from the earliest period of Christian assembly (and elements of that date well into the time of Moses), and there has been a strong "Liturgical Renewal Movement" since the latter part of the twentieth century. Here I wish to emphasize the manner in which worship leaders operate in ways similar to music therapists, military march leaders, and especially aerobics instructors.[6] These are all examples of roles that use music to coordinate human activity.

Music allows human beings to enact particular forms of agency. Music takes on meanings that become associated with emotions and, in worship, with our distance/closeness to God and our feelings toward the sacred. Daniel, a musician and pianist, said in worship, "There's always a different feeling with worship. It might be a feeling of weeping or something with joy. A lot of times I'm tearing up. I try not to bust out too much. I've got to be able to read the music still. Do you know what I mean? You try to hold it back but I get watery eyed constantly, almost every Sunday, trying to hold it back."

Referring to Roman Jakobson's theory of syntagmatic equivalence and Umberto Eco's notion of syntactic or grammatical signification, Richard Middleton describes how music provides a coordination or mapping, ways of framing and configuring, one's body.[7] In other words, "Music here is a medium of describing 'how'—how to move, how to think, how to include, how to begin, how to end, how to mingle."[8] For Middleton, music also contains 'secondary signification,' a wealth of connotations that motivate bodily conduct, "where it may be said to profile a range of subject positions associated with aerobic grammar... characterized by levels of arousal, emotional-stylistic orientation and bodily-gestural action such as the pace, force and style of movements and its stages of embodied agency."[9] Music therefore allows for an intimate, collective coordination of action. Worship leaders use music to coordinate action.

Similar to worship gatherings, coordinated aerobics in a gym also involves pre-scripted parameters of choreographed movements that are grouped into "chunks" and an overall sequential structure. DeNora continues, "Thus, and this point is key, over the course of a session, the musically implied aerobic body is configured, reconfigured, composed and de-composed as it is passed through and transformed by the series of changes that constitute aerobics and its grammar. Following aerobics' musical changes and the ways in which real bodies interact with prescripted musical bodily changes, bodily changes allow us to examine the body, moment by moment, as it interacts with, and is configured in relation to, music."[10]

Together, the design of a liturgical service constitutes an aerobic "grammar" that consists of certain phases, which are in turn characterized by the speed, degree of vigor, style of movement, and the mode of embodied agency required for the 'good' execution of the phase. Aerobic grammar, like worship times, is organized within "sessions" which are themselves "divided into sequentially organized stages, each characterized by a specific form of movement and energy level. To the extent that each of these components is associated with a mode of embodied agency, the aerobic actor is reconfigured as an agent in real time as he or she passes through the various stages of the session. This is to say that, at different times during a session, actors are configured as different types of subject/bodies, with, for example, greater or lesser degrees of cognitive awareness, emotionality and gender identification."[11]

DeNora writes, "Music is prominent as an orientation device within any aerobic session." In worship, as in aerobics, music is "placed in the foreground as a device of body constitution and bodily organization, a device upon which body coordination and conduct may be mapped." Musical devices include tempi, figures and gestures (rhythmic and melodic), harmonic structures, voicing, rhythmic/melodic packaging and chunking, and genre. In addition, many of the bodily moves are choreographed, "executed in conjunction with copious instructions from the class leader." It also involves a "return to cognitive consciousness... a returning of the class member to the embodied modality (the tension levels, energy and exertion levels and motivational levels) of everyday life in modern societies." Understanding the embodying aspects of music helps expand our understanding of music away from the merely acoustic elements.[12]

Music is a prominent orientation device within any form of liturgical worship. It serves to coordinate the corporate movements while providing a rich set of associations intended to direct people toward enthusiasm or contemplation, exuberance or meditation, over the course of a worship gathering. At times, music does not provide a "clear signal," but other times it does and can. Like aerobics, there is music that is produced and distributed commercially to be used in "highly specific circumstances" and for "particular segments" of the worship grammar. Indeed, worship music is catalogued by the intended affect such that worship music's position within the worship grammar is clear. Compact discs entitled "Celebrate" are designed for the "warm up" with a quicker tempo while "Meditation" or simply "Worship" are slower music for getting into "core worship." Variance in "beats per minute" express differences in intended use of the music. When it comes to music directors and worship leaders, they draw on these produced musical materials and resources in their own practical circumstances and modify them for their own liturgical use.

In aerobics, music defines the components of a session through its tempo changes and profiles bodily movements associated with each of these components. This profile is achieved through the ways that musical materials—melody, rhythm, gesture, genre—are deployed. In this sense, music is a device in the foreground, a means of affording aerobic entrainment. Here, music works at what Richard Middleton refers to as the level of "primary signification."[13] In the terminology of aerobics, DeNora describes the components as "warm up," "core," and "cool-down." DeNora writes, "Thus, over the course of forty-five minutes, music is used in an aerobic session to configure and reconfigure bodies and emotional-cognitive modalities as the aerobic agent is initially enlisted by the warm-up tracks (that feature emotional, romantic and fluid musical materials), launched on a trajectory of 'pure' movement during the core (where the beat occupies nearly all of the musical space) and 'cooled down' (recognitivized, resentimentalized, slowed down) into the more cognitive and less energetic mode associated with the precise forms of exercise at the end of the session."[14]

Translated into the terminology of worship, these aerobic components can be described as the three phases of an ideal-typical pattern for a musical worship set consisting of "orientation, "meditation," and "celebration." DeNora provides an idealized chart on beats per minute for music over time, suggesting that an idealized curve exists in the structuring of an aerobic session.[15] In the same way, an idealized chart can be constructed for the conduct of music in church services (see fig 5.1). Music provides an outline of a temporal structure of conduct over the duration of the worship service. DeNora notes in looking at aerobic workouts, certain rhythms were "like a hinge or switch" that shifted class members "into a mode of moving and orienting to musical materials commensurate with the core." The observation of such moves in accompaniment to music "illuminates clearly music's ability to profile movement style and to instigate movement trajectory." She noticed "rhythm thus provides a model for bodily action, one that also entrains the body and encourages it to begin a 'high impact' routine." Over the course of the class, "the music's quality changes: specific musical devices are introduced, gradually and imperceptibly, to induce participants to 'get into the rhythm'...." It is not only musical tempo but volume matters as well. A continuum between loudness and silence guides the states of worship. DeNora writes, "Played at full volume throughout nearly the whole of a session, the musical features of aerobics are thus designed to provide much more than mere 'backdrop' to aerobic proceedings, and they contribute much more than the all-important grounding of beats per minute."[16]

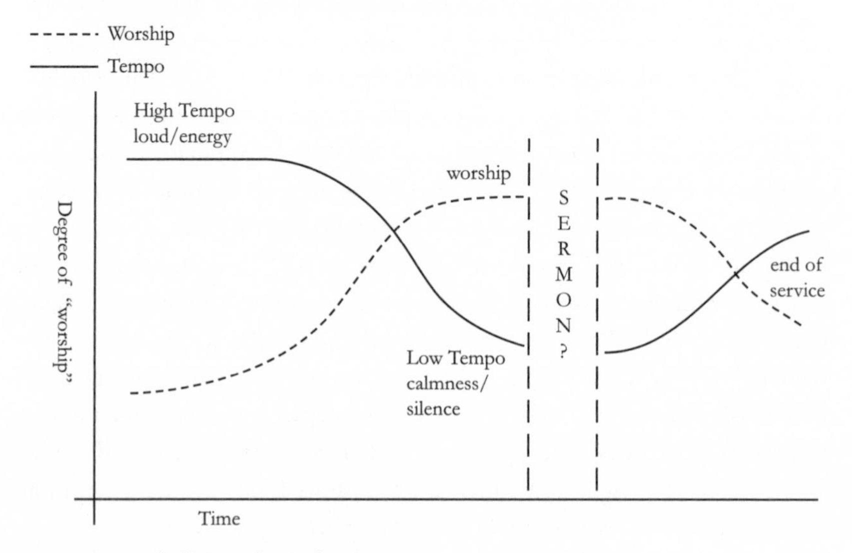

FIGURE 5.1. Ideal-Typical Worship Pattern

The ideal-typical worship pattern and its relation to the corporate experience of worship follows three phases. First is *Orientation*. Orientation is the start of the service and involves some type of opener, a "call to worship," that initiates, orients, and announces that the service has started. In "Free-Flowing Praise" services, it can be as simple as the worship leader saying into the microphone, "Good morning everyone, let's stand and sing together." In "Highly Liturgical" services, the call to worship can involve a grand musical opening through the sound of an organ or a choir. During the orientation phase, in both types of services attenders get themselves settled into a place in the room by finding a seat and setting their personal things down. Congregants stop talking and face front. In the orientation phase, the focus is on the sound of music and (if singing) the words being sung. The music is intended to be uplifting, with praise services having fast, upbeat, and "happy" songs in Free-Flowing Praise while in Highly Liturgical services it is more majestic, orchestrated, almost operatic in nature.

The orientation phase is usually quite short. Depending on the time available in the service, it can be as brief as two minutes, but not longer than ten minutes. Daniel, a white musician who plays piano, said services begin with someone praying: "It's very energetic, kind of 'get ourselves pumped up' kind of prayer, not a quite prayer where one person is talking and everyone silent but everyone is joining in, going 'Amen, yes,' and eventually it usually ends in applause or a clap among the choir kind of like, 'Praise God.' We praise Him before we even start the first song in order to invite the Holy Spirit there and be prepared from the first beat of the song." This is the epiclesis (sometimes spelled *epiklesis* from the ancient Greek ἐπίκλησις meaning "invocation" or "calling down from on high") or calling of the Holy Spirit into the service.[17] Larry, an African American, said, "We normally have four songs, but around the second song I'm pretty much engaged. The first song gets my attention."

In this "warm up" phase, the music is essentially "motivational," involving what Michel Callon calls "interessement."[18] These initial songs interpose church members between worship and non-worship "realities and so lead to their enrollment into the former, to launch them, imaginatively and physically, upon an aerobic trajectory, along the rhythm of aerobic grammar." Jeff said, "It's a shift of focus from yourself to God. By the time of about the second song, it ropes me in or gets me into that kind of spirit time or whatever, so I feel like I'm focusing." Kristy, a white worship leader, said, "Those really are just jumping off points to go to a higher level, but we need time. The whole thing with worship is that you need time to leave everything you just walked away from when you came in the door. You need time to allow God to work on your heart."

The orientation phase transitions to *Meditation*. While the orientation phase is intended to get people focused and centered on the platform, the meditation phase is intended for church members to center more on their relationship to the sacred. This is the portion of the service when worship leaders hope to have participants be "engaged," which means that their emotional connection to the spiritual aspects of the service is deepened in connecting their own private selves to God.[19] Wendy, an Asian choir member of her church, told me the congregation is encouraged to be more reflective: "They start off telling us to just kind of be quiet, be still and just seek God's presence." The music is more mellow and can even be quite calm. Often, the lights in the auditorium are dimmed. As the volume of the music goes down, worshipers are being encouraged to focus on the meaning of the words being sung and the collectivity of worship together. Wendy said, "I think the quieting of our hearts, our minds and prayer, intermingled with the worship and the scripture helps us to realize what a God we have."

Frequently, the mediation phase includes a point when all instruments stop playing; musicians on keyboards, guitars, or percussion are directed to take their hands off the instruments, as the corporate singing from the congregation becomes the only source of acoustics in the building. By turning off music from the platform, the focus is shifted on the experience of song through the congregation. Members in the auditorium hear each other and are drawn further into the sense of a collective group corporately worshiping together. Overall, the meditation portion of the service can vary from as short as seven minutes to as long as twenty.

From comments by both worship leaders and attenders, the mediation portion of the service is when their sense of "worship" is greatest. Hannah is among many who talked about how the meditation phase of the service is when the experience of worship was most powerful for them. "They turn the lights down, it's a little bit calmer, and it's a slower song." Members talk about a feeling of losing themselves and even being transported. Wendy said, "There are times when I just love the music so much that I am in a different place." Sometimes, the quietness of worship can be a lead into a transition to the head pastor's message for the service in a form that moves from quiet worship, to prayer, to speaker. While this is sometimes the case, most often the quietness of the meditation phase is juxtaposed with a louder, more energetic portion of the service. In other words, meditation can lead to a message but more often leads to a third phase of musical worship.

The third phase of musical worship is *Celebration*. In the celebration phase, musical worship is moving toward a close. It is the run-up toward the end of this portion of the service. Music is used to increase the overall energy of the room by bringing up the tempo and generating visible excitement about worship. In celebration, congregants are moved from inward focus back to a more outward focus. A fast, upbeat, energetic song is the most usual lead into the speaking pastor's message for the morning. The celebration phase delivers to the speaker an energized, enthused crowd that is "ready to receive the word" in praise services or to simply be in the right frame of mind in more liturgical services. (At other times, quieter and more meditative moments brings attentive listeners to the sermon.)

Seminary professor Robert E. Webber distinguishes between "sit down" and "stand up" music.[20] Orientation and celebration phases involve "stand up" music that rouses and stimulates enthusiasm, while the meditation phase involves "sit down" music that is more reflective and contemplative. Worship leaders plan for how to balance between these two ends of the continuum, and even members are aware of such differences. Cassandra, a white church member, reflected on her experience of the music of the service, saying, "I prefer softer tones of music before the message, because I think it helps me become more reflective, preparing my heart. It helps me to have quiet time in my heart, to allow confession to come through for myself. But the upbeat songs at the end, it's good to end that way, because you look forward to it and it helps you to leave, I guess, happy, or in a great mind perspective and a heart perspective too. So the upbeat songs, I think are good at the end."

The importance of a good ending places emphasis on how worship leaders also wind down services while keeping them an upbeat, inspirational time. DeNora notes that "shifting down" is important in the grammar of good aerobics, just as important as "shifting up" into the core. The shifting down moves to being "more self-conscious, and more sentimental." In this mode, "familiar melodies and lyrics are brought back to the fore, and rhythm is relegated to the background."[21]

The Continual Task of Introducing New Music

In talking with leaders about their regular responsibilities in the cultivation of worship within this structure, all talked about the process of introducing new music. Looking at the process of worship for both attenders and leaders, interviews repeatedly talked about the importance of familiarity. Laurie, a white worshiper in a "high church" congregation, told me she was not able to have a full worship experience because she did not know the music. Yet familiarity is not enough. When songs are too familiar, they are seen as repetitious and boring. Laurie said, "I find that singing a song I don't know doesn't move my heart like singing a song I do know. And if we sang the same songs over and over and over until we knew them, then it might have that moving effect."

Laurie is among many members who indicate a progression of experiencing worship that indicates a cycle in the music of the congregation. When first introduced, music is seen as "strange" and something to "get used to." As music is absorbed into a regular rotation in services, music is "familiar." DeNora describes this as the importance of "association." DeNora argues that music is not a "stimulus" but rather that individuals develop "associations" between musical sounds and rhythms and affective states. Francis, an African American woman, told me that in her worship experience "some of the songs that we have sung over the years have a special place in my spirit and my heart and it can set the tone for me in certain ways." Moreover, musical associations are particularly important when they connect with memories that relate to affective comfort, happiness, or relaxation. Musical associations are also connected with places in terms of the site in which music is consumed. There are thus associations "made between particular musical materials and other things (biographical, situational), more generalized connotations respondents associate with the music (for example, its style), perceived parallels between musical materials/processes and social or physical materials/processes (for example, slow and quiet, relaxed) and so on."[22]

Because various elements are involved in the creation of associations, it is not merely musical style, but also one's own situation as well as the social setting in which music takes place. DeNora rejects that associations occur regardless of context but rather emphasizes the importance of personal and structural context in the creation of associations: "A good deal of music's affective powers come from its co-presence with other things—people, events, scenes. In some cases, music's semiotic power—here, its emblematic capacity—comes from its conditional presence; it was simply 'there at the time.' In such cases, music's specific meanings and its link to circumstances simply emerge from its association with the context in which it is heard."[23]

So, musical familiarity is important in cultivating worship in that songs accumulate associations with congregational services that encourage the process of "letting go."[24] However, at some point, if the music is done over and over again so as to move from becoming comfortable to becoming repetitious, songs are experienced as predictable and mechanical such that these songs take on an affect of being part of the bureaucratic programming of services rather than a spontaneous encounter with the spirit of God. This leads us to an understanding of "the sweet spot" of worship (see fig. 5.2).

Worship leaders see a difference between the experience of congregational members who are "disconnected" because of music that is not known and the experience of boredom because of overfamiliarity. Worship leaders strive for members to be able to release themselves into worship, to get "lost" in the music. Mona, African American, said, "I wanted to let those songs envelop me. You know, I wanted to let them in." Music contains associations that allow the music to quickly (and efficiently) transform their experience from mundane to sacred. "It's that feeling that you are going to lose control. It's myself letting go to receive that ultimate worship experience. A song will start it, but ultimately it's within you. Letting yourself feel that." When her church introduced new songs, she found she needed to become familiar with them. "I had to kind of learn those songs. So I think that stifled me a little from getting that full worship experience and letting God come into my heart and letting the whole spirit work and just feeling that."

Music must be known well enough to be able to forget about it. Practice and familiarity can combine focus and letting go for musicians like John, a white musician, who commented, "When I am on and playing, I would say that it might be more full. Maybe because there is less distraction for me. Because I'm so into what's going on and to what I'm doing, that because I'm focused on one thing and making sure I go where the song needs to go and that's the only thing I have to worry about, for me, I think that is good because it also frees me up." John said, "It's interesting because it's like on the one hand, I am sort of there and paying attention to where the song is and what the leader is doing and that kind of thing, and on the other hand though, I am just so lost in the music and in my heart it feels like it's reaching out up to God while I'm playing. So I don't know, I don't want to say it's like euphoric or anything like that, but I just don't really know how to describe that because I'm in those two places at one time." John explained, "It makes it easiest to get into that experience when I'm comfortable with the songs that we are doing, and I feel like I can loosen up enough on paying attention to what is going on with the song and that kind of stuff, to be able to sort of allow my mind to switch onto what I'm doing for God."

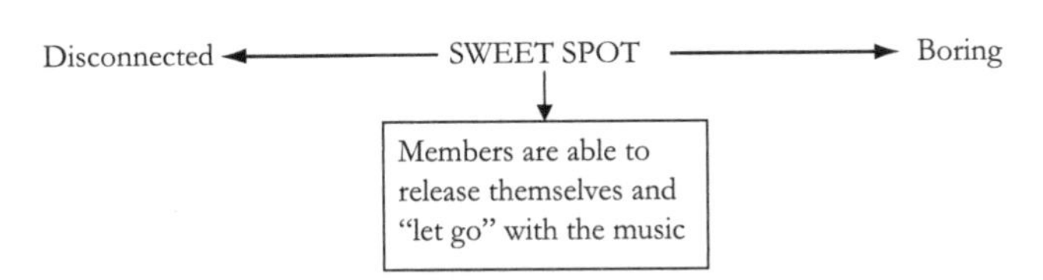

FIGURE 5.2. Balancing Familiarity and Innovation in Worship Music

Being "comfortable with the songs" is also key to being able to simultaneously lead worship and experience worship. Tina, a white member of the worship team, said, "I'm not thinking about anything else, usually probably my eyes are closed and I'm focused. Which doesn't happen very often because it's kind of weird to close your eyes on stage, I do it periodically, but I just kind of tune [out] everything else, and not necessarily look at faces or look beyond." Mike, a black musician, said, "You zone in on what you're doing so your whole world kind of collapses... I'm in the groove with the song. I don't have to pay attention to the song." Bernard, an Asian musician, said, "If it's fully happening, it's like I'm oblivious to other people around me... It's just free. It's just free."

Music must also be fitting enough into the congregation to avoid complaints. In the week-by-week planning of services, worship leaders face the criticisms of both their lead pastors and their congregations. Musical choices by worship leaders are rarely affirmed and often critiqued, and worship leaders learn to negotiate choices by avoiding complaints more so than by seeking complements. The most common source of conflict comes from congregational members. In her new role as worship leader, Jodi said, "Last year I probably got about nine e-mails a week with people complaining about the worship experiences." John said, "You are going to appeal to some people over here and some there... because not all of them are going to like it." When I asked him if there was any music that everyone likes, John said, "I wish there was."

The most important opinion leader in the congregation regarding music is the lead pastor. Older congregants are next, especially the ones who are long-time members. Not offending the older members of a congregation is a continual aspect of worship planning and transition. One pastor said, "You don't want to piss-off the old people." Many church leaders believe that age dynamics are an anchor that keeps innovation from happening more aggressively than church leaders would like. John said, "There are a lot of churches around here that are dying. The problem is that the people who are in control don't want to change. One of them had a congregational meeting recently and it was all about the organ. That's their biggest issue. One of the elders said, 'Those young people are ruining my church.' And I thought, 'That's the problem. He's thinking it's his church.'" In their minds, older and long-time members of a church do not provide *launch* points but *check*points for congregational change in music. Choices of style in services are often one of appeasing and not offending. Terms are couched in terms of quality, musical excellence, loudness, appropriateness, and godliness-sacredness. Comments are more often reactive, and suggestions for change are nostalgic, not innovative.

Music ministers are attentive to the criticisms they receive. Critique is ongoing, so worship leaders learn how to accommodate "complaints" in the course of the very public role they play in congregational services. Doreen said, "You know, Gerardo, I really don't want to be about pleasing people. I really want to be about pleasing the Lord and representing His kingdom. It's really hard when week-in and week-out you're getting stuff from people, "Well, that was too loud," or "Why can't we have more of this?" or "Why isn't there more of that?" because there's a tension between not wanting to just people please but at the same time do things that allow for people's hearts and souls to be opened to God."

In the midst of any discussions of religious conflict, my interviews did not indicate instances where racial issues were ever dominant. At no point did worship leaders or church members ever appear to complain about worship as having too much or an excessive use of types of ethnic or racially specific music. Although conflict over issues of race or ethnicity in music were not evident, several worship leaders and their pastors continued to attempt to cultivate music for church services that would appeal across racial and ethnic groups. In these particular cases, leaders worked from racialized assumptions rather than responding to specific desires or complaints from members about concrete issues.[25]

The Challenge of Worship Leading

Drawing on DeNora's discussion of aerobics instructors provides terms for understanding how music directors and worship leaders contribute to the design of worship using their own varying levels of "expertise," a combination of their accumulated knowledge and practical skills, to bring congregants into a collective experience of worship. These leaders "employ musical reflexive skills, they mobilize and deploy musical materials for specific purposes." I agree with DeNora when she states, "Music is an accomplice of body configuration. It is a technology of body building, a device that affords capacity, motivation, co-ordination, energy and endurance."[26] While the skills for leading worship vary from person to person, overall, the work of a worship leader, both paid and volunteer, is the preparation and production of a worship experience for gathered congregants. It is the overwhelming concern of worship leaders to initiate and guide attenders toward worship in the allotted time and space, and all other considerations are subordinated to this priority. Stephen said, "The way I look at it is that it's okay if this week we can get people wanting to worship God. Then the style becomes secondary."

The persistent goal for worship leaders is to foster fuller worship experiences in their parishioners, and not necessarily to enhance the racial and ethnic diversity of the congregation. Yet leaders are always satisfied when they see evidence of worship occurring across different racial-ethnic groups. Mark said,

> I think it's more just experiencing, not only diversity musically, just diversity, the diversity of God and celebrating that diversity. And one aspect of doing that is through music, the different channels of music that's out there—just to bring out these different elements of songs. Just to maybe incorporate one traditional-type hymn, whether you do a new arrangement of it or not, and bringing in a jazzy arrangement of a song, or bringing in a Latin element, or a black gospel element. Just to celebrate God's diversity, because I don't picture God sitting up there, going "I don't like this music, I'm not gonna listen to it." God's more concerned with the heart, and enjoying how we celebrate Him in different styles is to me more important. And a key element is bringing diversity into worship. I think the more we experience diversity in worship, the more we can connect to God. You know what I mean? No matter what your cultural background is, bringing those different elements can really help understand God more. So, to me, that's what's important about diversity.

More will be discussed in chapters 7 and 8 on this issue, but here it suffices to say that worship leaders and their head pastors bring many assumptions regarding the connection between race and music, ethnic orientations and liturgical forms, yet systematic analysis based on observations and interviews fail to justify the various assumptions brought forth. So, although church leaders carry notions of worship that guide their ministry activity, the actual workings between worship music and congregational diversity point to underlying structures of planning for worship that reveal how liturgical events in congregations create places for diverse people to interact, make relationships, and ultimately build corporate solidarity as co-members of their congregation.

6

Variety and Intentionality in the Design of Multiracial Worship

I don't believe worship music is going to make us diverse. You can't discredit it but then you can't say this is the element that's going to make it happen either.

—FRANKLIN, AFRICAN AMERICAN, creative arts team

ONE AFTERNOON, I traveled to a church near the center of Los Angeles where Terell, a worship leader in a mainline congregation, had expressed great enthusiasm for my project. "Race is so important," he told me over the phone, and we set a time for me to visit. I spent several weeks with Terell and his congregation, watching his leadership and experiencing their music. Terell is African American and had been the music director at the congregation for about five years. He spent much of his twenties and thirties as a jazz piano player playing bars and clubs in the United States and abroad, and found himself working in churches.

After leaving a paid position as a music minister at another church nearby, Terell offered to play Sunday services at his current church, which soon turned into a full-time job. The congregation is not affluent, and both his minister's salary and his financial resources for ministry are quite low, but Terell has an easy way of building relationships with others. Talkative, charming, and utterly committed to the beauty of sound, Terell actively networks with musicians attending his congregation and living in the city and draws them into expressing their musical expertise through church services and events. In hearing the congregation's live music and a few digital recordings he shared with me, I was impressed with the range of styles he played. "I can play all kinds of music," he said. But he was quick to say I should not be so impressed. Versatility for a musician is "a survival skill." His breadth of taste ranged from pop to classic, with a heavy dose of jazz instrumentation mixed in, and the spectrum of musicians introduced into the congregation is highly regarded. In his black-white congregation, hymns mingle with gospel, and a concert harp is just as much at home as an electric guitar.

When I asked Terell how he managed his role, he said the real work was not directing the music, but *selecting* the music. "I do the piano and such, but most important is choosing the music." Directing is the easy part; selecting is the challenge. He drew on his experience as a musician, saying, "The most important thing in jazz is to satisfy the people you are playing with." The back-and-forth feel between him and his congregation is subtle and complex. The conflicts are not readily visible, but Terell takes on himself the burden of maintaining racial harmony. "I try to do this," he said, "Have a European type of first song, then second a black song." Terell was clear that he thought of music in explicitly racial terms. "This is a very racial country. People look at music very racially." Even though he felt such separation is "really ridiculous," he stressed that the United States is caught in a fundamental racial divide. "You have two nations here," Terell said. The experience of worship is primary, yet he also believes the use of music in his congregation is critical to the management of solidarity as a sense of community is in part dependent on creating a balance of connection through worship.

Terell's management of music in racial terms brings to the center critical questions regarding the place of music in the management of religious solidarity. If Terell is right, then music becomes a vehicle for the management of social relationships. As Tia DeNora writes, "If music can affect the shape of social agency, then control over music in social settings is a source of social power; it is an opportunity to structure the parameters of action."[1] Racially diverse people who would otherwise remain disconnected or disaffiliated can be joined together on the basis of their connection (at least in part) through the sacred music available in regular worship services. I found myself asking if Terell's approach to music was typical. Are worship leaders uniformly concerned about the racial aspects of music and worship? How intentional are racial considerations in the construction of their worship services? For example, is the racial consciousness of Terell typical in the selection of music for all multiracial churches? Or are there other dynamics that govern the selection and performance of sacred music?

In the end, I find the focus on leadership intentionality and the demand for racial awareness typically discussed by scholars, "advice books," and church leaders like Terell to be flawed. It turns out that successfully multiracial churches vary widely in the musical styles used in services and the degree of intentionality for diversity present in the design of services. All multiracial churches are intentional about worship, but not all are intentional about diversity. Despite popular belief, intentionality in accommodating racial-ethnic groups based on racial awareness is not the secret to diversity. Nevertheless, we need to learn to recognize the sociological mechanisms inherent to the performance of multiracial worship services and appreciate the variety of approaches toward race and worship in multiracial churches.

Musical Style: Diversity, Variety, and Intentionality

The most prominent concerns publicly discussed among church leaders are questions about choice of musical style. Issues of music choice hinge on expectations of leadership intentionality, especially in acknowledging and raising racial awareness among worshipers. One of the most common approaches to worship music is speculation on the importance of style. Considerations of style include classic hymns of the faith, including negro spirituals (differentiated by denomination), with the most famous and most remembered hymns including "All Creatures of Our God and King," "Amazing Grace," "How Great Thou Art," "Holy, Holy, Holy," and "Rock of Ages." They also include contemporary praise music and recent gospel music. When discussing racially diverse congregations, considerations often turn to incorporating "ethnic rhythms" through instrumentals like a certain percussion for a Latin-Hispanic flavor. An associate pastor said, "If you try to reach African Americans, have a gospel choir, and have mariachi sounds for Hispanics." There is also an attempt to sing in different languages or add phrasing from other languages, especially Spanish or languages from the African continent like Zulu or Swahili. In practice, singing in Spanish is often done in the presence of bilingual people, while music from Africa constitutes an attempt to accentuate a global consciousness, usually a missionary imperative, by reminding people that Christian worship is happening in other countries as well. As one leader said, "The song words up in Spanish and reading in Spanish happens. On a couple occasions we may sing a whole song in Spanish because you're more comfortable with worshiping God in your own language and in your own style and in your own culture."[2]

In the cultivation of musical style, worship leaders can create different acoustic center points in the service time and alternate between them so that different styles can be played one after another, or leaders can overlap them to find a style where all of them can be accomplished simultaneously. In other words, in the general discussion of multiracial worship there is sometimes an attempt to have "diverse worship" where different styles happen in succession or an attempt to have "blended worship" that seeks to incorporate, interweave, or merge styles into a new sound. In addition, music can also be distributed over time such that styles are played on different days of the month. Some churches create special Sundays of the Month, or even Sundays of the year. One church features an annual "Super Salsa Sunday" with Latino-styled music and a "Super Soul Sunday" with gospel-R&B-funk-styled music, what was labeled "the African American flavor style of worship." At times, it may involve bringing in special musical guests, as when John, a white church member, told me how excited he was about a black musician performing African American hymns next weekend at his church, "He's going to bring some of his culture with him and it's going to be awesome."

The consideration of having different styles is based on the notion that different ethnic and racial groups require different sounds and rhythms to accomplish worship.[3] Many leaders actively incorporate a musical form of *ethnic signaling*.[4] One church leader said "the gesture" of musical style—even if it is bad—says to members "you matter." Even if the music is done poorly or the songs are sung badly, the "gesture" that it exists is believed to be important. Placing it in the service signals to congregants that church leaders value diversity in the congregation. George Yancey writes, "There is a subtle message that visitors to that church must either accept the racial cultural environment of that church or find another place to worship." He concludes, "Developing an inclusive style of worship is important because it signals a sensitivity and welcomeness to individuals of different races."[5] Playing different types of music is a symbolic expression of care and commitment. Joy, a worship leader, said, "If we really want to be hospitable to people who have different worship styles, we need to be intentional about music." She offered examples like "maybe playing pre-service music with a Latino beat to it."

Yet, different styles of music can alienate members of different ethnic and racial groups. A choir director was unsure of her worship leader's and lead pastor's demand for diverse music because of "a danger that you are running ahead if the congregation is not able to connect with the worship." For example, Yancey describes a church with "a distinctively African American gospel style." Because the worship "reflected the African American culture of the church," the church was racially homogenous. More interesting, Yancey asserts, "Having a predominantly black worship style was not conducive to producing a multiracial congregation." The church did not exhibit a welcome to nonblacks. "When a church limits its style of worship to only one racial culture, it is sending out signals about who is supposed to be comfortable at its service."[6]

Rebecca Y. Kim found in her study of Asian American ministries on a college campus that when blacks led worship with their "African American gospel style," whites left. She quotes a campus staff member: "Once the black student led, the style changed and as you noticed we also sang songs in Spanish, some of the white students just did not like it. They desire to worship in the way that is comfortable to them. They just weren't used to that style...." Students left to join another ministry that was white dominant. The "discomfort" was not solely among white students. Kim also reports that second-generation Korean Americans express similar moves toward homophily in worship, as one member said, "It is not like I can't worship with, say, a black person next to me, but it is just I am used to... being with Koreans all the time, you kind of get set... It is just more comfortable to worship with other Korean Americans."[7]

Music selection is a key element in liturgical planning. Churches have a high degree of flexibility within an overall ambiance of worship music style in the church. Yet worship leaders have as few as ten to as many as fifty songs that are done over and over again in a year's time. Churches end up singing just two or three dozen over and over again. This greatly simplifies the preparation of music since new music can be hard to teach and difficult to prepare and therefore not necessarily introduced every week. New music is mostly segregated to special music done by a subset of musicians (one player, one singer, or a small group) and rehearsals for new music often occur separate from regular worship music or choir rehearsals. It is unclear among church leaders whether to pursue "musical diversity" by introducing new music before having "attendance diversity." Kristy, an Asian choir director, said, "It's almost like the chicken or the egg, being which comes first. If you played black gospel music, would that attract more black people to come? Or do we wait until black people come first in order to do it?"

Not all church leaders welcome the attempt to diversify through new music in an attempt to satisfy racial overtones. David had doubts about the ability of churches to have equal representation among all racial and ethnic groups. "I don't know if there is a great way to have a megachurch with every nationality represented, hearing worship styles that everyone is going to connect to. I don't know if it's reality." Mark, lead pastor of a black-white multiracial church reflected on this practice, saying, "In a variety of churches, white churches try to bring in some gospel music, and then in some of the black churches they try to bring in some classical music. I always question the motives. I'm a little cynical. Behind that is something very, very good. But I was cynical about that because I wondered what the motives were."

While church attenders tend to assume worship leaders are intentional in designing services to achieve racial diversity, in actuality, the majority of worship leaders do not intentionally focus on race/ethnicity in the design or performance of worship music. This is similar to Yancey's observation, "Surprisingly, very few of the churches in the study made being multiracial a primary focus of their church." Nevertheless, Yancey suggests that intentionality is necessary and that churches must intentionally work toward sustaining diversity. "A successful multiracial ministry will intentionally work at becoming and maintaining its multiracial atmosphere." Again, Yancey writes, "Becoming multiracial is generally the result of hard work by the leaders and laity of integrated congregations. In those few instances where a church is fortunate enough to develop a racially integrated congregation with little work, effort is still needed for that church to maintain its racial mix."[8] Others also believe intentionality is necessary. Kujawa-Holbrook states, "Multiracial communities are not organic; that is, without intervention we instinctively build our congregations according to assumptions of racism and racial division rather than on a vision of justice and reconciliation."[9]

Intentionality is defined by purposefulness or willfulness. To be intentional is to be conscious of our actions and attempt to guide our actions by our intentions through paying attention to what we wish to accomplish.[10] As expected, there are congregational leaders who are highly intentional about ethnicity and race in the planning of worship services. Doreen, a white worship administrator, said the music of the services bring in a variety of "ethnic" musical influences, saying, "It's really an eclectic mix because I want to be deliberate about doing that so whoever is here is feeling that they are represented, that they are connected." For Andrew, the mixing of musical styles targeting different ethnic groups is critical for the church's diversity. The leadership of the church must be committed to playing a diversity of musical styles. And it should not be an occasional, half-hearted effort. It is not enough for leaders to think, "Well, I want to put a little bit of this." And then they will introduce one Spanish song of some sort. It is not enough to put a little bit of an ethnic "something" for diversity to happen. Andrew said, "No, they've got to be totally committed."

While there are diverse congregations that feature racially motivated diverse music, at the same time there are other congregations which are also multiracial who have no particular intentionality in their attempt to cultivate a musically diverse worship service. David, a white worship leader, said, "I love cultural diversity and I love being in the middle of it. I love to sing it, but I've learned to hate manufacturing it, and I just hate how it comes across." For

David, any attempt to isolate "ethnic" or "racial" musical styles and play those to accommodate or appease different racial-ethnic musical interests lacks authenticity. Such music is fake, and rather than bringing in diverse people will fail due to its lack of substantive connection to the real lives of people.

When I asked Dean, an African American worship leader, if there was such a thing as a type of music that every racial group likes, he said, "I wish there was." He thought it might be possible to include various types of ethnic-influenced music into services, but they had to be tamed or sanitized. This erases distinctive differences according to Dean, so that the differences no longer matter. For Dean, such fused music is also not satisfying to any particular racial group because it loses its base in the cultural circumstances of a particular people. When I told Dean about a church that believes Rock 'n' Roll is the universal rhythm and that anyone can relate to it, he said, "They are out of their mind." Dean believes that if the music is good, people can relate to the enjoyment of the performance, but they will not connect with the performance.

Jeremy, a white worship leader of another diverse congregation, also believed that the attempt to manufacture diversity through worship music was futile. He cited his own evidence, about a church "across town" who "wanted to do this gospel service." It was a "very Caucasian" church but they saw diversity there and there are some ethnicities in it that weren't represented so they "shifted the music" as a kind of catalyst to get diversity into the church. The effort was a failure. The story is part of his framework to avoid targeting racial and ethnic groups in the service. Angela is another worship leader who said, "I'm not geared to think racially. I'm not geared to think ethnicity. I just don't see it." When I asked Ken, a white worship leader, if there is any music that would universally appeal to all ethnic racial groups, he simply said, "I don't think so."

Philosophies Guiding Musical Choices in Diverse Churches

I found a variety of approaches to music selection among multiracial churches. To understand the philosophies that guide music selection among worship leaders, pastors, signers, and musicians, I categorize their decisions across two primary dimensions. The first dimension is the degree of racial awareness. How conscious are music leaders in considering race-ethnicity in planning the music selection for the worship gatherings? The second dimension is the degree of musical variety. How important are different types, styles, or genres of music in the worship gatherings? In answering these questions, I looked at responses from worship leaders, head pastors, vocalists, and musicians—all the people involved in guiding and performing the sacred music of their congregation. Combining both dimensions and distinguishing between leaders who have high racial awareness versus low racial awareness as well as leaders who emphasize exhibiting high musical variety versus a low musical variety yields a fourfold typology (see table 6.1).

Among the sample of congregations analyzed in this study, I found that about half of worship leaders bring no racial/ethnic awareness to choosing music. Depending on their commitment to musical variety, about half are *Traditionalists* who maintain a consistent style of music, while the other half are *Professionalists* who have a high value for bringing many styles of music into services and believe that ensuring the quality of the music helps the church overall.

When worship leaders design worship to appeal to a racially and ethnically diverse audience, they fall into two groups. In bringing racial-ethnic awareness to choosing music, about half of them are *Assimilationists*. Assimilationists tend to share a more generalized belief in the universal power of music in affecting individuals. As part of their philosophy of musical selection, they commit to one style of music believed to be universal. Assimilationists defend their choice of music style as best accomplishing worship among all people regardless of their racial-ethnic group. In contrast to Assimilationists are *Pluralists*. Pluralists are those leaders who are consumed with preparing and cultivating musical variety on the basis of appealing to different racial and ethnic groups. Although one-quarter of the churches in this study fall into this category, it is the pluralist approach that is most aggressively promoted in books and multiracial conferences to promote diversity. Pluralists believe music is racialized and will attempt to raise sensitivity to racial awareness. Music performance is driven by the attempt to enact a form of musical pluralism, a buffet of racially specific styles to provide every group a source of musical resonance. Among pluralists, incorporating diverse styles of music is

Table 6.1. Philosophies of Music Guiding Music Selection among Worship Leaders

	Low Racial Awareness	*High Racial Awareness*
High Musical Variety	Professionalists	Pluralists
Low Musical Variety	Traditionalists	Assimilationists

a critical means to enrich the program of music for everyone, not simply drawing in particular groups of people. So, while the philosophy of pluralism is not the one most commonly held by worship leaders, it is the style that is most popularly believed to exist among the worship leaders. Pluralism is therefore the philosophical approach to music that is most promoted in discussions in workshops, conferences, and publications addressed to worship leaders of non-diverse churches.

It is important to note that all musical forms in churches can "work" for worship, yet not all forms are promoted in every multiracial congregation. In addition, every congregation has "evidence" that their orientation toward music selection "works" since the evidence for diversity is "obviously" available for their observation in every worship gathering.

Professionalists

Professionalists in multiracial congregations are highly trained musicians who desire a sophisticated variety of musical sounds and rhythms in their church services. Professionalists try to integrate a wide variety of musical styles not necessarily with the intention of bringing in greater ethnic diversity, but rather to keep the music of the service of high quality. While these leaders regularly introduce a variety of music, everything performed has the same professional quality, which results in a type of homogenization of style. Professionalists have an abstract conception of "music" as a form of high culture that fuels the desire for the music is to be of high quality. Among music ministers who are Professionalists, music as a distinct arena of activity is something to be supported and nurtured.

Among Professionalists, the pursuit of a high level of quality on the style (or styles) of music is in itself an appeal to the universal human condition. Quality of music is a priority, not the racial or ethnic connotations that may be embedded within certain musical styles. Mike, a black musician in a Professionalist congregation, said, "I think that's what's awesome about music, is that it sort of transcends all that." Mike said, "I've never—race and music, I don't see that." Mike said, "Multiracial and music is kind of a weird concept because I would think good music is good music, playing good songs and putting some energy out there and doing it well." For Mike, the importance is in playing excellent music. "I think that's what's so beautiful about music, is it's so unifying, and the words and music touches your heart, and I don't see whether you're Japanese are black or Hispanic or whatever. I don't see where the difference is."

Traditionalists

Traditionalists like Angela, a white worship leader, say, "We don't cater to a cultural thing." Among these leaders, "Worship music is worship music." Another worship pastor said, "I do not see any evidence that songs we use are designed with an ethnic dimension built into them." Another African American worship director said, "I can't honestly say that I try to actively think about the diversity of the church as I plan worship—I just think about the songs and what I hope and pray that will draw people closer to God." Laurie, a white attender, said, "When you look at the congregation and you see five different cultures, I don't see that in music." Laurie added, "I don't think we are dealing with culture and diversity." Among traditionalists, there is no attempt to foster different styles. Instead, there is inertia of style established a long time ago. It is a simple, "common sense" understanding that the music that is found in services is the music of the church.

Authenticity takes on a specific meaning among Traditionalists. Lucy, a white worship leader, said, "All I really want the music to do is to be real and have it express a true relationship with God, and something that is compelling to bring them on and take them to another place in the music." Similarly, Raymond, an Asian worship leader, said there are people in his congregation who "want more Latin music, more gospel, more—just different kind of styles." He rejects a racially or ethnically targeted approach, saying, "Honestly, it's more about authenticity for me, it could be anything, whatever, as long as it's real and authentic." Don shares a conviction with other Traditionalists who said, "Good music is good music, regardless of what the style is, and everyone appreciates that." The style is not an "issue" for theses leaders because their only consideration is to foster worship in a simple, uncomplicated manner. As yet another worship leader said, "It goes back to being authentic."

Often Traditionalists believe the middle-of-the-road music that is at their church is appropriate and effective. This is the orientation used by Mark, a black choir director, to argue for the value and relevance of hymns, saying, "Hymns are important in pulling people together from all kinds of diverse backgrounds, just as important as reading the scripture or delivering the sermon." Michael, a black musician in another church, believes that "contemporary music... pretty much appeals to everybody." Mark said contemporary Christian music is "traditional enough that people feel comfortable with it, and it's simple enough to where everyone feels they can participate." The goal, as Mark stated, is "continuing a sense of community through the music, that is that in all the music that we play, it doesn't alienate anyone." The attempt to keep from "alienating" also fits into the orientation some churches have of appealing to the "unchurched." The priority is not diversity as much as bringing in people who are not familiar with church at all.

A white pastor believed that the middle-of-the-road contemporary music fit the congregation because the diversity of his church consisted of mostly acculturated ethnic groups who have become largely mainstream Americans. Jason said, "Even though we have ethnic diversity, people are acculturated. Most of the people who will be here are those who are closely related to Anglo [culture], and they aren't saying 'No, we're Hispanic,' or 'No, we're Asian.' They want this kind of music." According to Jason, contemporary "white" Christian music therefore fits the culture of his congregation. "They want this kind of music. They are comfortable here, and they are here because they are resonating with this style." One Asian male church member described the music, saying, "It's mostly just regular contemporary worship songs, maybe slightly jazzed up." It's all in the presentation. "Present it more so it would be appealing to that generation of people no matter what race they are." Others expressed a more surprising tone, as one drummer said, "One of the things I've noticed about this church, is how diverse it was. And I remember thinking the songs were too white and hokey."

Retha, a black female in a Traditionalist church, also distinguished between white and black styles of worship in churches, yet she resisted seeing these racial differences as significant for her own worship experience. Retha described African American churches as having "real hard core gospel with a loud, big choir. Even if they've got four people in the choir, it's loud and hard core." Retha immediately added a contrast, "As opposed to the white churches that tend to be more Integrity music (CCM) type worship." Yet, Retha does not insist that African American music is what is most important to her. "I kind of like a blend of the two." I also interviewed African Americans who explicitly rejected their ecstatic worship background, saying, "I don't want that kind of whooping and hollering." An African American musician talking about a popular CCM song "Our God is an Awesome God, said, "Where does it say, 'I'm a white boy talking to God?' It's just 'Our God is an Awesome God,' and it's a cool song." He was not convinced that musical differences are racially based. "It just sort of depends on the individual and what affects them." For Retha and other African Americans attending Traditionalist churches, race and ethnicity are not important considerations for selecting worship music. Their churches had a general, consistent worship style of music that fit the needs of their congregation.

Not only African Americans but members of other non-white groups also failed to accentuate racial or ethnic awareness in music. An Asian woman member of her choir said, "I wouldn't say worship styles are specific to an ethnicity." She says she looks out and sees different kinds of people all worshiping the same way: "As you are looking out at the congregation, you'll see somebody there and somebody there and somebody there, moving or raising their hands or whatever their expression is, or kneeling down. Because we have Chinese people and Japanese people and Caucasian people and probably every ethnicity doing that." They agree that people come from different backgrounds, yet they come together in worship. Daniel said, "Everyone has something to contribute in their own style of worship," and yet "everyone's there worshiping together."

Assimilationists

In contrast to both Professionalists and Traditionalists, Assimilationists are racially aware music leaders who intentionally believe a particular style of music achieves diversity because it is the "base" sound for all human beings. One attender called it "a standard kind of sound." C. Michael Hawn describes this approach to "cross-cultural worship" as "worship through cultural assimilation." Hawn writes, "This practice assumes a dominant cultural perspective that will become the common currency for all participants, regardless of experience or background."[11] For example, the lead pastor of Oasis Christian Center believes that "soul music" is the basic rhythm to human beings.[12] Soul is universal. So the choice of gospel-funk-soul rhythms is a strategic choice because it is believed to fundamentally connect all people. Mosaic in Los Angeles has a different musical strategy.[13] At Mosaic, the lead pastor believes that Rock 'n' Roll is the essential rhythm. Rock is the musical form that is most basic, the music that is most universal.

One Assimilationist leader in yet another multiracial congregation believed the base musical rhythm for human beings was not Rock 'n' Roll but Motown. "That whole era of Motown... there is this certain kind of soulful songs that are just what everybody sings. You know, 'My Girl' or 'Just My Imagination' or 'Sunshine on my Life.' Things like that that I think there's a universal appeal there but it happens to be grounded in this more Afrocentric sort of thing." Talking about R&B "soul" music, an Asian leader said, "I think whites love this kind of music too." For him, "The R&B gospel thing is more accepted by a wider audience than, say, rock is." Bradford said, "Style does matter. The rock stuff—Not even all the white people enjoyed that. But the more gospel kind of sound seems to involve more people."

Assimilationists have a grand concern over achieving a "real" worship experience that transcends racial and ethnic distinctions. Warren, an Asian American worship leader, said, "Music is one of the few things that is completely universal." The goal is to find a broad style with cross-over appeal. As one leader said, "More widespread: Asian, Caucasian, African American." For Assimilationists, accommodating to different racial and ethnic styles of music misses the point. The goal is not to pursue particularistic expressions but to provide opportunity for a universal experience. The irony is that although Assimilationist churches believe there is a base, human rhythm that touches all racial-ethnic groups, they disagree on the specific type of music that is supposed to be that fundamental rhythm.

Pluralists

I find Pluralists to be the most significant philosophical orientation connecting race and music in worship. Although found in only one-quarter of the churches studied, I consistently see this as the most actively advocated approach in discussions on worship in multiracial churches. This group had the most to say about the nature and process of multiracial worship. In many ways, this is the most interesting group of worship leaders because they are most explicit in adopting particular styles of music based on their notions of race. Andrew is typical of this approach in saying, "Music is key, music is crucial. I would skimp on other things." A black musician said, "You're not going to get a lot of diversity if the music isn't diverse." A choir director described her church's worship leader and lead pastor as "visionaries" who "will argue that once you diversify the music, the congregation will follow. It's an agent of diversification."

Pluralists are racially aware music leaders who intentionally attempt to incorporate a mix of musical styles based on beliefs regarding what music relates to what racial-ethnic group. They are also the most vocal and precise in describing their approach music selection for multiracial worship. Henry, an African American worship pastor, said, "We try to touch upon a lot of different styles here in our church because our congregation is so diverse." Henry said the church is doing all it can to "reach people," so the music is intentionally diverse. "This is our philosophy as a church, we want our church to reflect our community." One worship leader said, "Even if our teams do not reflect ethnic diversity, at least in our music we can do our best to reflect that."

This orientation is what some labeled a "shotgun approach" to music, like Joseph who characterized it as "a little mariachi to start, and then a little gospel, and then a little bit of this or that," yet always spoken of in a positive way. Jackson said, "In our church, we don't just do one style. We love the variety." Thad, a white member, said his worship pastor, "will mix all of them within one service." A choir member said, "They will try to do at least one kind of hymnal type song each week because we want to make sure that those who identify more with that type of music are comfortable but then also doing some other mellow music and also some other more upbeat music and that type of thing. Different styles." A white piano player often plays alongside an African American singer in their church and actively mixes between styles. "She's just singing it with soul and more of a gospel style, and I'm just right there playing along trying to give that gospel feel. And then the next minute we might switch over to something that's totally contemporary or straight type of music." Speaking of a previous music pastor, Aaron, an African American church leader, said, "He went across the whole spectrum even as he brought us into worship. He would use contemporary, he would use gospel sometimes, sometimes he would reach way back and use may be some old black style of song." Through the different leaders and musicians, "what we really try hard to work for is a balance. We didn't want people to walk out of here saying the service is this style or the style. The whole key is diversity."

Most significant among Pluralists is the cluster of beliefs regarding "their music." Jackie, an Asian church member, said, "When I think of the black and Latin people I think they have rhythm." June, a white music director, talked about Hispanics, saying, "Oh man, you go to a Hispanic congregation that is lively, and alive, and growing, and they are singing a lot of songs that have a tremendous beat to it. Their services are so loud and everybody's singing—now that's a style too." As a choir director, Kristy is eager to incorporate gospel music into the choir's repertoire. She believed African Americans should freely share their religious musical heritage. "It's a question of whether African Americans will embrace us as brothers and sisters and share their jewel of worship that they have." One black woman said, "African Americans go to church for the music."

Pluralists firmly believe every ethnic-racial group has a style of music best suited to them. It is part of their claimed sophistication in cultivating culturally sensitive worship. A white worship leader with many years of musical experience said, "We definitely are aware of—have concepts or ideas or guesses—about what kind of music is affecting the different cultures. The Hispanic culture, which is around and involved here, listens to a lot of upbeat music." A white worship leader said, "If you come from one kind of background, you might hear one song that resonates with you, but that song doesn't resonate with somebody else, but then another song is gonna resonate with them."

Representation is a core value among Pluralists. Henry, an African American worship leader, said his church was moving toward "making sure every group was represented at every service." Henry believed it was important to represent all styles in the same worship service together rather than "compartmentalize everyone." Henry said, "When I think of heaven I don't think of compartments, and I think that our worship service is a reflection of that." Although the styles are ethnically diverse, there is an attempt to "find songs and styles that everybody can embrace." A member of his church said, "He'll play some very contemporary Top 40 Christian songs, then some Latin flavor or Caribbean. He just mixes it up all the time."

An African American musician in another church said, "We have Latino people here, so I try to do something that would appeal to them. We have older black people, so I've done old gospel music from the '60s and '70s. I've done Japanese music; you know find Japanese hymns and things like that. I've always tried to consider everybody that's sitting out there and try to offer something to each person that's out there. I've played songs that have rap in it." Michelle, a choir member at another church, said, "You mix it up and you always have at least one song that they can associate with and then they get familiar with the other types of song." Vance, a black musician, said, "If you are going to do four or five songs, do something that the whites might be more familiar with and then something the blacks are. That way you get an opportunity to present someone else's culture and it becomes a learning experience."

Pluralists pay attention to rhythm and speed, as well as particular instruments like whistles, conga drums, or tambourines. One white church administrator was proud of "a woman in her nineties, a black gospel singer, who's singing a Negro spiritual" for the coming weekend services. Between gospels and hymns, this church attempts to mix "black" and "white" styles of music. "It's really an eclectic mix because I want to be deliberate about doing that so whoever is here is feeling that they are represented, that they are connected." Pluralists also pay attention to different forms of bodily expression in worship. An African American worship leader, Nora, believes physical expressions are racially differentiated, even "just raising hands and giving God the glory." When I asked Nora to explain, she said, "Because that's automatic for blacks when they are brought up in the Baptist churches. We find these white people who actually started our church were just raised on hymns, and they don't do all this, you know, raise your hands. We just worship differently. I think we've come to accept that from each other, that we just worship differently."

Among Pluralists, whites, blacks, and Hispanics have a distinctive musical culture. But there is ambiguity regarding Asian Americans.[14] Asians don't seem to share a distinctive Christian music to offer to the catalog of congregational worship music. Katy, an Asian choir director, said, "Unfortunately, I feel like Asians don't have much to offer. You have a Chinese harp or a Chinese guitar or the gong in worship. And yet I wish we could share stuff and I feel sad that we [as Asians] don't have much of a musical legacy like the Latinos do."

A Diversity of Styles for a Diversity of People

Among Pluralists, there is a great concern for playing music that would be familiar to different ethnic and racial groups and visibly demonstrating care and concern through musical representation. In promoting a Pluralist approach, Hawn describes this approach as "cross-cultural worship" and "culturally open worship." Hawn writes, "A culturally open congregation will display a spirit of receptivity toward the community's cultural diversity, even though the congregation has a distinctive cultural majority group." In this approach, the church "will also try to honor the cultural heritage of these newcomers in the worship life of the congregation. In essence, the majority group allows its worldview to be altered by the minority constituency in decision-making processes and in worship."[15] To fulfill the desire for Pluralist worship, some churches place all the musically diverse elements in every church service. One pastor of a multiracial church said, "We get new visitors every Sunday...and the first thing they are going to evaluate is the music style." Henry, an African American worship leader, said "It's incorporating different styles of music because if we just had a service where we just had one style, then it's almost like you're alienating certain aspects of your church."

A choir member confidently said, "If you have different styles, you are more likely to have a style that will jive with where somebody came from and traditionally it has been very—Churches have been ethnic specific and attached to that is a style specific to whatever they are comfortable with. So if you have a bunch of different styles of leading, you are going to get a bunch of different people feeling comfortable." Simon, an Asian attender, said, "They do try to change things up every now and then, more jazzier stuff, R&B, even rap, you know, to just kind of show OK, now we're down with that. Not like fake, as in, we don't really like this, but we're gonna try to use it as a tool. It's deliberate." Mark, a white worship leader in another church, said, "Bringing the classical element and the R&B element, I think that kind of covers a little bit of everything." Justin, a white member in another church, said whether it was "Afro-American" or "Hispanic," the important thing is "letting them be a part of certain things...at least you are including them. They feel included, and that's the trick."

An African American worship leader, said, "I try to incorporate some of everything in the worship set. I try to put a gospel song in there, a contemporary song, a hymn." Andrew said, "A lot of our music has somewhat of a gospel flair to it. But also we include with the percussion instruments or with the guitars Latin rhythm and phrasing. Also in the language, there'll be some songs where some of the lyrics are sung in Spanish, and so trying to address and embrace, if you will, African Americans, Hispanics and of course whites." Another white member said, "They sing a song in Spanish or put the words up in Spanish or a verse or two." A Hispanic worship leader said about her services, "I'll usually have a mix—I really try to mix it up. Do some contemporary. Do some gospel. Do some stuff in Spanish, of course. And the Spanish stuff is usually contemporary stuff, just translated so that they have an idea of what they are singing. And hymns. I try to throw some hymns in there too."

Pluralist leaders even have opinions on the type of instruments used by different racial groups. One leader shared a conversation with a few blacks in his congregation. "I talked to my African American folks and asked, 'So how do you deal with this soft-rock?' And they said, 'Pastor, have you ever been to a black church? There's no acoustic guitars.' That was like an epiphany. It was like, 'Yeah, you are right.' In fact, even if black churches have a guitar, and even if it's electric, it's not a guitar-driven worship. It's a very keyboard-driven worship, whether it's organ or piano."

In talking about taking his pastoral role, Curtis said, "Coming here we incorporated music from black churches that we have never had. Then you have Latin...taking one of these songs and doing Spanish words. Latin also is a Latin beat and instrumentation." One member told me his church brought in some songs that were in Spanish but at the same time "they try to add some contemporary white stuff to try to balance it out." A member from the same church said, "I appreciate the music since it's a balance. I feel like there's got to be an exchange because these two cultures [black and white] are coming together to worship, so it can't be all one way. It can't be all gospel or Vineyard or hymns, it's got to be a nice blend." She said, "It's like taking two families who have been married and are now divorced and putting them together. It's a blending of the two cultures."

Spanish is a target language for music among Pluralists. Daniel, a white worship leader, said in his church "We sing songs in Spanish as well. It's kind of funny sometimes because most of us in the choir, and the church doesn't speak Spanish fluently. So we're up there flapping our jaws trying to sing in Spanish, it can be pretty humorous, I'm sure. But we're trying." Another congregation said they brought up a Latino to participate in worship, "We put him up there and he starts singing and he helps us to immerse ourselves into the Latino culture with our worship."[16]

Some Pluralist congregations feature ethnically themed Sunday services. For example, I took notice when Aaron, an African American pastor, told me that "on Super Salsa Sunday we bring the Mariachis in and the congas and all things like that and we're just going 100 miles an hour." Aaron then said, "We also have a Super Soul Sunday once a year and that is the African American–flavor style of worship. Gospel songs, old spirituals and things like that." African Americans are featured prominently at this annual event. In this church, both "Super Salsa Sunday" and "Super Soul Sunday" constitute elaborate attempts to highlight diversity with the most easily stereotyped racial and ethnic groups present in the congregation.

Pluralists insist that expressing musical diversity is necessary "if we're serious about reaching the people with the gospel." It may involve sacrifice on the part of some people. Andrew, an associate pastor, said, "We need to set aside some of our own preferences so that we can minister to them with their needs, and some of their preferences in music." Andrew described the strategy of choosing music in a series of steps: "Who are the people that you need to reach, number one? Secondly, take an inventory of the people that are already attending your church. Is it second-, third-generation that maybe have others within the community of their ethnic background that could possibly attend? I'd take an inventory of that and identifying what some of the larger groups are, if it's African-American, or if it's Hispanic, or if it's Korean."

Having identified the target ethnic-racial groups in the community as well as the groups already attending the church, Andrew argues that musical choices come next:

> Knowing the demographics of our community and because we still have a significantly white membership, and because most of the praise and worship music and a lot of the radio stations and stuff that are heard is still somewhat kind of rock-ish music, my lead guitarist would need to be that. Because of the strong African-American constituency, I'd want a bassist that could do a little jazz and some funk. I would want a percussionist on congas that could do that for some of the Latinos. I'd want an acoustical guitarist who could also do Latin rhythms. Then I would want a drummer that could drive this thing…

Having different musicians who can build different styles, the group would have the resources to play ethnic-racial styles for various groups. Andrew said,

> We could take whatever song we want, but as we develop the roadmap, and this is where we start, we're gonna do a bridge here, I want to feature this soloist, I want you to really slap it, give me some funk. I want you to get down. You've got 15 seconds. So in your 15 seconds, go for it, or 20 seconds or 30 seconds. And then we come back to the chorus, and every different song that we do I'd want to be able to feature that some of those instrumentalists and give us some of that, because that will help those within the congregation engage.

In another church, the music director was proud to have brought in a professional Latino singer. He said, "His heritage helps to bring in that kind of music that is just amazingly energetic and different." Another worship leader was especially hopeful that as the congregation would "continue to grow in numbers" the church would also incorporate more diverse musicians "whoever could bring whatever to the plate, so to speak. Styles particularly."

Maximizing an Exotic Mystique

The ability to switch styles within a church service demands great musical skill by musicians and great openness on the part of visitors to learn a repertoire of songs as they join the church. Even when music is perceived to be racialized among Pluralists, it rarely means that music alternates radically from one style to another within one service. Instead, worship leaders nearly always use a strategy that maximizes an "exotic mystique." In this strategy, most leaders select worship music that has a basis in "Rock 'n' Roll" rhythms and then incorporate other musical influences like salsa or gospel.

Describing the style of music in his church, Bill, a white attender, said, "As a whole it's mainly a white kind of style" that is "flavored" in different ways. Henry also described "flavoring" music, saying, "I will take a song and we will flavor it Latin or we will make it more funk, but it's maybe a traditional song that we will flavor at a certain way, Latin or gospel.... That's why we have this middle-of-the-road approach in our main services, and then we sometimes touch upon others." A drummer who is part of the church worship team said, "If it's not songs themselves then I would try to arrange what we're already doing into something that they [non-Anglos] relate to more, namely it would have more aggressive bass lines, it would have more aggressive drums, a little bit of funk, a little bit of more of the groove factor." Another musician talked about adding a "black beat" to music, saying, "It wasn't written that way, but we'll change it, the beat will have a little bit more syncopation type thing." David, a white worship leader, said, "We'll add some congas if it's gonna be a little more Latin so it can be flavored in that way."

Practically speaking, even when a diversity of styles is played, there is always a base style that constitutes a musical center for Pluralists' services. And there are two choices: white CCM music or black gospel music. LeAnn, an Asian church member, believed CCM has universal appeal and that Blacks can relate to it and enjoy it. LeAnn said, "Contemporary is more for all cultures. It can be black, it can be white, it can be yellow, whatever. It suits everyone." So, is gospel music only for blacks? According to LeAnn, "Yes, [but] black people like contemporary songs, too." But is gospel music only for blacks? June was proud of her congregation's inclusion of gospel, saying, "For congregational singing, we love some of the African American spirituals." Kimberly, a black choir member, says "No, because I think everyone enjoys it." And when I asked her about white, "Vineyard" music, she again said, "No, I think it's for everyone." Simeon, a black worshiper, was more ambivalent. At one point, Simeon said, "I think there are different kinds of music for different kinds of races." Yet, Simeon also said, "I'd say black people do mostly enjoy gospel music, but I think everybody enjoys it really." For Simeon, "The service does a really good job of having the gospel music and then having the contemporary music in a good mix where it'll make a racially diverse group of people comfortable and at the same time." Nora, a black worship leader, said, "We do do gospel, and then there are just a few songs, maybe just a few other hymns and we kind of make it that style. But for the most part, we do gospel." She believed the church incorporated gospel to attract African Americans, saying, "Musically, yeah. By incorporating a little more gospel songs." And for Hispanics? Nora said, "I think the more passionate songs, because they are a passionate group. I think they really love the more passionate songs." Then Nora contradicted herself in saying she did not attempt to incorporate different songs for different racial groups, "I just say everybody is going to relate to the songs."

The mixing rhythms and styles within a consistent musical base is often emphasized by Pluralists. Bill said, "There is something about rhythms. Latin American rhythm is different, you know? African American rhythm is different—the way it's presented." Michael, an African American member of the worship team, said, "Black people are doing the same contemporary music that white churches are doing; they're just doing it differently. They're using the same...contemporary songs that you might see in a white megachurch, but with the black beat." Daniel, a white musician, also characterized his church as "kind of a hybrid between different styles...pretty much a mix of the three styles, Latin, gospel and contemporary," with contemporary being the base style. Mark, a white worship leader, said, "Acoustic rock is the foundation of everything we do, but I try to change it up a little bit, incorporate different instruments into that, give it different sounds, you know, trying to incorporate different styles or bring in different elements to give it some diversity."

Essentially, Pluralists do not radically alternate rhythms and styles in services but rather use a base musical rhythm that is mixed with ethnically tinged elements. Songs are arranged to accentuate stereotypic musical styles, as one Asian worship leader said, "to give it that flavor." These are "spices" that allow people to experience a variety of (tamed, homogenized, and accessible) styles of music. One music director said they "overlap the styles." Moreover, these are styles that appeal to many people. In other words, these are styles of music that already have a broad commercial base and possess broad familiarity and appreciation.

Andrew said, "If you take three circles and you overlay them, there is an overlap in the center of all of those where our worship pastor takes us, not to target the preferences, otherwise we'd be in venues, but to take a little bit from everything where it all overlaps is our mindset, that's how we've developed our worship services and our music" (see fig. 6.1). A choir director said, "I wouldn't characterize our sound or our music or worship as African American. I think if you took somebody out of a black church and planted them here, they would be like, 'This is not black worship.' But we take elements of it, that's for sure." An Asian musician in another church said, "It's never supposed to be hip-hop, it's never supposed to be gospel, it's never supposed to be rock; it's supposed to be this medley of different styles and just celebrating

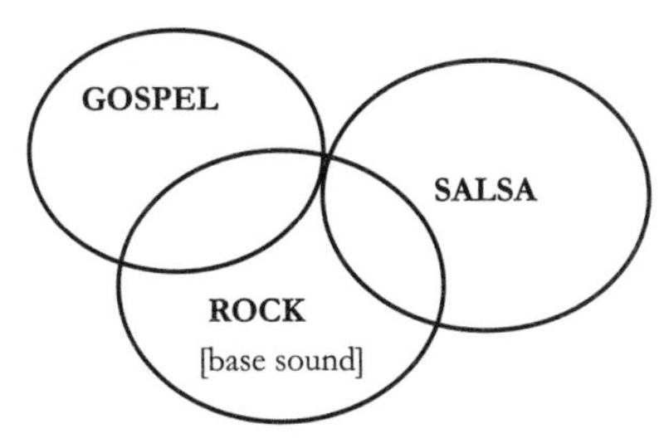

FIGURE 6.1. Worship Leaders "Spice" Base Musical Rhythms to Maximize an Exotic Mystique

that." One choir director described her desire to create this type of "blended" style, saying, "I would actually hope we don't define a dominant style. I know our pastor thinks once we get all gospel or R&B, then we are diverse but I don't know. I would like to incorporate all the different styles."

One church leader considered their music to be "70% gospel," and that they were drawing on their "background" as musicians "because they are used to that." The gospel style is a base for other styles also incorporated into the service. Henry, an African American worship leader in another congregation, said, "Mainly we have gospel. We incorporate gospel music, and some of the latest contemporary Christian styles, passion type of worship, praise and worship music, and then, we incorporate on top of that some of, whether it's Rock 'n' Roll or jazz styles, things like that."

Racially Specific, Broadly Inclusive

While bringing in the "different" musical styles based on "cultural heritage," Pluralist church leaders often insist that even racially specific music is for everyone. A black choir member was attracted to her church for its "gospel service." She said, "The service is for the African Americans predominantly" because it featured "more gospel." Yet as she experienced the variety of music in this Pluralist church, she emphasized how she can to accept that the music was not solely gospel. She said, "I like different kinds of music. I don't just like only one kind. When I listen to music, I listen to classical music. I love Mozart; he's my favorite composer. I listen to Christian radio, it's a little rock. I can hang with that." Mike, a white worshiper, said, "We sing some in Spanish and have the Afro-American gospel, but we all enjoy it. I enjoy singing in Spanish. I enjoy all the types of songs. All of them."

Moreover, playing different musical styles "exposes other people to other cultures." People tend to see such musical exposure as an educational experience. Such education can help (in their minds) build bridges between racial and ethnic groups. Music provides privileged access to "the exotic other." As one choir member said, "A lot of people if you've been in one style your whole life, one style of worship, it's like the type of song you are used to your whole life—it's a lot harder to try and absorb different styles of music and enjoy and appreciate them the same way you have the other."

More often it is not just an emphasis on exposure to cultures but an expanded sense of the presence and power of God in seeing it expressed through "the other." Travis, a white music director, said it is all about "experiencing not only diversity musically, just diversity, the diversity of God and celebrating that diversity. And one aspect of doing that is through music." He said the goal is to experience "the different channels of music that's out there, to bring out these different elements of songs. Just to incorporate one traditional type hymn, whether you do a new arrangement of it or not, or bringing in a jazzy arrangement of a song, or bringing in a Latin element, or black gospel element. Just to celebrate God's diversity." For Travis, diversity of styles contributes to an expansive ability to worship God. "God's more concerned with the heart, and enjoying how we celebrate him in different styles is more important to me." Diversity is "a key element" of enhancing worship. "I think the more we experience diversity in worship, the more we can connect to God. You know what I mean? No matter what your cultural background is, bringing those different elements can really help understand God more. So, to me, that's what's important about diversity." Ilene, an Asian member of her church, said, "The Lord put people from different countries and different races together and they are worshiping at the same time even though each of us have different experiences. It acts like we are a family and also helped me to understand and to witness other people's stories." The experience of diversity worship "helps to strengthen our belief and faith in the Lord." Even more, "When you get to be around other people you get to see how they worship the Lord and that will build you up."

Sometimes the demand for Pluralist music creates tensions of ethnic performance. In one church, a musician talked about "this Asian guy but he is singing the gospel" and attempted to downplay the need for racial authenticity by suggesting that ethnic performance was no longer necessary to achieve true musical worship. He said, "It made the transition easier. Now it doesn't really matter who's singing it. Music is music and we are all able to connect with it." This is another attempt within the intentional practice of diversity to emphasize that the diversity of styles is meant to not alienate anyone but include everyone.

Enforcing the service being for everyone means that among Pluralists no single style is intended to dominate. Aaron, an African American pastor of the diversity service, said, "We didn't want people to walk out of here saying the service is this style or the style. The whole key is diversity. The service has its own unique identity but it can't be characterized by one particular style of music." Melody, a white worshiper talked about her the gospel music of her church, said, "There is a place in that music for everybody."

GERARDO: Because of the styles?
MELODY: Just the joy. It's the joy of the Lord.

Danny, another white member, envisions in the midst of different styles a more universal musical experience in worship where people are united by a simple desire to "dance and praise" like in the Bible. So the Pluralists emphasize different styles as being performed by people of specific heritages and for people from particular ancestral backgrounds, and yet they firmly believe stylistic changes are not forms of "turn taking" but that all music is for everyone. Peter, an Asian member, said, "Music's universal, so whether you play it with a Latin beat or with turntables or whatever, I think, ultimately, if you love music you'll enjoy the music."

Finally, Pluralists assert that diverse worship is "spiritually healthy." Using an analogy to healthy eating, participation in multiple styles of worship are intended to keep a balance and vitality in spiritual life. Daniel, a white musician, said, "You can't be healthy if you're going to just eat one type of food. You just can't eat meat all day long. Do you know what I mean? You have to have some vegetables in there. You've got to get your minerals and all your nutrients and vitamins. Different styles of music play a part in giving you a well-rounded, healthy worship experience. If you limit yourself to one thing, you're going to be malnourished."

Musical Selection is Not the Secret to Diversity

Is it possible for leaders to simply "decide" they want diversity and therefore implement a plan to do so? Is racial awareness in music selection the "key" to diversity? Workshops, conferences, and advice books assert the importance of willful agency and racial awareness by church leaders. Leaders must decide, plan, and implement a musical strategy for their worship in order to attract and retain diverse congregants. In the effort to provide answers, church leaders often seek formulas that abstract out particularities in favor of a set of general solutions to the "problem" of homogeneity. Yet as George Whitfield Andrews argued a century ago, "We cannot undertake to decide in a dogmatic way what music a church should sing."[17] The experience of musical styles is not deterministic, such that the associations that come with the acoustics of a sound do not automatically imply that all individuals sharing an ancestral heritage will automatically connect with certain rhythms. Musical styles are ambiguous and therefore lend themselves to multiple associations. And worship leaders find the ability to accomplish worship is not dependent on a particular approach to music.

Remember, all four approaches to musical styles described here (Professionalist, Traditionalist, Assimilationist, and Pluralist) come from successfully diverse churches. Taking into account the variety of approaches to musical selection among multiracial churches, I find no specific approach to the sound or genre of music that is most effective for accomplishing diversity as all of these approaches are found among them. Any approach to music selection can work, and leaders do not need to be racially or ethnically conscious in their musical selections in order to create services where people of all ancestral backgrounds can truly worship.

However, the final chapters reveal how racial awareness does enter into the consideration of church leaders and members in terms of recruitment to participate publicly in the worship services. Chapters 7 and 8 demonstrate that it is more significant to understand how the belief in racial and ethnic differences creates structural processes for the engagement of diverse people. Music, then, relates to the overarching structures of congregational life not by acoustics but by encouraging and stimulating churches to actively staff visibly diverse people in both volunteer and paid positions in their regular ministries of worship.

PART III

Negotiating Race and Achieving Congregational Diversity

7

"Have You Seen Our Gospel Choir?"

CONSPICUOUS COLOR IN MULTIRACIAL WORSHIP

If you are just trying to change things through music, the music alone won't do it.

—BEN, ASIAN AMERICAN, church staff member

IN THE CULTIVATION of a diverse ministry, gospel choirs take a privileged role. A lead pastor said, "I really feel like the gospel choir is the lynch-pin in this whole thing." The "gospel choir" shows up in a surprising number of diverse congregations and has become the most significant organizational component introduced into congregations with a value for diversity. Among the multiracial churches I observed, about half have instituted some form of "gospel choir" even when few or no African Americans attend. The gospel choir also was discussed by several pastors in the context of goals to introduce more "black" music, most often African American spirituals or a more general notion of having more "soulful" music in the church. One female pastor said, "I try to make it happen very often." Because of expectations of racial authenticity and racial performance, it becomes necessary for churches to strategize a means to accomplish "black music," and the vehicle becomes forming an "inspiration" or "gospel" choir.[1] Even if it appears only occasionally, the question, "Have you seen our gospel choir?" becomes a point of pride, an indication that the church is firmly committed to the principle of diversity.

Worship leaders and music directors make choices regarding the music they choose to include in their services, and they are increasingly pressured to make musical choices to accentuate the potential for diversity.[2] Since diversity in the United States is largely defined as the successful integration of blacks into non-black settings, the goal for diversification often reduces to the attempt to attract African Americans to non-black congregations. And gospel music is generally understood to be the music required to successfully bring

African Americans into a congregation.[3] Yet, because only blacks can authentically do black worship music, congregations must find ways to bring in at least a few into the congregation as performers in the hope of attracting others who at least will become regular attenders. Moreover, specifically introducing a gospel choir is intended to stimulate a more intimate understanding of African Americans. Linda B. Walker, a professor of music at the University of California, San Diego, writes, "When students participate in gospel choir, they experience another culture firsthand."[4] And ethnomusicologist Margaret Dilling states that participating in a gospel choir "causes students to think about race and race bias in a structured and diverse environment."[5]

From a casual understanding of "black church culture," the only aspect of black churches that is consistently desired—even envied—is gospel music. Chris, Hispanic member, said, "And that's what Benny brought. He brought a gospel choir. They called it an 'inspiration choir' but it was a gospel choir [chuckles]." Chris said it was the emotive style that stuck him in the gospel choir. When the new black pastor came, "He brought a gospel choir. Brokenness is the key thing of being before God and knowing you're broken and being able to uninhibitedly praise and worship God and to rely on him." Manner of preaching, forms of dress, length of services, or any other aspect of black services is not even mentioned. The appropriation of black religious life is highly selective and reduced to what is seen as a readily assimilable aesthetic form. Margy, an African American member of her choir, said, "Black music has more of a rhythm to it a beat to it, something that has a little beat to it. The kind of thing that goes on in the black culture." John, a white drummer, was critical of his church saying, "It seems like to me it would make sense if we did more things, if we did once in awhile a kind of gospel kind of thing." The genre, then, that is most widely believed to be able to accomplish racial and ethnic diversity in churches is gospel music, even if it is only performed poorly and sporadically in a congregation.[6]

Gospel music is accentuated due to the pervasive stereotype of the African American worshiper. It was a surprise for this researcher to see how pervasive black stereotypes are among devoted, pious church goers who are eager to embrace the agenda of racial equality and racial diversity. African Americans remain iconic for worship, even within the African American community, because they are universally believed to experience authentic worship more profoundly than any other racial-ethnic group. The ideal of multiracial worship is consistently described by members of multiracial churches as African Americans singing gospel music. What makes this shared belief of African American worship significant is how it is deeply influences the social norms of worship among churches seeking to achieve greater diversity.[7]

What is most fascinating is how members of diverse congregations feel the need to incorporate gospel music, regardless of whether there are blacks in the congregation or not. A black worship leader who helped build their church's "inspiration choir" described the style of music as "Wospel" (or perhaps better spelled "*WASP*-el"). He said, "For lack of a better word I call it Wospel. It's kind of an imitation of gospel. You have certain songs were they try to do in a gospel style but it's not quite there." He said, "Because of our diversity we aren't just trying to do the stuff you would hear in a black church." In another church, a white worship leader said, "Even if we've got half Asian, half white, we want to have some African American gospel music because we want to attract all types."

The benefit to the congregation is that "black worship" enlivens the service. Melody, an older white member, said, "The inspiration choir has more of the uplifting type. You could feel the power of the worship." Kenny, an Asian member, contrasted Asians with African Americans in worship, saying, "What they [African Americans] bring to our corporate worship time, the service feels a lot more alive and has a lot more energy as a whole compared to my experience of when we were predominantly just Asian." Kristy, a choir director from a pan-Asian church, said, "There are some blacks who are open to share that [gospel music] and there are others that think its offensive because it's specific to their culture." The performance of gospel music is protected. Kristy said, "Like, 'Those outsiders, they are not doing it right. They are just using gospel music to get a spiritual high because it's so upbeat and uplifting.'"

Even without African Americans, the incorporation of a gospel choir is an extension of the African American spiritual mystique and serves the function of showing how worship should actually happen.[8] Shawn, a white worship leader, said, "The choir is demonstrating how you can worship." Shawn said, "It really matters a lot that their emotions are driving a lot of it, that there is a real, what would you call it, just a sincerity, authenticity. You can see that in their faces, you know?" So, even in the absence of African Americans, blacks singing gospel remain the model of worship in multiracial churches. Doug, a white member, said, "The gospel pieces always sound the best and stir the congregation—the exuberant, enthusiastic, joyous singing of the choir really encourages the congregation in its singing."

Priority of Visual Diversity

Even more important is that the "gospel choir" provides opportunity for conspicuous color on the platform. All multiracial churches believe that visible and diverse ethnic and racial presence up front during church services is critical to accomplishing diversity. Leaders frequently provide anecdotal evidence that seeing diversity matters for people feeling welcome. Doreen, a white worship administrator, told me, "I had a conversation with a black man not too long ago that said, 'Yeah, I can come in and I can worship anywhere; but if I come in and there's somebody black on the platform, that just feels like home to me.'" Kristy, an Asian musician, believed visible diversity mattered "because when they see people up there of different backgrounds, they feel less intimidated because the people are different colors." An African American pastor said the visual presence of diversity works "because they will look up front and see African Americans on stage, and they will see some in the choir, and then when that first note hits with the worship style and our four songs, by the time we come out of it, they start making up their mind to stay."

All multiracial churches confront the challenge of cultivating a racially diverse presence in public services. Church attenders often talk about it, and church leaders express the imperative and desire for visible diversity. Visible diversity is the most prominent issue addressed in my interviews. One member called it "diversity on stage." Moreover, scholars and "advice literature" push for presence and visibility. Diversity in worship comes to mean the presence of performers who are "obviously" different from the majority of attenders, usually based on skin color, hair texture, facial features, and noticeable foreign accents. By accentuating "otherness," "orientalism," and "exoticism," visible difference affirms and legitimizes the congregational goal of diversity.[9] By invoking racially specific notions of music, congregational leaders become obligated to find singers and musicians who can legitimately perform the music. Since only blacks can sing gospel (or only Hispanics can sing in Spanish, etc.), they are sought out to actualize the music and fulfill the mandate of bringing diversity through the liturgy.

The effort to bring diversity up front leads to diversity being proportionally greater on the platform than in the congregation as a whole. One white member said, "I notice on stage that it's very multi-ethnic. You have different races on there. And you have different races singing solos, playing different instruments." For this member the diversity on the platform is simple: "We want the church to be diverse, so we're going to mirror the diversity of the church." The "reflective mirror" between platform and pew is often discussed among both leaders and members of diverse congregations. "I think it's reflective of what the congregation is."

In actuality, the diversity on the platform rarely mirrors the diversity of the congregation. A Latino member acknowledged this, saying, "You won't see as much diversity in the pews as you will see up on stage." An Asian attender in another church said, "The worship teams are probably the most ethnically diverse groups in the church." An attender in the same church said, "You can definitely see diversity up there." Another Latino attender similarly said, "If you want to see the biggest diversity in this church, it's the worship team because that's the main focal point. That's where you'll see the most diversity." The intentional placement of diversity makes the platform of multiracial churches proportionally more diverse than the rest of the congregation. In my observation, the worship teams publicly exaggerate diversity on the platform, including racial and ethnic groups rare in the congregation, highlighting their presence up front. The desire for obvious diversity in the local church connects with complex issues of exoticism, authenticity, and globalization.

Worship teams take on significance for diversity because they consistently offer church leaders the opportunity to consciously manipulate the visible diversity of the congregation. Leaders make it a priority to recruit for diversity, and any further diversification is tied to the visible incorporation of differences up front. This propels the pursuit of a greater presence of diversity up front in contrast with the diversity observed in the pews. One African American member of the worship team simply said, "We're going to have to get more ethnicities involved in our worship teams." Diversity on the platform provides visual evidence of the "diversity" of the congregation. One lead pastor talked about how he actively cultivates a diverse presence, saying, "The people that you put up front really send a message, and I think that's leading the way." The most obvious benefit of displaying visible racial and ethnic diversity is that it reinforces for the congregation a value for diversity. In talking about seeing the diversity of the worship teams, one attender said, "I like that because having them up there says something about who we are and who we want to be." Another leader said, "As we plant new churches, we want to have mixed teams of Anglos, Asians, Hispanics, and African Americans leading... If you do that, then that tells everyone, 'Whoa, people are in the front, people are worshiping, they are multicultural.' That's the message that comes at you right from the get go, more than the music."

The obvious presence of diverse performers is a priority by both leaders and attenders and indicates underlying practices within the music ministries of the congregation to support the crafting of a diverse image. Ken, a white worship leader, said he makes an earnest attempt to diversify those involved in music and worship ministries, "getting that leadership there so you don't have all white people and bringing in those that already naturally speak foreign languages." Daniel said, "Every ethnicity and style of worship plays a vital role. We are not really complete as a body without having all those components be at least in some ways part of the worship experience." Daniel means not just musical diversity but insists on the physical manifestation of diversity in the enactment of worship. With Ken, Daniel, and others, diversity "on the platform" indicates structures of diversity "off the platform." Scholars and practitioners often "push" for diverse racial presence and visible diversity, and structures of integration must be present beyond worship services in order for this to occur. The imperative for diversity stimulates the recruitment of diversity as well as the practices involved in musical worship, both on and off the platform, which effectively promote cross-racial bonding in successfully multiracial churches. So, participation by diverse racial-ethnic groups in the public performance of worship does not stimulate diversity but rather indicates the existence of cross-racial/cross-ethnic structures of interaction in the preparation of these performances. Finding, articulating, and accentuating those structures becomes the true secret for cultivating diversity.

In sum, while neither styles of music nor philosophical orientation toward approaching the relationship between race and music are consistent among all multiracial churches, what is consistent is an emphasis on having diverse bodies among people involved in the worship services.[10] *The priority for visible color stimulates diversity by actively recruiting and accentuating obviously diverse people on the platform.* So music does matter, but not in ways typically believed. Multiracial churches do not achieve integration by diligently accommodating to supposedly distinct racial music styles or by constructing assumed universal forms of worship; rather, they successfully diversify by stimulating unobtrusive pathways of cross-ethnic and interracial interaction through multiracial worship practices.

Colored Bodies Conspicuously Placed

Many leaders admit that they deliberately place people in prominent places. Daniel, a white worship leader, said, "We intentionally had people in spots where when you walk through the door, you saw something diverse first. You saw that there's all different kinds of people in the front." Another church placed a white and an Asian pastor "up front a lot" and included a prominent mixture of Asians "right up front" so that attenders saw "the look of the church had that mix." Racial presence is actively managed in churches that value "diversity" itself and seek that as a type of branding for their congregation.

The deliberate placement of "colored bodies" is expected by lead pastors but actively managed by worship leaders and music directors. One worship leader talked about the relationship between music and diversity explicitly in relation to the visible color of people up front at church services. "It's the visibility of our teams, what they look like, that matters. I'm usually pretty conscious of having an ethnically diverse looking team." An Asian woman in anther church said, "The first thing you see, besides the pastor, is that the worship team is ethnically diverse." The visual cue of an integrated congregation up front compliments the music being played. It's a priority, as Lawrence said, "just that people see."

For church leaders, what is intended to be visible is not only people from various racial and ethnic heritages but also a physical manifestation of diverse styles of worship. Doreen said,

> Both the Hispanic and black population are more demonstrative in their worship, so that affects the people that are leading it, that are seeing that. It's human nature that you are going to react to somebody or respond to somebody that's responding to you. They are more likely to clap when there's a good beat in the music or more likely to raise their hands. Diversity brings some of that. There's less inhibition in their freedom to express their worship, whether it's to stand and sway or raise their hands or clap or move their bodies or shout out in the middle of a message, to shout "Amen" or whatever it is, there isn't that same need to be so appropriate. That affects worship for everybody. If you see other people feeling the freedom to express themselves, it gives you the freedom to do the same.

One African American pastor said having gospel music led by African Americans "has a strong influence in how we worship. I try to be careful with it in that I don't go overboard with it or that it doesn't become the dominant thrust of it. I always try to think of others, again multicultural, multiracial, and try to think of them also. With my presence in the service, I understand that I rub off on people in some degree or another. How I worship rubs off on them."

The priority for visible diversity is so high that churches are willing to bring in colored bodies from other ministries to support diversity initiatives. One music director looks for blacks and Latinos serving in other areas of the church hoping to persuade them to join the worship team, even temporarily. "I want to find somebody else—can we borrow somebody from another team?" Other leaders bring in diversity from other local churches or hire vocalists and musicians to play in the band every week. Yet, "borrowing diversity" has unintended consequences. One attender said, "I was bugged by was the fact I would see people up there that I would never see before coming on Sunday morning. We were hiring musicians who are Caucasian to play." This attender did not see diversity on the platform as supporting goals for racial and ethnic integration as much as a push toward greater professionalism in the performance. "Our staff sees our worship service as becoming real professional." But from the standpoint of hiring staff, hiring others is yet another opportunity to promote diversity.

In many ways, the interviews lend support to the importance of visible diversity. Miriam, an Asian attender, talked about "different people, different instruments up there, contributes to my worship experience and reminds me of the diversity." Asking Chris, who is Hispanic, about his experience, he said, "When I look at the success of our services, one of the things that really helped was the fact that there was diversity represented up front. That has been one of the key things that has helped keep the service diverse and make everyone feel welcome." He described a "multiracial" lay leader who welcomed people at the beginning of the service. "You have those kind of leaders up front representing diversity, it grabs you." A white pastor was convinced attenders connect with the church on the basis of seeing people who represent their own ethnic or racial background, saying, "When you are walking through the door, people are seeing themselves." An Asian worshiper also emphasized in having visual diversity up front, "People would say, 'Look at the people up there that are like me.'" Racial presence is related to what one attender called "comfortability," the idea of people feeling a sense of welcome and comfort rather than being isolated or alone based on their ethnic heritage. Tammy, a white choir member, said, "It is that the feel that everyone is welcome, everyone is accepted, we are going to turn our back on you a white, black, Hispanic, Chinese, whoever you are. You are welcome here." An Asian attender in yet another church said, "It's a very good experience to have [people from] different backgrounds and people from different races worshiping under the same temple."

Encounters with people of similar backgrounds is intended to attract people. But also, I was intrigued to find that the presence specifically of blacks for non-blacks can be especially comforting. Daniel, a white worship leader, talked about his first experience with the diversity of his church. "It was just cool to see an African American guy leading worship." Because the church was "mixed," he did not feel racially excluded. "It wasn't like walking into a complete gospel church where I would probably be the only white guy. So I guess it took some of the pressure off. In coming to a church with a mix of everybody, you don't feel isolated." The encounter with visible difference is ameliorated by occurring in an integrated context, such that the difference is not inherently stigmatizing. The physical diversity signals a place of acceptance and openness. Chris, a Latino, said, "It gives you the ability to open up and feel like you are not being judged on anything because it is such a diverse service. There's no dominant culture here. It gives you the ability to really open up and worship and feel comfortable and feel like this is a place where you are not being judged." In another church, a member said, "I looked around and was like, 'Hey this is neat, they're not all one color, they're not all one ethnicity. Well maybe I can fit in here,' because usually I'm in the minority." Visual diversity also aids in recruiting more diverse worship teams. In one pan-Asian church, a leader said, "Now that we have more colors up there, colors of skin if you put it bluntly, people come up to me and go, 'Wow! Can I be part of the worship team? I always wanted to be part of it but I thought it was only for Asians because I only saw Asians up there.' "

Not everyone agrees that presence of visible diversity matters, like David who said, "I've been in a situation before where we're trying to reach a certain target, so we put those people up front and I think it's insulting to people." But reactions like this fall in the minority. Most leaders and members, like Aaron, place great priority on the visual presence of diversity. Aaron believes visitors evaluate their place in the church based on whether they experience a resonance or comfort with the diversity of people on the platform: "They will look up front and see African Americans on stage, and they will see some in the choir, but then when we hit that first note, and the worship style and we do our four songs and we come out of it, I think they start making up their mind. They would probably think this is not the full African American thing I'm used to, I did feel some, but it's different. So they are processing it." Another church leader focused on the imperative of bringing in people who did not already attend the church, saying, "We want to be more missional and as the community comes here just to test the waters or to see what's going on and asking 'Why would I got there?' that they feel a connection when they come in. That's much more of a concern to me." Achieving that visible connection is the focus of their strategizing the worship services.

Visible diversity affirms for multiracial members that their church is a place where the ambiguity of their own backgrounds can belong. One Latino talked about the "a pain in my life," that his white father and Mexican mother "went through the racial discrimination that they had gone through." He said that his family "from Oklahoma and Nebraska . . . were never fond of his father marrying a Hispanic to start with, and so I always felt like part of me was not safe around any of my family. That was a big deal." His stepsister married a black man and her stepbrother married an Asian woman. "My family is very diverse, so the thought of having a place where everyone would be welcomed, and even beyond that, a place where I saw God providing an environment that was complete in representing all of what God is in its diversity. That was exciting."

Hiring Black Worship Pastors

The deliberate exaggeration of visible diversity is not just about bringing "colored bodies" but especially "black bodies" in the performance of "black music." The incorporation of African Americans is at the core of achieving visible diversity. A lead pastor of another Asian-dominant congregation said, "The band and the performers for the most part are African American. I do think that's helping us a lot." Diversity is not sufficient if it does not include blacks in the mix. One church leader said, "I don't want it to be just a Caucasian-Asian worship band." Sociologist George Yancey is one among many writers who put great emphasis on the presence of blacks in public leadership roles as key to stimulating diversity.[11] David, a white pastor, said, "We need to have an African American leader occasionally to help lead if we want to really make it a multicultural thing." Similarly, a member who characterized his church as "mainly a white kind of style," said, "I'm pretty excited about this guy that's coming this weekend. It's African American hymns. He's going to bring some of his culture with him and it's going to be awesome."

Leaders and attenders inevitably bring out memories of African American involvement in the music of their churches, even if it consisted of "special guests" or members who are no longer involved in the congregation. One member talked about the church ten years ago when "there were some exciting things going [on], when there was a black choir director, when a black couple, the Robertsons, were very involved; she played piano, and he had a great voice." In conversations and interviews, blacks are consistently highlighted in worship, Latinos are occasionally highlighted, while whites, Asians, and other groups are never mentioned in terms of their minority status in their involvement in worship services. John, an African American music director, believes that in order to diversify churches must play black music. "Absolutely, yes," he said. "I'm convinced that in the white world is far more accepting of black music. The white people would say, 'Come on, we'll play their music.' But how many people in the black church would say, 'We want to integrate this church, let's play white music to bring them in'? I don't think too many." John added, "I can't get young black kids to listen to our church music, they look at it as white."

Blacks continue to be stigmatized in multiracial churches as leaders and members continually assert an overly homogenized religious image of all African Americans, one that is ecstatic, holistic, and generally seen as "naturally musical." Will, a white male musician, serves in a church with very few African Americans. Nevertheless, he expressed strong opinions on the mix of white-black music that was important for his church. Will said, "There's just a real distinct culture in the black church, a real distinct way that they do things." The music for them, "It's like the language of church for that culture." Will even stressed that "the quality of the music isn't as important in a white church, and in a black church it is critically important. They are super hyped up about it." So the attention to detail on not only *what* was played but *how* it was played becomes important for Will in planning his services. "I don't want to be stereotypical, but there are ways that black musicians play that you notice." The exoticization of African American religion even in a positive light perpetuates notions that have oppressed and radically separate blacks from other groups since the historical understandings of African American religion were constructed amid exploitation, segregation, and injustice.[12]

The priority of appropriating black bodies motivates the most prominent "strategy" for diversification: hiring a black worship leader. One African American member talked about a dominantly white congregation he visited with a black worship leader who said he really enjoys the "gospel flare" he brings to the service. Yet, when I asked if having a black worship leader mattered to him for his own worship experience, he said, "No, I don't think so." Even when he recalled "times where we've had people sit in with the worship team that are black," he remained ambivalent whether the presence of people from his own racial group affected his connection to the congregation. Despite such ambiguities regarding the effect of visible diversity, most churches hired—or expressed the desire to hire—an African American musical leader.

A black staff member of a mostly non-black church told me that in order to "reach black people," presence on the platform was not optional but critical. "You have to have a black man coming in here." Some churches have had guest appearances by black musicians that fueled the desire for a black staff person. In talking about an African American musical "guest," one member said, "Hopefully they'll hire him." David, a white worship leader in another church, said, "We have a lot of African Americans coming in, so we need to have an African American leader occasionally to help lead if we want to really make it a multicultural thing and spread it. We're going to really need to do it—not me pretend to do that...."

In one church, I asked if there was discussion when hiring the African American pastor now on staff. How racially conscious was the hiring of this black pastor? "Of course, it was brought up that, 'Yeah, he's an African American guy. Great to have him here. But he's also a pastor that has a real passion and we think that we need this kind of a guy to help lead.'" No church would say they would hire pastoral staff simply because that person was black, yet the intentionality of bringing an African American on staff is viewed as directly supporting efforts toward diversity. "It wouldn't help our diversity if a whole bunch of whites tried to do something. It's a social barrier that's out there." There is a consistent effort to materially show the uniting of racial and ethnic groups in public services. Musical involvement on the platform unites visual and audio aspects of diversity.

From conversations with lead pastors and others involved in hiring decisions of their churches, it is clear that churches with non-black pastors would rather have a black worship leader. Repeatedly, the most consistently intentional action among church leaders for diversity is hiring a black pastor. For example, one church hired a black pastor to oversee the "diversity service." And Shawn, the white music director who hired him, said putting him up in front of the congregation at the beginning of services "is intentional." Shawn said in his church, "I'll open up with one song and he'll come up and greet the congregation." Other visible "color" is also brought forward. "We'll have guys like Manuel coming up, and he's more Hispanic background, so he'll come up and do that too in the morning services. We're trying to be intentional about that too." One Asian member talked about their recently hired black worship pastor, saying, "Hiring him set the tone for more diversity." In essence, the visible placement of a single black person is viewed as a critical symbolic marker for the value and welcome of diversity on behalf of the congregation to all ethnic and racial groups.

The goal is to visibly place a symbol of diversity in a high-profile position early in the service. A pastor said, "They'll come in the door thinking, 'This is pretty cool.' That's what their eyes tell them first." Hiring an African American worship leader brings visual diversity on the platform for every church service, as one church leader said, "The fact that he is black, that he is African American, lends that visual diversity to the team that is up there." Yet, the imperative of bringing a black leader is based on the notion of their musical authenticity. Some worship leaders told me their pastors ask, "Can we bring in some gospel music?" and "How about adding more funk?" Another pastor told me he was hired to incorporate "more of an urban-gospely-R&B type of style, and that was very intentional on our pastor's part because he wanted to go in that direction." Yet another worship leader told me her pastor had been dreaming about a gospel choir for twenty years. A member of the worship arts said, "Although members would say, 'Pastor, we are just not gospel,' he just waited patiently for the day when God would start up a gospel choir." Yet another worship leader told me about a conversation he had with his pastor before he was hired: "Pastor said, 'I want worship like the black church.' I said, 'I can't offer you that because I'm not black.' He definitely wanted something that had a lot more groove, harmonies.... So that was my main directive." Another pastor described the desire for incorporating "more music with syncopation and soul." Another pastor simply said his leader wanted "Motown." In nearly all cases, the primary directive was integrating some form of "black music" as a means to incorporate more blacks into worship. The directive to include more "black music" is shaped by the racialized climate of the United States where the black-white divide dominates issues of diversity, so it is no surprise that the directive most often comes in some variation of "we need more black music here."[13]

The need for a visible black leader is always tied to the need for racial authenticity in musical performance. A Hispanic member, for example, said prior to the hiring of their black worship pastor, "African Americans felt like, yeah they enjoyed the music, it was okay, but from their black church culture, expression in worship and that full gospel, you know, what they were used to, it wasn't quite there." He felt that the incorporation of the "black church culture" and their "expression of worship" was necessary to bring them into the congregation. Simon, an Asian church member, said, "At one point, we had an African American worship leader and for a while music drifted into the more—I'd say stereotypical—gospel music, a lot more upbeat, and we had a choir up there." The hiring of an African American is based on a profound belief that blacks have a "worship culture" that is clear and distinct. One white church leader said, "I can say, 'Let's do something that's more gospel feeling or that's more Hispanic feeling,' and we could find those pieces of music and we can play it, but do we really hit the target audience? I don't know because I'm not black and I'm not Hispanic. So I could say, 'Boy, I really enjoyed that,' but I'm still just a white woman enjoying it. I don't know. Is the black person feeling like, 'Hey, that felt great. I loved that'?"

In short, most churches believe they could solve their diversity issues, especially in attracting more African American members, if they were just able to hire an African American worship leader. Indeed, after conducting interviews in several churches, I stopped being surprised to hear they were "planning to hire" a black worship leader. For example, one staff member said, "We are looking for a new permanent worship leader coming in, somebody that has that diversity and that ability musically to push us out to a new place." In the context of the interview, it was clear being "diverse" and bringing people to "new musical places" meant hiring an African American worship leader to incorporate more gospel music. Shelly, a white worship leader, said, "We've identified an African American man that at least from a senior leadership standpoint would be ideal who has his PhD in music. He can play very traditional classic music that would be more the style of what we have in our early service and has studied and is very proficient in jazz and contemporary music, so he would be able to bridge those different areas. As well as the fact that he is black, that he as an African American, lends that just visual diversity to the team that is up there." Another church had begun to diversify whites, Latinos, and African Americans and hired an African American "from Chicago" who came from "an all-black gospel type of background." I was told "he brought a different flavor to the service." The spicing of the service also included creating "what we call an Inspiration Choir." Another church talked about a white worship leader who had "no soul in him." His replacement was an African American. Because of hiring a musician with "soul," the quality of worship was perceived to have changed, "the enthusiasm [has] grown a lot because of what he brought to it."

The importance of the conceptual presence of blacks in shaping multiracial worship is that blacks' performance of "black music" represents striking, visible racial difference and therefore provides affirmation in the progress and achievement of multiracial goals for their congregations. Among leaders hoping to hire diversity, they want that obvious, visual diversity accompanied by what they anticipate will be a broadening of musical styles. In contrast, one leader who was frustrated with trying to further diversify her church lamented, "We haven't had many African Americans up on the stage." Of those churches that have hired a black pastor, all discuss it as a core component of their efforts for diversity. Another church leader talked about hiring Benny, an African American worship pastor, saying, "Benny was a key component in bringing diversity because what Benny does is he brings an African American presence. The former worship leader was white and he had a great heart, but his worship experience is limited to his culture." When it comes to worship, whites are perceived to be "limited" in their ability to craft an ambience sensitive to other racial and ethnic groups in such a way that they would be able to fully worship God. "Benny had been enmeshed and other cultures, even though he has a strong African-American background, he knew the reformed church and knew the reformed culture, and he is also very adept at other Christian songs by white artists and so forth and brought in a broader background for us to engage."

Black worship leaders (whether actually present or not) are consistently idealized as "experienced" and "well-rounded" musicians who were not solely tied to the gospel music tradition. Leaders assume a high level of musicianship in different genres that makes that black worship leader "able to bridge those different areas." The person would bring a broader range of musical styles, especially in bringing gospel music. Lauren, a white church leader, said, "My hope is that having somebody that is different than what is generally on that platform, meaning white middle-aged predominantly male, will allow for that [ethnic/racial] expression and that broader experience." An attender in commenting on the visual diversity of the teams similarly said, "I hope that [the worship] it's fuller, like we are going to incorporate more different styles of worship."

Hiring a black worship pastor is viewed as critical for diversity in bringing not just African Americans but all other non-representative racial and ethnic groups. What may seem to be a hiring for a specific racial group is actually believed to tie into the potential of bringing in diversity more broadly. There is little worry from church leaders that bringing diversity on the platform would threaten the larger demographic base within the congregation. "I'm not worried that we're going to lose something that appeals to the white population," said one church leader. However, the styles of music being considered are always those that are already welcomed by the dominant group. Specifically, gospel (and often salsa) are forms of "ethnic" music that are viewed as culturally acceptable. So the incorporation of such musical rhythms only adds to the value of the services for the dominant group. Leaders believe if they can add the appeal of "crossover music," then they can diversify church.[14]

So, in multiracial churches, hiring toward diversity involves staffing appropriately. When I spoke with one church leader about the effort to incorporate more Asians in his congregation, he said, "If we want to be intentional about it, we'd have to bring someone on staff. You put your money where your mouth is...." Another church leader simply said, "To reach black people, you have to have a black man coming in here who loves leading music."

"Black music" takes on a mythic quality in multiracial churches. For example, in a pan-Asian congregation, church leaders often spoke of "Motown" as the rhythm, sound, and feel they sought in their churches. One leader of an Asian-dominant church believed that he had a deep, personal connection with black "soul music," saying, "The Temptations, and the Delphonics, and Chicago, and Blood, Sweat, and Tears, and Santana. That's my soul music." He strives to bring the "Motown Sound" into his congregation. "I started dreaming that one day we were going to have a more R&B, a more funk, a more black appeal with some Latin like Santana-ish sort of thing because I grew up with all of that." He believed the music was universal to all Asian Americans. "I lived a divided existence, which I think a lot of Asian Christians do." The difficulty with requiring "black music," like "soul" or "gospel" in his church is the pervasive belief that only blacks can truly perform this music. Non-blacks have an inability (a racial inability) to worship properly.

An interesting twist in this predominantly pan-Asian church is how proudly they talked about hiring a "gospel artist" who is Asian. A musician said, "He can do eclectic styles but he's led us in our worship with much more of an urban-gospely-R&B style. That was very intentional on our pastor's part to hire him because he wanted to go in that direction..." In this multiracial church, the authenticity of racial performance was less important than at least having the style of music; nevertheless, hiring for this style was intended to diversify the congregation. The hiring of an Asian gospel musician is an ambiguous strategy that affirms the ethnic base of the congregation while attempting to attract other racial-ethnic groups less representative in the congregation. "We wanted to go toward opening up to our African American and Latino community because, well, we've got the whole East Asian thing down."

Hiring a worship leader in support of diversity therefore includes the complexity of who the congregation will accept as a musical leader. In other words, who "fits" the congregation? This is further complicated by the common practice of churches to hire those already acculturated to the doctrines and practices of the congregation. As one pastor said, "We tend to hire from within." For most diverse congregations, hiring from within will most likely mean hiring a person from the majority ethnic-racial group in the congregation, and this can unknowingly accentuate the dominant ethno-racial group in the internal power structure of the congregation.

Racially Specific, Yet Radically Inclusive

Taken together, the thrust of adopting African American styles of music, encouraging the racial performance of blacks, and the racially directed hiring of black worship directors indicates that the weight of structuring worship experiences in multiracial churches is decisively toward an idealized ecstatic black culture of worship. Through sharing anecdotes, personal reflections, and programmatic vision, a constant subject among all non-blacks I talked with was the African American worshiper.[15] When I asked how the diversity of the congregation affects the worship experience, Daniel, a white musician, confidently said, "Well, it definitely enhances it. I think everyone kind of learns from everyone. I mean, let's say there is some white person that's more conservative and then he's sitting next to some African American person that's jumping up and down, and I think as long as the person is open enough, they might see that and go, 'Hey, maybe it's okay for me to clap my hands,' or whatever." In a pan-Asian congregation, a church leader said, "I so love it when I look out there and I see the non-Asians, especially the Hispanic, especially the blacks, moving like they would in a black church." Another leader boasted, "We just recently had a girl and a guy, African Americans, that sang up front, and I felt like they brought more diversity to the music because they were adding more soul." Incorporating African Americans and black styles of worship are fundamental to the structure of multiracial churches as they implement intentions for even greater diversity through worship.

African Americans carry the burden for diversity among congregations—even those congregations with few or no African Americans. As the imperative for racial and ethnic diversity continues to expand, the universal sense of the power of "black worship" will especially shape the structure of liturgy in churches across the nation. It also makes worship for blacks a unique arena of envy and privilege in the United States. This religiously tinged notion of race deeply affects the practice of worship in all multiracial churches, especially in the creation of "gospel choirs." The simplest formula for diversity came from a white associate pastor who said, "If you try to reach African Americans, have a gospel choir."

In one pan-Asian congregation, the presence of a gospel choir is extremely important to both leaders and members. When I spoke to the gospel choir director, she said, "I felt it [gospel music] was such a great way to bring community together and it was a great way to diversify people, experiences, and expressions of worship. I loved it. And our pastor recognizes the choir intrinsically to be a diversifying tool." We talked about hiring, and she said the pastor "could have hired an African American worship leader." Churches with diverse membership have enough anecdotal evidence to support whatever strategy they adopt. Jodi was proud of a moment in her Asian-dominant church when an African American started coming recently to church, saying,

"Of all the songs we played, when we played the one gospel song, he went, 'Oh my gosh, a song I know.' And he just came alive, and he immediately told me afterwards, 'I didn't know any of the songs, but when I heard that one song, that was a song I knew, and I knew the words and I knew this was a church for me.' Because he felt a connection here." The church is firmly committed to moving in toward gospel styles of music. The church ended up hiring another Asian gospel choir director. "What a great fit," said one of the leaders. "She is an Asian woman who does gospel and leads a gospel choir. And she says, 'See, I was raised in Hong Kong and look what God made me.' Yeah, we are the church of possibilities." Such vision-centered language that combined ethnic affirmation while seeking simultaneously to transcend it toward an African American (and some Latino) direction is a means to sustain a diverse vision that conforms to idealized notions of what "diversity" should be.

The gospel choir in this multiethnic Asian church comes from a deep sense that diversity must be created intentionally. Jodi, the worship director, said, "It's intentional. You have to be intentional about it. As awkward as it is and as weird as it is." Yet the congregation had experienced this Asian gospel choir leader as "a shock." She acknowledges that gospel directed by an Asian woman is odd, as people tell her, "'There's nothing gospel about her.' And that it's awkward, and it's weird." When I asked if an African American would be even more of a shock, she said, "We are taking baby steps in that direction to ease people into it." She remains committed to the principle of having a gospel choir. She lives in the interim of hoping to recruit a true gospel singer (i.e., an African American) who will take over the position. An "Asian" gospel choir director is a transitional figure for a hopeful future hire of an "African American" gospel choir director.

For most congregations that are diverse (and the many that want to become diverse), the gospel choir has become an absolute necessity. Doug, a white member said, "A choir shaped by the African American music for the church is very important in letting folks of ethnic backgrounds know that this church is open to their participation." In the minds of leaders and attenders, the gospel choir signifies openness to such a degree that even Latinos, Asians, and other ethnic groups would feel welcome as well. Doug said in his church, "Fortunately, we have usually at least one Hispanic family worshiping, and although there are no tangible signs of outreach to folks of Latino background, I have to think at least they know it's not a white church."

The sense of "at least it's not a white church" gives concerned members the confidence that the church is moving in the right direction. A Latino talking about his worship experience with the gospel choir said, "This is not our world. It's still a white man's world." He said, "You feel that with propositions and things that are going on. People can feel oppressed and to be able to give them that. The inspiration choir gave them a voice. Even in the white church, it was nice to see diversity come in and people have a voice here. To feel like they weren't afraid to worship, to be who they are. And nobody has asked them to change." The gospel choir allows permission to experience full worship without the "oppression" or burdens of being a minority. A gospel choir marks a church as is "a place that's diverse." As one white member said, "The gospel choir is all different [people], not all the same." She was proud of her choir and believed the visible diversity in the choir encouraged acceptance. "Being all ethnic groups, it just shows that everyone is accepted." For Chris, gospel music emphasizes the oppression and heartache of non-white people in the United States. Gospel music is not just for blacks, but for Hispanics like himself as well. He said, "Brokenness is the key thing of being before God, knowing you're broken and being able to uninhibitedly praise and worship God and to rely on him."

In the end, the priority of the gospel choir is that it is seen as a means for including all people, not just African Americans. Evan, pastor of the "diversity service" at their church, said, "It's not a gospel choir. We particularly stay away from that word 'gospel.' We don't want to give people the notion that we are trying to turn that service into a gospel, black-oriented, music-style service." Nevertheless, music leaders of diverse congregations like Evan depend on racial stigmas and try to leverage them productively. And these productive stigmas only work if racialized beliefs are general enough such that everyone acknowledges the power of the visual presence on display. For non-black church services, this means incorporating African Americans on stage, sometimes Latinos, especially if they are darker skinned, speak with an obvious accent, or conform to other ethnic stereotypes. In other words, a person must fit into the role of the racial other in order to fulfill the value for diversity. One church leader talked about a Latino man in his church, saying, "This guy Carlos comes to the forefront because he's got a great voice and a heart, so we said put him up there." Because Carlos conforms to a stereotype of "lively Latino," he helps represent a Latin flavor through his presence. "We put him up there, he starts singing, and he helps us to immerse ourselves into the Latino culture with worship." The phrase "we put him up here..." signifies the strategic use of people like Carlos for their ethnic distinction as those who accentuate the badge of diversity on the platform.

Both leaders and members of these choirs assert that the music sung in a gospel choir is intended for everyone. One black choir member said the music is not intended only for African Americans. She said, "We know that we have a melting pot in the service and we want to feed everyone through the music." In another church, Asians singing gospel is celebrated for the ability to transcend racial differences. When a musician recounted an Asian singing gospel music in their church, he said, "It kind of made the transition easier. And now it doesn't really matter who's singing it. Music is music and we are all able to connect with it." An African American musician said, "If you just have a gospel choir, if you have a multiethnic church and you just have a black, gospel choir, it's going to turn some people off, and all they do is one type of music, but it's going to attract people that like that. But if you have a choir that's doing all different types of music, then you're going to attract all different types of people."

Racialized Ritual Inclusion: Gospel Choirs Get Diverse Members Involved

In Christian churches, worship is almost always accompanied by music and often led by a choir. The presence of a choir can be defined quite specifically as a group of music performing some form of "choral" or what most may see as "classical" music. Nancy Ammerman found such choirs are more likely if the majority of the members have college education and high family income.[16] She cites Paul DiMaggio and John Mohr in stating that knowledge preferences and habits instilled through higher education are often linked to the consumption of classical music, a pattern especially notable with mainline Protestants where religious tradition and demographic trends coincide.[17] Ammerman summarizes, saying, "Having a choir is an organizational strategy that reflects a complicated mix of religious tradition, local priorities, resources, and cultural preferences."[18] Conservative Protestants are more likely to have worship bands and praise teams, although in my observations many of these congregations are redefining their mixed-race musical groups to be called "gospel choirs." Of course, choral music is notable with African American churches. According to Ammerman, two-thirds of black churches have at least one adult choir, and many have multiple choirs.[19] She cites James Abbington who asserts that African American churches typically have five or six choirs even if in small congregations.[20] Regardless of their denominational tradition, choirs are part of the collective religious experience of the Black Church. More than simply the experience of hearing the choir sing, choirs in all these churches allow opportunities for members to be involved in the ministry of their churches.

Similar to Ammerman's findings, Mark Chaves also indicates that participation in an adult or children's choir is an important spiritual activity in American congregations.[21] Besides being in the congregation and worshiping, participating in the choir is certainly the most common musical involvement in a church. It is an involvement members tend to enjoy. Wendy, an Asian choir member, said, "It's a great experience and as we rehearse for the gospel choir, I just can't believe that God would allow me to do it. Even if I don't go and sing on Sundays, it's just such a joy to be in the choir, the gospel choir."

In an analysis of a church that successfully diversified, Penny Edgell Becker describes how congregations that seek to change the frame of how "race" is resolved is a practical problem that needs to be solved. The first effort in City Baptist was to change the weekly ritual, the worship service, by placing racial diversity in front of the church. Music was also changed, to add variety. She emphasizes that while race is a social and political problem, in practice it is a problem of interaction. While she discusses the role of pastoral sermons for framing personal attitudes, her analysis also accentuates the importance of people from diverse racial and ethnic backgrounds being included in church services.[22] "Racialized ritual inclusion" is central.[23]

Racialized ritual inclusion is what I label here as the process by which church leaders change worship services to incorporate members of different racial and ethnic groups. Racialized ritual inclusion through regular, public, and sacred actions is a means to create an inclusive symbolic environment. So, while attitude change is important, the focus on music and worship leads me to further emphasize visibility, materiality, and practice in fostering the racially and ethnically interactions evident in multiracial churches (a view also emphasized in my studies of Mosaic and Oasis).[24] Racialized ritual inclusion is therefore consistent with a view of seeing culture as consisting of rhetorical, interactional, and material tools that are organized into strategies of action.[25] It involves understanding how social action is constructed, rather than merely the issues or ideas of what is being constructed. It also involves understanding the pervasiveness of racial and ethnic notions of difference, rather than merely stressing unity on the basis of religious similarity.[26]

The gospel choir occupies a unique intersection between the intentionality for diversity by leaders and the activity of church members who may not be aware of the direction of their leadership. "I love trying to meet people where they are and challenging them," an Asian gospel choir leader said. "The choir is a really great intersection. We're talking about musical diversification, but also bringing the congregation along with the diverse music." For her and other leaders, the gospel choir serves several purposes. First, it pursues aesthetic enjoyment both for the choir members and the congregation. Second, it creates relationships between strangers. Third, it provides a missional component as the choir performs in venues outside the congregation. Finally, the choir is a place where Christian discipleship is modeled and expected. As this Asian gospel leader summarized:

> Gospel music is fun, so that attracts people initially. It builds community because it's in a group. And there is an outreach factor to it because we get to go outside the church—we've been invited to sing out in the local community. So there is a witness factor. And there's more interfacing with different people than normal. And it's a ministry of accountability too. So I think it's just a great place for so many things to just converge. It's exciting. I'm really excited all the time.

The choir allows for a profound sense of "togetherness" that accentuates the life of the congregation in a focused, relational, and enjoyable manner. Monique, a Hispanic, said that "with the gospel choir, it's just so contagious." Consistent involvement of diverse people in the music ministries of a church—like joining the gospel choir—is a pathway to fostering interracial community in multiracial congregations.

8

Interracial Community through Multiracial Worship Practices

> No one at this church believes the music is responsible for the diversity. Community is established through the people. They love each other. They care about each other. It's small enough that they all pretty much know each other.
>
> —THERESA, WHITE, lead pastor

ONE SUNDAY MORNING, I took a seat right in the middle of a diverse congregation, anxious for the music of the service to start. Over the past week, I had interviewed several members from the "gospel choir" of this church. They were so proud of their choir, the music, their diversity, and the importance of the choir to their church experience and to the identity of the congregation that I became quite excited to hear this choir perform. The service began, and after several congregational hymns sung together, it was time for "special music." I watched a group of eight singers (a much smaller group than I expected) take their places up front and a man hurriedly shuffling sheet music at the piano on the side. With a moment to gather their collective composure, the choir director nods to the pianist and the choir begins to sing—and the music was horrible. The piano was out of sync. The vocalists were out of tune. The bass singer was much louder than everyone else, making an awkward harmony throughout the entire performance. When it was done, I looked around to see the reactions of fellow congregants to what I thought was a terrible performance. To my utter surprise, everyone clapped. But what were they clapping for?

When I spoke later with members of the choir, I found that they themselves were quite satisfied. Ronald, an older African American choir member, said, "We don't get no complaints from nobody. Like I said we have all nationalities. There are so many songs we select from, but anyway, the whole church, after we got through, the whole church clapped because they enjoyed it." When I followed up with attenders over the following week, about half of them praised the choir, saying something like, "Oh, it's soooo beautiful." But I simply could not bring myself to believe them. Instead, I believed the other half when, with a smile, they would look at me, shrug their shoulders, and say, "Well, you know, they're *our* choir."

Seeing the connections between performance and appreciation unlocked the unseen bonds that existed within this and other congregations. Among all congregations, while I found some members who said they like the music of their church, I generally found that members are reluctant to say anything critical about the music of their churches. As the gathered congregation comes to represent for each member "my people," there is an appreciation for those who perform the music of the church as "part of what we do." The aspects of the service that help to draw people together have little to do with the quality of the sound produced. Maybe notes are missed, and the music is not perfect. But this is "us." Through participation in worship music of the services (both in following direction and hearing performances) members come to feel connected to each other and are supportive of each other. Is it music they would buy off the shelf? Maybe not. But because this is "us" there is an appreciation for what comes through.

Music alone does not integrate people. The force of the music does not come through its professional quality but rather through the relational connections members share. By analogy, most of us have had children or grandchildren, nieces or nephews, who have performed a musical piece in public. The violin might have "squeaked" more than played, and the piano may have "eeked" out more than a few missed notes, but in the end the performance is still cheered because of our connection to that person. The relationship, not the music, is celebrated. The music gives occasion for building relationships.

How Worship Music Structures Diversity

Amid all the well-articulated beliefs and confidently asserted worship programs described by leaders and members of multiracial churches, observation shows that there is no formula for successful multiracial worship. Even if some (certainly not all) multiracial worship invokes a racialized paradigm of musical pluralism in their congregations, this is not a sure method for stimulating congregational diversity. And given the variety of approaches to music among diverse congregations, the focus on musical style is not the most important element of worship practices responsible for stimulating the integration found in successfully multiracial churches.[1] Even when the model of musical pluralism is implemented, there are other factors involved in the cultivation of diversity.

If music is not the answer, why is there so much attention given to music? It is easy to see why church leaders bring such optimism to their belief in the efficacy of worship music. Throughout my interviews, I found church leaders believe they have complete control over the musical environment of their congregations. Churches have no control over their demographics of their neighborhood or geographic region, but they can control the style of their musical worship. Since music choices can be manipulated, then perhaps it can be a manageable element of the congregation that could change the demographics of the congregation. Yet what leaders and members most often fail to understand is that it is not the style of worship but the social system in which worship is embedded that actualizes the diversity of the church. While the acoustics of music are obvious, the social system of worship is not. Music plays an important role, but superficial changes in style are not sufficient. And from the standpoint of systematic analysis, stylistic aspects of church cannot explain the source or sustenance of congregational diversity. Understanding how music and worship structure diverse relationships is more important than simplistic notions of "racial worship experiences" or "intentional integrative leadership."

For many multiracial congregations, the attempt to diversify worship involves both music selection and the people performing it on the platform.[2] Daniel, an Asian worship leader, said, "We will do Latin style and we will do gospel. Especially for our large gatherings, for Easter services, anniversary services, we'll make sure that our music is diverse and our teams are more diverse." When music directors and worship leaders begin to consider the manner in which diversity is played out in terms of actual people, it is hard to get away from the underlying belief that different musical styles are believed to relate to different groups. A worship leader from a pan-Asian group said, "If I were to describe our style—If our style were similar to another ethnic style—it would definitely be more of the Caucasian style. I think that's why Caucasian people have been joining our teams." He said, "Our vision has been that we will not limit ourselves to one style for worship. We want to do more—There have been a couple times when we would do a Spanish song or the lyrics would be in Spanish and teach that to the congregation, and things like that. So we'll try to do things like that. And I think we are just now entering a time when people of different ethnicities will join." There arises a pressure to place people of different racial and ethnic backgrounds in prominent positions. The mix of acoustics and visual cues proclaim diversity and inclusiveness.

The recruitment of diverse people to visibly showcase diversity in church worship creates the structures of diversity. This is a process I label *racialized ritual inclusion*.[3] To actualize music, people are needed, and the intentional recruitment and incorporation of diverse people creates the possibility of involvement and relationships that ensures diversity happening over time. By highlighting ritual inclusion, we reframe our understanding of how music works by privileging the practical over acoustical dynamics. A significant form of ritual inclusion is through intentional staffing for public diversity in the liturgy. George Yancey echoes the belief of many who actively advocate the increase of racial diversity that the desire for congregational diversity must accompany the commitment to staff leadership positions (both paid and unpaid) with racial diversity. In most multiracial churches sampled by Yancey, "Leadership tended to reflect the racial diversity of the church members. If the official clergy leadership was not always racially diverse, then generally the lay leadership (elders, deacons) was racially integrated. This diversity was generally not an accident since these churches tended to be aware of the importance of diverse leadership. Multiracial leadership is important because members of different racial groups desire to feel represented by the members of the church, especially racial minorities who historically have received a lack of respect for their opinions and perspectives."[4] Intentional diversification toward representation is viewed as an important component of achieving and sustaining diversity.

In terms of intentionally recruiting and staffing for diversity, I found that notions of African Americans as worshipers to be especially important to the structuring of worship and music in diverse congregations.[5] The belief in the superiority of black worship and the necessity of black inclusion drives the construction of diverse church services in practice. The push for black inclusion through hiring black staff and forming gospel choirs inadvertently serves to diversify the congregation.[6] It is not music but rather recruitment and participation in musical structures that fosters relationships, community, loyalty, and a sense of connection—the bonds that create a sense of what "church" is together.

Visible diversity is a seductive aspect of believing the vision for diversity is being actualized.[7] But many of the more astute observers of their congregations see that visible diversity is not enough. I found one conversation particularly enlightening. An Asian choir leader said, "It's easy to measure results and progress with something like the worship team because it's so diverse.

I mean, it's up there and it's visible." She said that dealing with "one-on-one relationships" is "harder." Having rich sets of cross-cultural relationships "is like several million years down the road. But building our worship team, that's something we can do now. And it's something we can do immediately, and we can feel good about the results we get. So I'm afraid that people would just stop there and say, 'Okay, that's enough,' and not go beyond. A diverse worship team is a starting place, but it's not the end."

Conspicuous diversity is to be followed up with "genuine relationships and community." Once the presence of diversity is "what their eyes tell them first," the next thing is to encounter "the warmth of everybody greeting them." Visible diversity, greetings from diverse people, and the togetherness of worship through music, these all go together into constructing a holistic experience for new visitors as they come through the door. "The whole kind of thing starts to operate within itself like that."

The motivation for conspicuous color and visible diversity is not intended to be "racist" but rather to fulfill a religious mandate to complete Jesus's call of reaching people with the message of salvation and realize a truly global ambition to bring "the world" to Christ (Matthew 28, Mark 16, Acts 1). Rafael, an Hispanic associate pastor, said the "foundational point" is: "You've got to have the right heart. You've got to have the commitment to ethnic diversity, not for the sake of ethnic diversity, but simply because if we're going to be faithful to the Great Commission and the Great Commandment." For Rafael and others, ethnically diverse music and worship is not just a gimmick. It is the task of people to reach out and build relationships with others who are in their neighborhoods, workplaces, and schools. Rafael said, "If you're in an ethnically diverse community, the church will naturally become ethnically diverse." An African American pastor in another church agrees. "Our wholly evangelical thrust is to the community that is diverse." He and others focus on the missional imperative. "It starts with a leadership that says we're going to stay and reach out to our community. So we are a community-oriented church. Strongly so."

Multiracial churches, therefore, structure for diversity in ways that actualize the racial and ethnic integration of their ministries, but not in ways they intend. While musical choices can communicate the value of diversity to visitors of a church, this is done not merely through promoting styles of music but by expanding the structures of participation and involvement. So while leaders and members may believe that the display of visible, racial difference is important for members of groups to feel "welcomed" and "at home," in actuality the desire for diversification leads dedicated staff, lay leaders, and committed members to actively recruit and incorporate difference out of their intense desire to "see" diversity happen. In the process, these people come to have relationships, share successes and sorrows, and come to commit to each other in ways we typically associate with familial church community. Aside from (and even in spite of) the varying beliefs of attenders and church leaders, diversity happens—even without the intention to diversify—because music and worship create practical spaces of interaction where cross-racial bonds are formed and sustained.[8]

Music as Congregational Involvement Besides Merely Attending Services

To see how the practice of music in multiracial churches actualizes cross-ethnic and interracial interactions, we must recognize how interpersonal relationships are embedded within the worship ministries of congregations. Steve, a young Latino, said, what "draws anybody to a church is the worship and music and personal relationships." The order of Steve's observations is the same order as my own. I began my research with a focus on worship liturgy, specifically the music, and eventually moved out to focus on the manner in which interpersonal connections are built and sustained through the musical practices established in the congregation. Music and worship of a congregation stimulates diverse relationships in a congregation. But it can mask how relationships existed before new practices were instituted or obscure the manner in which relationships are made in the midst of current, intentional practices for diversity. For example, Chris said, "I love salsa music, but they've mixed in some salsa stuff, you know. But Latinos were here before the salsa music. Before Dwayne knew how to sing a couple Spanish songs, they were here. Yeah, I don't know if it's so much ethnic as maybe it's social. You know, as maybe it's—I mean it was community. Just being with each other. So when it comes to the church service, it's a service. When they created the diversity service, they were saying it's a service. And people came." Chris emphasized that Latinos and whites participated together in the church before there were Spanish songs. For Chris, his congregation's diversity was not created or sustained through a mystical bonding of listening and spirituality in worship but rather through connections that were further accentuated through musical involvement and performance. Music provided an opportunity to create more opportunities for diverse involvement.

Other musical forms that highlight race or ethnic distinctions also create opportunities to build community. For example, the creation of gospel choirs in multiracial churches institutionalize a legitimate and desired presence of African Americans through the music ministries of multiracial churches. The intentional, racialized ritual inclusion of blacks in the formation of gospel choirs publicly highlights their involvement. At the same time, gospel choirs and the inclusion of African Americans are not intended solely to attract African Americans but rather support a much broader vision for diversity as the creation of gospel choirs stimulate involvement of both blacks and non-blacks not represented in the congregation.

In talking about the diverse music of her church, Kimberly, a black choir member, emphasized how music becomes an event for members and guests to mingle together. She said, "We will have Super Salsa Sunday, and I appreciate that. We have food, which is important to culture. And then we have Super Soul Sunday, and we'll sing a bunch of gospel songs, and then we'll eat and go with the food again that's very important to culture. Music and food are bringing us together." Kimberly sharpens our observations to look not just at the sonorous aspects of music but its social aspects. Just as food involves more than the sense of taste, music is more than the sense of hearing. Music and food are center points for social occasions that create space for interactions between people both familiar and unknown. Music and food provide focal points for interactions and allow new forms of community. And just as taste is not equal for everyone, so is music not equal. The "musical buffet" of a congregation is mirrored in the church meal set up for everyone to enjoy.

Another way the practice of music in congregations incorporates difference through racialized ritual inclusion is through partnerships with other churches, usually Latino or Asian homogeneous ministries who share a church building. In one mostly black-white congregation, the church attempts to sing a few Spanish lyrics in the music and even read Biblical Scriptures in Spanish, even though services are conducted mostly in English, "before the sermon almost every week." Few in the congregation are fluent Spanish speakers, yet they will bring in a Latino pastor, "Pastor Roberto, the Spanish noon service pastor," to speak in Spanish and then a translator will translate into English. The actual incorporation of a native speaker is one of the most obvious practices in creating diversity through programming in church services.

All Multiracial Churches Create Spaces of Community through Worship Practices

Racialized ritual inclusion is critical because members are more likely to stay in a congregation if they find ways of being involved and feel connected to others in the church. The most important aspect of music in stimulating diversity is how music fosters places for participating and opportunities to connect with others. For example, if a non-black church introduces a gospel choir, it essentially communicates that there is a possible opportunity for African Americans who had been involved in a choirs in a previous church. The gospel choir provides a readily recognizable way to be involved and participate in the ministries of the church. Even more, the performance of music provides opportunities for church members to recognize others and be recognized publicly, initiating a context for interactions beyond the service.

Recruiting Singers and Musicians

The music ministries of a congregation demand a considerable amount of planning and preparation. Once there is a commitment to having a choir or a worship team, it requires work on the part of leadership, especially in recruiting singers and musicians. While recruitment is an issue in any worship ministry, a particular challenge emerges once diversity becomes a criterion for who is on the platform. Jeremy, a white worship leader, believed that the best way to diversify the music was to include musicians from different ethnic heritages, "getting people involved and people giving critique and critiquing the music and hearing the influence." The effort becomes not selection of music but rather recruitment of musicians. "They can draw in talented musicians that are really diverse and bring what they have to the music. On my part, it involves a daily attempt." It is a pastoral challenge of assimilation in "figuring out how to get the right people involved and opening up and giving freedom. For me it's trying not have my grip on music style and the leadership of all that stuff so much that I'm not freeing other people to be involved and try different things." Others simply believe that including diverse people is important in order to publicly manifest the diversity of people in the congregation. Overall, much of the diversity of the church is believed to be dependent on the ability of music leaders to continue integrating diversity into the worship teams and their public performances.

Most church attenders are quite naïve about the manner in which diverse people are incorporated into the worship ministries of their diverse congregation. Sharon, an Asian and member of her choir, stressed that the diversity of her choir was "not intentional." She said, "Not intentional. I think it is just happening... because we are God's people. It's great here at church we see each other as just part of God's community. So it's not like, 'Oh, you're black, you're red, you're green, you're purple.' It's not like, 'Oh, no, we need to have more white people here.' God brings them." When I asked about specifically about recruiting for diversity, Tony, a Latino musician said, "I definitely don't hear anything of that. I don't know why people are picked. I don't hear anything like we need to tailor to this type of crowd. Because I've heard about some churches that do that, you know, tailoring to this type of community. I never heard of that." Illene, an Asian attender in another church, said, "You can only think what an amazing thing that the Lord would bring all these people from different countries to the same place and only he can do such things, only he has such amazing power to do such things. That actually helps to strengthen our belief and faith in the Lord." Another Asian attender said, "To me, I see with my own eyes how the Lord put people from different countries and different races together and they are worshiping at the same time even though each of us have different experiences."

But these church members are wrong and would be surprised to find out how much time staff and lay leaders in their own churches spend trying to add "conspicuous color" to the public persona of the congregation. Multiethnic church leaders spend considerable time recruiting specifically for diversity. Malia, an African American member of the choir, told me she was involved as "soon as I got there." She "wasn't asked," she laughed and said, "NO, I was told to join." On visiting the church, "Once people found out I sang they invited me and said why don't you be a part of this." She was pressured to join the choir, although she did not seem to mind the attention. As a black woman, she became an important asset to the public musical profile of the congregation.

Explicit talk of bringing diversity becomes the subject of staff meetings and sessions with lay leaders. A Latino full-time staff member said, "One of the things our pastor talks to us in staff is that we need to make sure that we have ethnic diversity reflected in our ministry teams. In other words... make sure that the key leaders are not all white, because what are we saying? Only whites can have the key leadership positions and blacks and Hispanics and Asians aren't capable of holding those positions? So he's constantly telling us, 'Hey, evaluate the people on your teams. Make sure that there's diversity.'" In another congregation, Adrian, an Asian lay member of the worship team, said her ministry leader "gave us a challenge to look for non-Asian musicians." The effort to recruit diversely is verbalized and made an expectation. "There's a conscious effort to purposely seek out non-Asian people with that kind of gifting." In another church with a significant percentage of black choir members, a member said, "It was important that we saw not just black people. It's really hard to find that balance, it really is. We've really looked...." Racialized ritual inclusion is a conscious effort in all these churches.

One white worship leader described the challenge of recruiting and retaining musicians in a service that tries to display a variety of styles. Robert said, "It's maintaining the kind of musicians we have now" and then adding even more. "I think it's going to actually help us not only to continue to grow in numbers but also in maybe different styles of music too and adding whoever could bring whatever to the plate, so to speak. Styles particularly." A diverse congregation for Robert offered the opportunity to recruit diversely trained and experienced musicians who could expand the musical palette of the congregation.

It is not merely visual color but the belief that members of different racial and ethnic groups bring with them different musical heritages. As Robert, a white music director, told me about a Latino in his music ministry, "His heritage helps him to bring in that kind of [Spanish] music that is just amazingly energetic and different." A white musician in another congregation agreed. He said, "Because of the diversity, we are able to do all kinds of styles of worship. Within the worship ministry and the worship team, it's probably more diverse than the actual congregation is." In this congregation, the drummer believes the concentration of diversity in the worship team is not only greater than the overall diversity of the church—as if the diversity of the congregation was more concentrated within the worship team—and by doing so, contributes to the overall diversification of the church.

The degree of plurality in musical styles is dependent on the quality of the musicians available in the congregation. An Asian director of worship said, "There's an intentionality to the songs we use to reflect the ethnic diversity, but it depends on the level of musicianship, because different rhythms are just different styles." Here is a leader that intentionally selects songs to reflect ethnic diversity, but feels dependent on the ethnic capability of musicians to play those types of music. "Certain drummers, for example, may not be able to hang with a Latin rhythm." The idealism of bringing a vast variety of music styles often runs straight into the technical skills available among musicians. "There's a lack of resources." It is difficult for non-musicians to appreciate the degree of difficulty involved in moving from one musical rhythm to another, a fact I was frequently reminded of when discussing this issue with professional artists. An associate pastor described how hard the director of the gospel choir works with the team of "untrained voices." He said, "She gets a pretty good sound out of them, and everybody tries real hard to do it in more of a gospel style."

It is fascinating to note that the presence of diversity can also inadvertently hinder recruitment efforts. One worship leader told me about church members who said they were disqualified because they believed they could not sing in the ethnic styles desired by leaders. She said, "As far as multicultural worship, there are a lot of people who said, 'I can't be in the worship band anymore because I can't sing like that.' " The church was creating a new "gospel choir," and church members believed they did not have the ethnic qualifications to sing like African Americans. A co-leader changed the rhythm and tempo to demonstrate to choir members that they did not have to quit. "Marcus had to come alongside and put a little bit more time into them and show them they can sing like that." The co-leader feigned a technique that allowed them to "fake" a gospel-style: "He put a lot of words in a really quick repetition if you are singing a gospel song or something, or really high beat song. We told them, 'You know you can do it. And we are going to help you do it.' You know, it's like the guy who said, 'I've got no rhythm.' Well it's like, 'You do. It's just a different rhythm.' " The concrete limitation of musical skill often creates frustration among lead pastors in congregations who might have believed that adequate time for practice or better recruiting would solve this problem. Some worship leaders continue to emphasize rehearsing and retraining their volunteers, while others come to rely on extensive musical networks in their city to supplement their volunteers. Todd said, "That's one thing we've been really blessed with in Los Angeles, and then from my background of playing in the L.A. scene and different things is that I know a lot of really talented players."

A musician in a pan-Asian church said, "They are working really hard right now to make it more diverse." It remains a challenge. "They say, 'Oh, we are all about diversity.' And then I come and everyone onstage is like black-haired. So it takes away from the whole vision—I don't believe them." Leaders face limitations in actualizing diverse styles in looking at the musicians available to them. Thad, a white drummer, said, "Because of the diversity, we are able to do all kinds of styles of worship." Nick said, "Music is contingent upon the musicians that you have, unfortunately. (Pause.) We have one of two choices. If all you have is a keyboardist and an organist, you know they're in their sixties and seventies, they're not going to do much for you with regard to diversity, because they have this style of playing, and they have their repertoire. So you've got to do the one thing. You either have to recruit individuals that are starting to come, which is tough, because you've got to build the congregation to get there. Or you can hire the musicians."

Several churches pay studio musicians to play for the services because the congregation simply cannot sustain certain instruments through volunteers. In Mark's church, "It's bass and drums, because we don't have a bass and player or a drummer." Churches at the time of my study will pay between $75 and $250 for each set of weekend services they come and play. Everyone else is a volunteer, unless worship leaders bring in special artists for special guest performances. Guest performers of various racial and ethnic backgrounds are almost always friends of the worship leader brought in to play quality music that the normal ministries of the church could not bring. There are also bands that actively promote themselves to churches for services. Mark is one of several worship leaders who told me, "Sometimes people contact the church, saying, 'We're gonna be in the area, we'd like to play.' " Mark went and listened to their songs on a website and compared them to other contemporary Christian bands ("They're like Delirious, which is a band out of England. They kind of have that sound, and they said that's one of their influences, and some other stuff"), and so he decided "It'd be nice to have them come lead us." Worship leaders are motivated to bring guest performers in part to broaden the musical palette of the congregation, and in part to get a break from their responsibilities. Mark said, it's "great for me because I get a week off"—and then quickly added—"but I still feel like I work twice as hard, because I go in, I help set up and make sure everything's done right." The bonus is that racially and ethnically diverse musical guests further accentuate a congregational value for diversity.

Rehearsals and Relationships

Lead pastors and music directors are often concerned about the quality of the musical performance in worship. Yet I found it important to distinguish between the performance of music and what leaders and members do in preparation for the performance. In other words, I found it important to pay less attention to the choir *performance* and more to what happens in choir *rehearsals*. To understand diversity is to understand how music creates opportunity for meaningful relationships.[9]

As a social group in any congregation, the choir (or praise team or worship band) is a bounded, manageable set of relationships. Monica's choir group normally meets on Monday nights. "We get together and sing." She emphasized over and over again that her choir is "small," saying, "It's nice also because it's a small group. I've been in a big group before, and it's a headache. But this is a smaller group, and you don't have too many people to deal with. It makes it much nicer because everybody works together. It is small, and I like it. It's intimate because it's a smaller group of people." Tammy, a white woman active in her choir, said, "We have close relationships, and I know the people standing next to me, and we have prayed for each other. It's not so necessarily true with the people in audience." Tammy makes a distinction between the group of people she knows in the choir and the larger crowd of the congregation. When she is not singing and just in the pews, she said, "I may know the person sitting next to me but not having a close relationship like that I have with the people on stage. So it's a difference."

Toby, a white choir member, said, "We're a pretty diverse choir, we have African American members and European Americans and Hispanics." In our conversation, he emphasized the togetherness of the choir in facing a challenge together, saying,

> When you talk about diversity sometimes I think it's more important to talk about things that don't divide us but things that unify us. So you've got this diverse congregation and we've all selected say one song to sing, and let's say one week it's a piece of Mozart's, a sacred piece, a very traditional European piece of music. And everybody in the choir is committed to that piece and nobody says, "I don't like this music." Everybody gives it a fair chance. And by the same token there are some pieces I've never heard before that we've tackled that are more like an African American spiritual, or maybe part of Pentecostal hymn, something I'm not familiar with. We'll all embrace it, we'll all tackle it, and we'll sing it. Sometimes I think that way, just bringing these diverse songs together into one unifying moment; I think that can make a difference.

Rather than the exposure to different cultures as relating to different styles of music, he emphasized that there is a fundamental approach to music that involved people working together to master a piece of music regardless of personal aesthetic taste. The mastery of music for performance is a basic goal accomplished within his diverse church.

I laughed when one choir member admitted, "There are a lot of times on a Sunday where we're not really prepared." This was not cause for disappointment. Instead, it manifested the priority of the choir lies not in the skill of the performance itself. "We just do the best we can. Our leader is really supportive and says, 'You guys really sounded great.' It's really a nurturing environment." Involvement in the worship teams in congregations is not about performance, it's about the togetherness. Will, a musician, said, "At the root, I feel like the church is meant to be a community of people that get together and share with each other. Share life with each other. I feel like music is kind of secondary in terms of that. What's at the top of my list is do I connect to these people, do I feel like they are welcoming people, and can we share similar experiences, and things like that."

Rehearsals provide some social interaction but it does not stop there. Kristy said, "We don't have much rehearsal time. We try to go out to lunch sometimes. It's difficult to know each other one on one. Sometimes we break up into groups, smaller groups, and we pray together. And prayer is a big thing too, just sharing. We laugh a lot in rehearsal too. We laugh more than we sing. There's something about humor that breaks barriers. I just try to get to know people one on one. It's hard to get to know everybody in the choir, but I try to make that effort and a lot of friendships have developed within the choir." For Kristy and others, the choir is the most important connection they make in the congregation. According to Russ, "It's a sub-set of the congregation, and I certainly got to know my fellow choir members."

Mike, a white man, shared with me about a woman he came to know through involvement in the choir:

> My wife told me there was a funeral for a woman named Dorothy. I can't remember her last name, but I remember the news didn't really strike me. "Dorothy's funeral is Saturday, she just passed away." And then she said, "You know Dorothy, she was a little old woman with grey hair who used to put out the chalice cups." And then I remembered her, and I remembered her face, and now I knew who she was and how I hugged her and embraced her on Sundays and I really didn't know her. Oh, that was her. And I realized she's gone, she's not alive anymore. It makes an impression on you.

Mike then talked about a choir member, an older Asian woman, who had recently passed away:

> I'm sure somebody probably told you about Mrs. Chang. That was tough because it's one person that sat in front of me for a long time, for

> the three years that I sang, and she was there most of the time. She's such an interesting person, and she had so much energy and life. I wouldn't have gotten to know her if I hadn't sang in the choir. She had a personality, kinda prickly in some ways; but singing with her every Sunday you got to know her. You can actually come to understand her. So in that way it was good.

Mike's long-term involvement in the choir, including rehearsals, preparation, and performance, fostered a building of connections with others different from his natural affinity group. The diversity of the congregation is actualized for Mike through the connections made with other people involved in the worship ministries of the church. Involvement in the choir was the core of his congregational commitment. Mike said, "Before this church I never went to church enough to really know people and know if people were here or not or had passed away or moved away or what. Being part of the church for several years, we're starting to see that. It's something new for me."

For those who have never committed to participate in the music ministries of a church, it may appear that once-a-week connections are shallow. Even members talk about how occasional their relationships are. Clara is like many who began telling me she did not have active relationships with people in the choir because they live too far away. Yet my interviews with her and others reveal that even weekly meetings can be significant because they occur in a highly affective context. Talking with Clara in her home, she brought out her wedding album where I recognized several people from the church. "They got married the same year we did."

GERARDO: Have you made some friends that aren't white?

CLARA: Yes, Cheryl is in the choir, and Mary.

GERARDO: And you just get to know them from being there?

CLARA: Uh-huh. I get hugs from them every Sunday.

GERARDO: When did that start?

CLARA: I've always had that! We're very touchy-feely.

GERARDO: I think it's a very warm church, but still, was there a sense of adjustment or surprise at having these different friends that come from different places or backgrounds than you do? Did you ever think about that at all?

CLARA: No. They're just like you and me. You know? I don't think of them as being different.

Talking with Clara, she told me about how members of the choir would celebrate birthdays and take meals to people who were sick. Glen, a white member of the worship team, also talked about the caring relationships among members of his diverse group, saying, "There's a genuineness in this church that I haven't any place else, and people in this church are very sincere, warm, and caring. I think they truly love each other, myself included. I think there's some real strong feeling for one another. I've grown close to a lot of people here." The racial and ethnic diversity of Clara's and Glenn's friendships come from their involvement in the choir. Being in the choir gave them a supportive network of friends who rely on each other.

Corey, a white worship leader, talked about making connections among people, saying that in their mostly commuter church "the hardest thing is it's so spread out that people don't just come to the neighborhood church. They'll drive a long way, I mean we've got people driving from an hour away on Sunday mornings, just to come to church here, and people from the next county driving up. And because of that, there's people on the worship team that are like that, you know, they're driving and all this, so it takes a lot more effort to get everybody together outside of church sometimes for an event." Nevertheless, Corey immediately went on to describe how frequently choir members get together socially, saying, "I usually try to do lunch after church with the worship team, just to get everybody together and do something outside of church, because I find that that's really important to build those relationships and encourage people and stuff like that." Members overemphasize the "hard" commitment of being in the choir or worship team and casually forget the "soft" relationships that happen in less structured, unscheduled ways.

Overall, I found that members tend to underestimate the amount of interaction that happens outside of weekend services. Randy, a white member, said, "Sunday morning is pretty much who we are. That's where the interaction takes place," before highlighting other ways he connects with people in the congregation. I asked Floyd, an African American member, if he spent time with people in choir outside of rehearsals and worship time. Floyd said, "We do from time to time. We're pretty geographically dispersed. I stop by to see one couple and their kids from time to time just to see how things are going. Another person and I are in a small group together, so I'll fellowship with her outside of the Sundays and Thursday rehearsals." During an interview, one husband started telling me, "We don't see anybody from church on a personal, friendly basis. I don't think we've had people from there to come over here on a one-on-one basis at all." Then his wife sitting nearby corrected him, relating how people had come for an event they hosted last year, another couple who had come for meals, when the pastor and her husband came, and so on. The husband then readily admitted that there had been quite a few occasions. Every person mentioned was either part of the choir or a paid staff member.

Over the course of my research, I came to realize that when a person is recruited to serve in a choir or worship team, they take on a concrete commitment to the diversity goals of the congregation. Jesse, an Hispanic in a pan-Asian congregation, told me he had been thinking about leaving the church until the lead pastor approached him about being involved in the Sunday morning worship team. "It was just the fact that my ethnicity and my background wasn't represented at the church. I told him I could leave here and nobody would even notice I was gone." His new role in the ministry of the church allowed him to feel valued as a person by taking on the mantel of diversity. As a person who believes "music helps you have a sense of identity in the church," he said the worship ministry was how he came to have a sense of belonging to the church and its purposes.

There are many stories like Jesse's. I found that as members like Jesse become involved in the musical ministries of their church, they do not necessarily see themselves as working to diversify their congregations, but they do see themselves as contributing to their church. Yet by being part of their church, they succeed in accentuating the diversity of their church through their involvements. Over time, Jesse began to understand that his ethnic-minority status in the congregation was significant for the value it indicated to people watching his involvement. His involvement was directly connected to the missional goal of incorporating other diverse people into the church. Diversification in the music ministry as a form of outreach became a goal he embraced and could work toward. "I still don't feel we are fully represented. That's why I'm on this worship team, to make it more friendly for non-Asians." An Asian attender said, "There are people who are involved in worship teams, even though [they] wouldn't be at our church otherwise."

As recruitment for diversity is intentional, those who are not of the dominant race (especially African Americans in white congregations) are more aggressively targeted for inclusion in worship ministries. With new purpose and specific focus of involvement, these new recruits are more likely to remain. For them, the togetherness experienced in playing music together is often seen as part of a larger project, in what one white worshiper called "doing this racial reconciliation thing." Through the process of racialized ritual inclusion, they are supportive of their leadership as they don't disagree with the nobility and desirability of the goal. As one choir member said about her music director, "She is really striving for diversity, specifically, and she really feels that is done by getting diversity in styles of worship and even styles of playing."

African Americans and other "minority groups" therefore do not necessarily see having representation of their specific racial or ethnic group as critical to their own involvement in a congregation—as long as they feel connected to the congregation as a whole. The interview data instead indicate over and over that those who are in dominant ethnic groups in a congregation who have caught a value for diversity emphasize that it is important for "the other" to see their own people on stage. Non-majority members—even first time guests—are therefore recruited for conspicuous diversity. Yet these non-majority members accept that they may be less represented in the congregation. One member is typical in seeing his involvement in accentuating the diversity on the platform as an attempt by church leaders to engage a particular goal that he believed was not only commendable, but actually sanctioned by God. For him, the music was "balanced" because the worship leaders "try to make it seem like it's not for just one group." And he believed this came from the best of spiritual motives. "I think they are doing that with the best of intentions and I'd like to think they are seeking God in those things." Joining in the cultivation of visible diversity through conspicuous color becomes a way to affirm their own value for diversity and support the goals of the congregation.

"Like Family": Being Seen and Making Friends

As members become involved in the public ministries of the church, they place themselves in a position to know and be known by others. Monique, an Hispanic woman, talked about people being involved in the gospel choir, saying, "The more people you have up there, the more people that they relate to up there and it's like, 'Hey, that's my friend.'" In another church, Becky, a Middle Eastern girl, said that she's gotten to know people up front, "I see them every Sunday, so that's how I know them." It is interesting to note the ability of music to command attention. It creates a centering point, a place of social orientation, that overwhelms the workings of a group. Recognizability and relationships between people through music are more important than the acoustic sound.

Conspicuously colored members experience racialized ritual inclusion as an opportunity for connection and relationships. Even the poor incorporation of language in services can be viewed as an aspect of relational care and concern. Jesse is among the few Latinos who expressed a firm belief in the importance of Spanish language for a deeper worship experience. He believed he "could have more of a worship experience because you hear more in your own language. And when I do hear it—like that girl Monique that will speak in Spanish or sing in Spanish sometimes, even that will kind of give me a little tug on my heart because I hear words that I understand, I know are not exclusive to the mainstream of the church." It's about a feeling of incorporation or belonging. "In other words, I know that is for our people. So it will have some effect on the worship experience in that the identity makes you feel more tied in to where you are at." Another example comes from Chris, a Latino member of the church, who talked about trying to incorporate Spanish or Latin music in the service; Chris said, "The gesture is always a feeling of, 'Wow, they are trying to speak to me.' And it's the same feeling I felt when we came in. They were a little overly excited to see us because we were darker than them, but it was a feeling of, 'Wow! I matter here!'" Chris said how Spanish was incorporated into the service:

> A couple weeks ago, Paul was taking Spanish classes because he wants to be able to communicate to us better. He says, "Okay, so I'm going to try this." And then he spoke some Spanish words. And he just butchered them. And I kind of looked around and thought of how people would respond to this. But the reality is Paul speaks love always and everyone knows Paul's heart, and it comes out, so when he tries to speak Spanish, and it's horrible, it's coming across as, "Paul loves me enough that he is really trying." It's not a gimmick and it's sincere and it's authentic. And that is beautiful. So I think that's the same spirit that is felt when even now our predominantly African American inspiration choir, when they sing a song in Spanish or do anything like that, because it's a safe environment where people really feel loved, it's like, "That's just another gesture of love." It wasn't done perfectly, but, "Thank you for trying to speak and try to reach me."

Caring connections become more important than the actual presence of diversity. In this way, music is not merely a source of unity, but a source of *community* as involvement in music gives members something to do as responsible persons in the congregation and a group of people to which to belong.

The persistence of diversity therefore comes from sustained relationships built between congregational members. One choir director challenged my questions about music saying, "Are you just looking at the music because it's the most visible thing? I think people need to diversify the kinds of relationships they have in the congregation, you know, the relationships that people are accountable to." She emphasized the unseen relational connections between people. "Look at the friendship groups. I would start there and encourage people to have cross-cultural friendships." A pastor firmly believed the music was not responsible for her congregation's diversity. Her belief is that it is "the welcoming, we welcome the neighbors whoever they may be." One lay leader involved for over twenty years in her church said, "We do a good job, I think it's one of our strongest points, of connection with one another, making lifelong friendships in supporting one another and that is what keeps people coming."

A member in another church said, "The whole music thing is great, but it's not the reason I stayed. Because music comes and goes. It's the people." One comes to find threads of involvement laced throughout the congregation. Beverly, an African American, said, "Everybody is sort of involved in one way or another." Among the majority of church staff and members I interviewed, people feel like they are cared for in the congregation. Not just that they are accepted; rather, members really express feelings of deep connection that these are their close relationships and this is their "family." They reflected an underlying sense that "I know people and they know me," an intimacy discussed in a very positive way. At times, members in the smaller churches will especially prize their connections to each other, saying "In those big churches, no one knows anyone, but here we know each other. That's a big draw." Alice, a Latino member, said she never really noticed how many Latinos are in the choir or in the band. "No, but I never even realized it. It's not important to me. It's what is coming across not who or what race is up there." What she emphasized was a feeling of mutual connection rather than a sense of racial distribution. "I think the message being put out is a good thing and I never even thought to think how many Hispanics are up there."

Certainly worship is more than just music. Alice, a white member, said, "When we leave here, we'll all be together and there will be no race anymore, so start here and now and not wait until then. The interaction, you can see it." Leo, an Asian member, said, "All of the fellowship before and after worship all of that is part of the worship experience for me." Illene, an Asian attender, said the diversity of people worshiping in her congregation "helped me to understand and to witness other people's stories and their testimonies and it was very good." She said, "We are a family."

Relationships Signified and Reinforced through Performance

Scholars who study diverse congregations seem to agree that if we left congregants to their own desires, congregations would remain almost wholly homogenous. Therefore, congregational diversification will be accomplished only if there is a deliberate structuring of opportunities that occur which is sponsored and encouraged by corporate leadership. As a site for racialized ritual inclusion, the music ministry of the congregation is an important resource for structuring diversification. George, a Hispanic member, said once "you reach a certain social level, you move away from where you grew up. Somehow your culture changes." He listed some of his relationships, saying, "This guy who is Filipino, there's a Japanese guy in there, a Chinese guy, two Hispanic guys in there and four white guys." He said, "We made so many friends there and we met so many young families and all our kids are starting to do this and we are throwing them together and we do all kinds of weekend activities, camping, barbeques. It's a really neat connection and I'm glad I'm here."

One middle-aged woman, Heather, told me she had stopped coming to church for awhile and finally came one Sunday morning. She immediately ran into the "die-hard" older members who "never go anyplace." She felt younger, but this "older crowd" was always there and "they opened their arms and just took me in, and then the hug thing we do in the morning when we first get here, that just—once I started crying I couldn't stop. And I knew I was home." She added, "This is home for everybody."

Music alone is not sufficient; it is relationships and a sense of belonging that bind people to their church. One member said, "Everybody was saying that our church was noted for its music and its barbequing." John, a Middle Eastern attender, said he and his wife "went to another church as very similar to this music, but when I got a cold feeling from those people, so I said I don't want to go to this church." Music is a pathway to involvement, a means for others to connect to the congregation. The sense of being "like family" came up constantly. Lester, an older African American, said, "It's a nice church. The people treat you like a family." After talking about forms of care and relationships, he later again said, "To me it's most like a family church. Everybody knows you and loves you. It's like a family." Aida, a Latina, said, "I've missed a lot of Sundays, but I always come back because it's more like a family." Lucy, a white worshiper, said, "What we have is very, very strong and very, very satisfying. We are all family. We care about each other personally…here I know everybody and their children." A Native American told me what was most important is "the people. You're like family. And it's not just my extended family. Because most of them I feel like they're family no matter where I see them, or what day I see them." The sense of family was especially important to him. "When we make a mistake, we do it as a family. When we disagree on something, we do it as a family. When we all agree, we celebrate as a family, we mourn as a family." He added, "We can all support each other as a part of this family just from different ethnic backgrounds." Charlotte at another congregation said, "Everybody is really friendly with everybody, everybody hugs everybody, it doesn't matter what color you are. They talk, they go out with each other, have lunch together, little functions like picnics, people interact very well with each other."

In the novel *Moby-Dick*, after an evening of conversation with the "savage" Queequeg, Herman Melville puts words in the mouth of Ishmael about his newfound affection: "See how elastic our stiff prejudices grow when love once comes to bend them." The accentuated presence of visible diversity alone is not the secret, but the practices inherent to the performance of music is. Music provides sites to be recruited. Music provides regular, ritualized places of involvement and belonging for participants as volunteers give up to ten hours or more a week to their church. Music also provides places of corporate memory and familiarity that accentuates corporate identity through familiar songs and favorite tunes. And music provides opportunity for relational connections that extend far beyond performances and rehearsals. So, it is not about the performance, but the relationships signified and reinforced through musical performance that help sustain the diversity of a multiracial congregation. Even if the music is bad, even "terrible," the cross-racial unity comes out of caring relationships people share together.

Conclusion: Mystical Worship and the Reality of Practice

People need something to connect them, something to have them come back, and I think music is very important as it relates to that.

—RUBY, AFRICAN AMERICAN, member of Praise Team

WORSHIP IN MULTIRACIAL churches is always connected to the promise of unity. Shauna, a black choir member, is one of many who expressed a belief in the power of worship to heal racial divisions. "It's amazing to me how we've come together for the sake of worshiping God, for the sake of God himself, to worship together, because to me it's an insult to God when all blacks go to one church and all whites go to one because we are all created as one." I found leaders and members in all multiracial churches expressing Shauna's belief. The purpose of worship for them is to overcome earthly imitations and achieve a shared, transcendent experience of God.[1] A corporate connection to God will surely erase the arbitrary separation between believers in favor of a spiritual unity.

I entered this project seeking an experientially based answer for the overcoming of racial and ethnic divisions through worship. I thought I might come to grasp something of the emotional power of sacred music, how music "tugs at the heart," "lifts the human spirit," and "transcends our earthly concerns" by "stirring the passions" of a diverse crowd. Music would be "soothing," "inspiring," or just plain "worshipful," and the experience of music would create a profound human connection. As I began the project, it quickly became evident that while the virtuosity of the music can sometimes stir an otherworldly, yet deeply personal, communion with both the spirit of God and the gathered saints, most church members revealed that it was an effort to achieve a deep worship experience. And worship leaders, vocalists, and musicians seldom "worship" at all due to their responsibilities in performance.

I soon found that many members and leaders do not believe music is universal but racially specific. They believe only certain music truly connects with certain racial and ethnic groups. For them, accentuating and incorporating diversity is accomplished by building a musical repertoire of styles and genres with crossover appeal. They invoke a musical pluralism to justify and promote a buffet style of musical programming developed for liturgical services. Pluralist leaders select worship music that incorporates "diversity friendly" musical influences such as "gospel" and "salsa" to "spice up" their music. Like a chef preparing a musical casserole, worship leaders and musical directors add selective aspects of ethnically oriented influences to provide people a variety of idealized and racialized styles of music.

Yet, not everyone is convinced that incorporating "multicultural music" is the key to stimulating diversity. One Asian choir director said, "I wouldn't say you are racially reconciled just because you sing a Spanish song every once in a while."

As I continued to pursue my research, I came to understand that it is not the acoustics of musical style but rather the visible presence of diversity—a racialized ritual inclusion—that stimulates integration of different racial and ethnic groups into their churches. Katsuo, an Asian musician, said, "More than the music I would say the ethnic make-up of the people on stage probably has a bigger influence." He's right, and articulating my understanding of the unstated motivations, social workings, and extensive impact of visible diversity in the liturgy of multiracial churches became the core challenge of this book.

Worship Practices and the Promise of Racial Unity

Much of the research presented throughout this book supports that music is racialized and that churches often reinforce rather than challenge fundamental racial barriers. Indeed, part of what needs to be grasped about worship music is the extent to which both church leaders and churchgoers commonly assume the necessity and unchangeability of racial differences. With worship music, people tend to accentuate racial differences, often unknowingly polarizing musical differences as a way of demonstrating their assumptions of the polarizing differences between racial groups. In this way, worship music can and often does merely reinforce the racial differences believed to exist in the world—whether they are religious or not. Such musical absolutism and racial essentialism is quite common. Worship in multiracial churches largely exaggerates racial and ethnic differences at the same time it attempts to overcome it. So, what allows for music to encourage diversity rather than simply reinforce differences?

All multiracial churches share notions of "black worship" or "Latino worship" and believe racially based musical preferences lie at the root of the challenge to cultivate integrated congregations—even among those that do not incorporate diverse musical styles. Leaders and members in multiracial churches as well as the growing number of advocates for incorporating diversity saturate their programmatic intentions with an inherent racial essentialism. For them, the key is to include musical styles that are recognizable (even if in a stereotypical format) as long as they appeal to a mainstream audience. Musical leaders invoke an exotic mystique by bringing in gospel and/or salsa rhythms to welcome and appeal to non-white ethno-racial groups.

While not all multiracial congregations orient themselves around racially or ethnically sensitive musical styles, all of them are highly intentional about visibly including "conspicuous color" in who leads and who performs music up front during church services. In short, belief in the need for racially specific music is not universal, but a belief in the need for the presence of diversity is. Churches recruit along racial and ethnic lines as musical leaders are motivated to integrate people who are "visibly diverse"—especially African Americans. *A persistent, racialized ritual inclusion is the engine that drives diversification through worship.*

Beliefs of racial authenticity and performance promote profound assumptions of racial difference, however they simultaneously drive the imperative to include people of diverse racial and ethnic backgrounds into worship ministry structures. The performance of music is a structured social activity that requires planning and recruitment. As issues of diversity are heightened in a congregation, the music ministries of the church attempt to expand the inclusion of people from various racial and ethnic backgrounds. Actualizing visibly diverse worship music serves to accentuate the diversity of congregations. In this process of racialized ritual inclusion, the active incorporation of diverse people in the performance of worship music creates structured opportunities for the creation of community.

Multiracial churches ironically reproduce notions of racial and ethnic differences at the same time they try to eliminate them. More specifically, racially essentialist ideas affect the musical practices that are eventually implemented in churches and the interpretation of worship practices church members see on display. The coordination of diversity-affirming musical worship involves recruiting and incorporating performers, both paid and volunteer. Beliefs of difference lead to recruitment and involvement on the basis of difference. In the end, diversification of churches is not about racially accommodating distinct music styles or enacting simplistic notions of leadership intentionality but rather about stimulating cross-racial interactions through musical worship practices. As conspicuously colored people enact worship practices, a connection is forged between racially diverse performers and the congregational "audience." The choir may be off-key, but the choir is a social group providing a place of belonging and sacred connection to the congregation as a community. The occasional dissonant chord of the pianist and the ill-placed harmonies of the vocalist still connect the performance of a fellow church member who has with reverence and a sense of duty agreed to serve on behalf of the people gathered in that place for that occasion. Intertwining attitudes of gratitude and corporate solidarity draw people together regardless of style or form. These diverse members may only see each other once a week, yet members through corporate worship come to know each other and have surprisingly deep relationships with each other.

Worship as Inherently Social and Situational

Many will be disappointed that this book largely ignores stylistic differences in describing congregational worship. They will say I neglected crucial dynamics by pursuing a more "practice-based" approach to multiracial worship. However, it is imperative to acknowledge that music is never simply acoustic.[2] The effort of guiding congregational singing and putting together a sacred performance involves a mix of staff and lay volunteers. Even when professionals are enlisted to play the organ or backup the lead singer, the great majority of "worship" is pragmatically oriented toward moving the service along, sometimes filling gaps, sometimes highlighting the pastor's message, and sometimes accentuating a value for bring disparate groups to see themselves as connected into a single whole. Music is part of a church, and thus all aspects of the music from preparation to performance, from engagement to evaluation, are part of a process that affects the relational connections members make with one another.

A more expansive notion of worship and music is required. Worship matters because it is a central Christian practice. Across congregations in the United States, Nancy Ammerman and her colleagues find all congregations have some form of regular worship gathering and, for most, participatory worship is a core component of their mission.[3] Individual attenders of Sunday morning services list the style and quality of worship and preaching as the two most important factors that attracted them to their congregation.[4] For most Christians, going to *church* is going to *worship*, and even in some languages "to go to church" means literally "to go to worship." Many congregations are called "houses of worship." Although churches are not completely dependent on musical singing or performance for the conduct of their ministries, music remains one of the most important, most contested, most treasured, and most controversial elements of Christian practice. Music is not a mystical element of the worship service, but a ubiquitous presence that defines part of what it means to "do church" together in corporate assembly. Music is not just the sound communicating to a group of individuals; it is an inherent aspect of the rites and rituals of the corporate activity of congregation.

Participatory worship is therefore inherently social, providing an ideal ground for examining broader sociological dynamics in congregations. Worship music is not "a part of" the culture of a church or "embedded within" the culture of the church. Music is a practice. Music does not add to the community of a congregation; it is, in the moment it is done, the community of a congregation as it continues to move forward in life as a whole. Music is a performative element that actively engages the community in its very existence.[5] Music not only engages our emotions; music involves physicality. Congregational worship is a physically engaging process involving not only the ears and minds of people, but also their whole bodies in socially shaped activity. Spaces for worship are designed with a deliberate focus between worshiper and worship leader(s) up front. Indeed, the modern move toward projection screens is the attempt to remove all obstructions between pew and platform. Worship is not just how one sings or what the types of music are practiced. Worship encompasses the entire liturgical event that occurs within all church services.

Coming to terms with the social nature of music and its place within the life of a congregation helps sensitize us to understanding how music works in multiracial congregations. Church services are important for the achievement of a worship experience. Tia DeNora follows Pelle Ehn's discussion of Joseph Weizenbaum in seeing music as a prosthetic technology, material that enables capacities to allow actors do things they cannot do independently.[6] Although worship is so often considered an individual dynamic, the private experience of worship is triggered in the public place of worship. Daniel, a white worship leader, talked about how emotional the experience of worship was every Sunday, saying, "It's just an energy or a presence that comes down on everyone agreeing. Especially in a multicultural service, everyone has something to contribute in his or her own style of worship.

I might be a little more reserved while the next person over is shouting out, but I think altogether it's all part of the Body of Christ. Do you know what I mean? We all need each other and we all play an important role in strengthening each other, strengthening the whole church." Members of different racial and ethnic groups are not distinguished in their experience of worship. Instead, I found great similarity in their process of worship. In the end, it's the togetherness of worship that stands out.

It is often true that Christians have been conditioned to associate particular forms of music with Christian worship. Moreover, it is also true that music can be believed and reinforced as connecting with particular racial and ethnic groups (gospel music is for blacks; salsa is for Latinos). Yet, such meanings are neither static nor deterministic. The appropriation of music on a personal level involves not only the music but also the recipient who attends to it, the memories and associations brought to it, and the local circumstances of consumption. Some may be shocked to learn that not all blacks connect to gospel, nor Latinos to salsa. Nevertheless, the racialized meanings of music come to be anticipated and actualized in multiracial churches, often as Caucasians attempt to enact supposedly "non-Causcasian" music forms. A musical form combines with listeners' contextualization of that music and the situational context in which it is heard. Lifting considerations of music from its auditory phenomena to accentuate both what a person brings to the experience (memories and associations) as well as how meaning of music is ritualized within a context (liturgy and practice) all affect the momentary response as well as later recollection of the meaning of that music in multiracial churches. In multiracial churches, different forms of sacred music often take on heightened racialized associations. Music becomes the avenue to address concerns for attracting and connecting racially and ethnically diverse audiences.

I emphasize the process of racialized ritual inclusion in my understanding of diversification through liturgy because the sociological significance of worship music is found in its impact on social structures rather than on individual meaning. Too often, a belief is expressed that singing the right kinds of music will produce the right kinds of people as the meanings embedded within the songs initiate proper attitudes and perspectives. In multiracial churches, the belief is often racially specific such that ethnically targeted music will speak a person's "heart language" causing them to emotionally connect. I agree with DeNora, who argues "against determinist explanations of meaning" that "depicts actors as enactors or 'cultural dopes' who are frozen in to their cultures without the possibility of reflexive behavior (or insincerity, alienation etc.)." Musical meaning, to the degree that it exists, is enacted by an individual or group to the degree it is attributed significance. Musical meaning is an active part of corporate production in how "the social world or *Lebenswelt* (or 'Nature') is produced through the scenic practices, interpretive procedures, members' methods or 'work'; how through interaction (collaboration, conflict, collusion) actors come to construct an aura of naturalness bout the object, utterance, act, 'as if' the properties perceived *in* that object are actually and intrinsically *of* it." The work of scholarship is "to tell the 'local history' of how the phenomenon was 'realized,'" and includes how meaning is produced by "forces, relations, and available technology" involved in production. Moreover, social contexts of music production provide "cues" that consist of "various conventions or ritual practices that, through experience, come to carry certain con-notations [*sic*] which, one could say, serve as 'tools' for the work of sense making and meaning construction." In short, "the meaning of objects, utterances, and acts is neither inherent nor invariant but socially constituted."[7] The force of music in multiracial churches is not found in the musical form alone; rather, "music's powers" (as DeNora calls them) derive from the way people interact with musical material.[8]

Worship music, then, is never simply "worship music," but rather a conglomerate of musical experiences engaged by particular church members who engage that music in particular places and within a framework of ritualized understandings and corporate practices.[9] The musical worship of a multiracial congregation is one aspect of an overall interactive-performative space that stimulates interracial relationships and even encourages cross-racial mutuality-identification. A sociology of worship, then, examines how music is enacted within multiracial churches rather than attempting to prescribe an ambitious (and even inspiring) program for how to bridge the cultures of the globe through worship.

A Sociology of Multiracial Worship

In theorizing congregational worship and the centrality of music, I emphasize with DeNora the manner in which individuals exercise agency in a collective and collaborative manner in "materially and aesthetically configured spaces that are created—by actors themselves or for those actors by other actors (such as retailers, social planners or employers)—prior to and as part of action's scenes." The set-up of worship is arranged beforehand through worship leaders and music directors in conjunction with lead pastors and a bevy of volunteers. In the planning and performance of worship services, musical materials are mobilized "in an attempt to define the parameters of social scenarios, to provide cues for crafting agency in real-time social settings." Worship provides the occasion "to regulate and structure social encounters, and how it lends aesthetic texture to those encounters. Music provides, in other words, a resource for establishing the prospective parameters of agency's aesthetic dimension." Sacred music produces and structures individual and corporate initiatives. Through practice and performance, music initiates "the construction of subjectivity, intersubjectivity, co-subjectivity" and emphasizes "the rich domain of the precognitive, embodied, emotional and sensual bases of social action and order."[10]

Worship in church services is a largely pragmatic affair in which music is used to organize people in the service for how to understand themselves and each other.[11] Although church attenders do not have command of their aesthetic environment, music is an inescapable aspect of the collective environment that orders their actions. DeNora reminds us that "social order is an achievement, an effect of temporal action" and articulates a perspective on "music's role as a device of collective ordering, how music may be employed, albeit at times unwittingly, as a means of organizing potentially disparate individuals such that their actions may appear to be intersubjective, mutually oriented, co-ordinated, entrained and aligned."[12] As individuals enter voluntarily in multiracial worship, they do so in ritualized, ceremonial ways. While members enter worship knowingly, the do so in ways that are socially established through practice, habit, and routine.

Analysis is complicated even further when we realize that there is no single "culture" of multiracial churches, and a diligent researcher quickly learns that any multiracial church is the site of rich investigation rather than smug assumption. However, it is interesting to note that among the congregations I studied, I found a significant structural similarity. Since the great majority of multiracial churches are monolingual, designing services to appeal to a mainstream, English-speaking audience is largely assumed. None of the churches I observed feature more than one language in church services, and none feature simultaneous translation to other languages. While there are multiracial congregations in the United States that do this, they appear to be rare, require special equipment, and demand highly dedicated volunteers.

Among fluent English speakers, and therefore often largely acculturated Americans, my interviews reveal that leaders and members carry in their minds similar ethnic and racial categorizations. With respect to worship, the notion of "blackness" dominates discussions on diversity and worship, followed by Latinos. When it comes to Christian worship and music, Asians are seldom mentioned, Native Americans are completely excluded in conversations on diversity, and Middle Eastern barely so. Because music is a form of social ordering, it promotes congregational structures dividing members along racial and ethnic conceptions of difference. For example, diverse congregations in Los Angeles are often concerned with incorporating Spanish. Songs are often sung in Spanish along with verses from biblical scriptures. But any growth of Spanish speakers in a service is never fully accommodated into these services. Two churches told me that although their most diverse services attempted to maintain "a bilingual environment" of English-Spanish for a period of time, services were done primarily in English and all preaching was in English. In both churches, a Spanish-only service was eventually created to accommodate Spanish speakers. One pastor said, "As they continued to grow within us, our Spanish brothers and sisters, we noticed that no matter how much of an effort we put forth to try to honor them and present a gospel or worship in their own language, we would always fall short." At no point was there consideration of shifting the primary language from English to Spanish; instead, Spanish attenders are siphoned off into independent ministries which meet either at another time of day (or another day of the week) in another (usually much smaller) room at the church "because you're more comfortable with worshiping God in your own language and in your own style and in their own culture." Styles and cultures in these multiracial churches are accommodated as long as they are in English, and these linguistic divisions are justified on the basis of people being "more comfortable worshiping God in their own style and in their own culture."

Any discussion of worship style in congregations today often includes orientation to the significant changes happening in worship service music in America around the turn of the twenty-first century. People have been in the throes of passionate debate on the nature of worship music, often dubbed "the worship wars," in which the appropriateness of different forms of musical styles are being argued, with different camps asserting the biblical, historical, and aesthetic imperatives driving their philosophies of congregational music. This is not the place to debate the pros and cons of sacred music being produced today.[13] Suffice to say that among some writers in support of hymnody and rootedness in church traditions of sacred music, there is a harsh disdain for "popular, media/market-driven forms of music."[14] These same writers often criticize American popular culture while simultaneously idealizing the popular culture of non-Western nations. Pragmatically, what this means is that in avoiding spiritualized American pop music, these advocates often uncritically accept the Christian music of other nations—no more than a form of "noble savage" argument—which results in an idealized exoticism played out by well-meaning church leaders.[15] Easy to sing and simple to reproduce, songs in Hindi, Farsi, Swahili, and other languages make their way into workshops, conferences, and church services that promote diverse worship. Yet, theologically speaking, the "thin" Christian folk rhymes from other nations are not any deeper than the "thin" lyrics of contemporary praise music simply because they originate among non-Anglo people. We should be aware also of more sophisticated enthno-hymnody in which ethno-racial groups reflect hymnody from their own cultural perspectives while staying within the Christian tradition.[16]

They "hymn explosion" of the 1970s produced new music, many of which thoughtfully include more contemporary music, Negro spirituals (rarely used in black churches), and Spanish "coritos." Editors of contemporary hymnals have greater desire to include diversity of musical choices with a concern to stimulate solidarity with the global church. However, regardless of the intentions of producers of hymnals, we know the diversity of songs within a hymn book may not be utilized so that the intent of the editors is not fulfilled. Not all songs are equally emphasized, and the multicultural aspects of any particular hymnal can be completely ignored in the ongoing musical experience of a congregation.[17]

C. Michael Hawn writes with intelligence and passion about his desire to broaden the Western hymnal traditions to the music of Christians around the world. He forcefully and persuasively argues for "global music" that would remove Westerners from "liturgical ethnocentrism" and open them up to "liturgical interpathy."[18] I find Hawn's analysis and recommendations to the church compelling. I see Hawn as focusing on a diplomatic exchange between global cultures, a hymn-oriented exchange, perhaps made mandatory, by the globalization processes bringing groups together in the same pews that had almost always been separated by geography and language. In Hawn's vision, the church would be able to create a malleable musical repertoire that allows Christians from any country to feel at home. In a way, Hawn proposes a grand United Nations approach to the construction of worship music that favors a highly intentional, and highly committed, exchange of world cultures in a way that would undoubtedly provide greater texture to the musical tradition of Christian churches in the Western world.

Considering my own research reported here, none of the multiracial churches I visited had a large contingent of attenders that had recently come from a foreign country. Instead, all the churches that I observed are incorporating either blacks, whites, and Latinos who have been in the United States for at least a century, or Asians who have been here since the beginning of the twentieth century. A few members were connected with the opening of American immigration in 1965. But what this means is that the racial and ethnic cultures routinely segregated in our nation's churches are not people who have just come "off the boat," so to speak, but rather people who have been segregated by vast mechanisms of institutional racism that sociologists are still working to understand fully. The breaking down of global rhythms from Africa, for example, have little relevance to the worship lives of African Americans whose ancestry lies in the distant past. Thus, while Hawn strongly encourages an incorporation of "global" rhythms of music as a means to diversify churches, I believe these global rhythms may only be distantly connected to the lives of hyphenated-Americans living their religious lives in an urban-suburban context of North American cities.

Some practitioners insist on an enculturation of liturgy and worship to reflect a particular ethnic or racial group. But aggressive, unreflective commitment to enculturation may so veer in the trajectory of a particular non-Anglo culture that the church becomes unable to accommodate the cultural specifics of still other cultures as they move into the region. Take, for example, a church in the eastern part of Los Angeles. It made spectacular breakthroughs in the 1960s and 1970s incorporating African Americans that had moved into their dominantly white community. Pastors of the church were aggressive in making connections with their new neighbors, and the first African Americans that committed to the congregation helped shape the musical content of the services and stimulated the greater attendance of a growing stream of blacks attending the church. Forty years later, the neighborhood has again changed. Hispanics have come to be a sizable percentage of the local population, but the ambiance of the services has not changed. There is much greater commitment (and even assumption) of the "African American culture" in comparison with barely a mention of the Hispanics that have recently settled into the area.

Another example of how ethnic accommodation can simultaneously alienate is a church I visited in Chicago that aggressively enculturated toward the immigrants from central Mexico in the midst of a neighborhood that has slowly revitalized over the years. Undoubtedly, the work of the church over many decades have helped shape the climate of the neighborhood, raising property values, and making the area a pleasant place to live. Yet now "the neighborhood" is defined specifically as the Mexican-Americans that live in the area, and not the wealthier whites who are beginning to move in. The church enculturated so many aspects of the church toward Mexican American symbols, language, and culture, that it appears that the Anglos moving into the gentrifying area feel the church is a haven for immigrants rather than a church serving the entire neighborhood.

This is not to disparage the work occurring in churches across the country desperately attempting to serve the needs for the more marginalized in our cities. This work is important and necessary. Yet, it is also important to point out that the bias of culture works both ways; churches serving the marginalized may in turn marginalize those of the vast variety of races and ethnicities who have "mainstreamed" into the broader society. This may be a tension the Christian church may be forced to live with for the foreseeable future. It is highly unlikely that a uniform, globalized culture will ever emerge, which means that with the vast mobility of peoples around the world, the church will always be faced with creating hospitality for the stranger among us. And perhaps thinking through the theology of the stranger, the alien, the foreigner, the widow, and the orphan will have far greater consequences for dealing with racial and ethnic diversity for all of us.

In my analysis connecting music and worship to diversification in multiracial churches, I find that the worship of God is not nearly as important as the notions of difference and diversity being promoted through worship. For example, self-affirming, self-congratulatory experience of music from "the African church" is used in ways not intended by the original producers (and certainly from the original context) as in the use of an indigenous African hymn among a mostly white American church audience. In the majority of my cases, that means dominantly white and Asian churches appropriate musical forms labeled "black" or "Latino." Blacks and Latinos then willingly participate and come to assent in their role as representatives of diversity in support of the religious mission of the congregation. By recognizing the "pragmatic theories of meaning in use, meaning in interaction," an avenue is opened to investigate the manner in which sound, movement, and coordination in multiracial churches are both "determining and determined."[19] The key point is that "music's semiotic force—its affect upon hearing—cannot be fully specified in advance of actual reception."[20] Worship music that may have been meant for one purpose (for example, the affirmation of a specific ethnic identity) may be reappropriated for a different purpose (the affirmation of a welcoming diversity). Most important, regardless of the seemingly stable semiotic meanings of a piece of music, the analysis of "music in practice" highlights how "music may be reappropriated, reclaimed for different interpretive uses according to the configuration of its mediators." Music directors and worship leaders as mediators between production and consumption can utilize musical forms in unexpected ways since music can be "repurposed" to create or support initiatives in their own congregational settings.

Worship music is a form of social order in multiracial churches that structures both individual subjectivity and collaborative action. An alternative analysis might privilege the individual tastes of members and therefore assume that musical styles are responsive to the willingness of members to tolerate different forms of music.[21] Yet this overemphasizes the importance of listeners entering a musical environment over the structural characteristics of the environment itself. Church members work with the musical materials available, following cues for what to do with their bodies but also signals for whom they can connect with for relationships. The efficacy of music for diversity is not so much in enriching individual experience as in its capacity to structure relationships. In my analysis, I move away from individualized meanings of worship to focus on music's role in structuring multiracial congregations and their environments. I also avoid a musical technologism that insists that human beings react to music in predetermined ways.[22] Instead, multiracial churches provide an opportunity to investigate ways music and meanings come to be clustered in particular places.

"World-Building" a Diverse Community through Worship

To more fully understand multiracial worship we must take into account a more complex approach to local church community and individual identity that encompasses broader social factors that takes into account the immediate social context and, to the extent possible, issues of class, nationality, generational placement and urban dynamics. Some sociologists emphasize personal identity formation and group unity as formed through the social practices involved in the production and consumption of music.[23] Following these analysts, I find the role of music in cultivating multiracial groups and the formation of distinctive group identities implicit to the consumption and production of music in multiracial churches.[24] Music is not universal or timeless but emerges from social interaction and changes as the sociocultural environment within which it is embedded changes. And the distinctive cultivation of unity can be seen as an aspect of "world-building."[25]

Since music is so central to the ritual gatherings of congregations, music is invoked toward world-making, that is, for the creation of a shared reality. Music can, in other words, be invoked as an ally for a variety of world-making activities. It is a workspace for semiotic activity, a resource for doing, being and naming the aspects of social reality, including the realities of subjectivity and self. Focusing on congregations, music is a prominent focus in many church services, racially framing the event and accentuating the emotional and symbolic significance of the service. Shared musical practices both establish and transform cross-ethnic and interracial social relations. Music plays a dynamic role in symbolically organizing a space in the expression of personal identity, including ethnic identity.[26] Participatory music can make the event of worship a celebration of the group itself, which helps socialize the participants to values and ideals that help hold themselves together as a moral community.[27]

Church leaders use music as a resource for organizing corporate worship. Thomas Turino writes, "Musical sounds are a powerful human resource, often at the heart of our most profound social occasions and experiences."[28] When used in worship, it is certainly used for "world building," by which I mean that it is used to create an ideal sense of what human relationships are to be like. When racial diversity is a corporate ambition, it is enacted in a variety of ways through worship. Among racially diverse congregations, music takes the ambiguous and contradictory meanings of church life and centers them on core notions of diversity. Music in multiracial congregations becomes meaningful because it is seen as an arena for cultivating and displaying unity. DeNora states that "music is a referent" in that it serves to clarify "the otherwise potentially polysemic character of non-musical phenomena (social circumstances, identities, moods and energy levels, for example)." Worship music can in multiracial churches become "routine identity work" that regulates "the parameters of collaborative and collective aesthetic agency."[29] It is used to "articulate the collective identities that are fundamental to forming and sustaining social groups."[30]

Other researchers emphasize musical unity as occurring only during special occasions. For example, an early study of religious interracial contact by L. Maynard Catchings looked at Southern churches and found that a significant number of churches, which reported interracial participation, indicated the practice of interracial contact was rare and oriented around occasional events a few times a year.[31] Considering the role of music in forming and accentuating a multiracial community in church services, we could draw on Émile Durkheim and subsequent scholarship building on these insights regarding shared identity through regular corporate worship.[32] Corporate ritual creates a strong sense of bonding and identity that defines a group with particular intimacy who share sacred duties to each other and to the world. Through this perspective, worshipers are drawn into a community and become obligated to live a communal existence as extensions of each other, even when away from intense ritualistic experience of the sacred cult.[33] What draws all of this research together is a recognition of the manner in which worship in multiracial churches can define a "musical milieu" as "a relatively stable configuration of action and meaning in which the individual actively maintains a distinctive degree of familiarity, competence and normalcy, based on the continuity and consistency of personal disposition, habitualities and routines, and experienced as a feeling of situatedness."[34] Drawing from a phenomenological perspective, a musical milieu is defined by a system of relevancies and typifications that act as a scheme of interpretation and orientation that constitutes a universe of discourse amongst participants. To the extent that the orientation and interpretation of the musical system is institutionalized or standardized, a socially approved system of relevancies and typifications will provide a common field through which individual members live and order their lives.

In all these approaches, the priority is on the shaping of individual action in relation to aesthetics, one that associates with imaginations and emotions, that affects the movement of bodies, that coordinates the actions of groups, and that creates unseen connections among people across racial and ethnic lines. Music, then, carries connotations. In regular meetings, the coordination can be infused with associations regarding the sacred mission of achieving multiracial unity. Furthermore, music becomes "part of the cultural material through which 'scenes' are constructed, scenes that afford different kinds of agency, different sorts of pleasure and ways of being."[35]

In emphasizing the local construction of a shared identity through music, is it possible to isolate musical patterns of church worship by racial and ethnic group? Perhaps, even though the overall emphasis in this work is a warning to not generalize and typify music per group so as to predetermine the types of music that will or should be present in diverse churches. We know that through regular interactions human beings come to create their own systems of status and identity within particular "spaces" or places and that these social systems can be competitive or cooperative.[36] Jonathon S. Epstein, Andy Bennett, and Martin Stokes are among the scholars that look specifically at how music tastes create "space" and "place" and form ethnic communities within communities.[37] Place essentially transforms through music. Stokes surveys youth post-war (post-Vietnam) counter-culture music and how it was shaped by and continually shapes various ethnic societies.[38] Bennett demonstrates how music gives everyone an identity (he focuses on popular music among young people) and that a person's musical identity can challenge mainstream culture.[39] Epstein similarly argues how music is part of constructing a youth subculture distinguished by distinct values, beliefs, symbols, and actions, which certain youth employ to attend to, and cope with, their shared cultural experience. By extension, racial and ethnic subcultures are "generally in opposition to, and often indirect contradiction with societal values, norms and expectations."[40] Particular churches can be characterized by ethnic-specific musical styles, and their worship music can provide a means by which people can take on an oppositional identity that sustains itself against mainstream culture. Nevertheless, for the understanding of how music and worship work in successfully diverse congregations, rather than isolate particular ethnic styles that reinforce particularistic identities, it is more fruitful to postulate the manner in which worship music works in practice to foster and sustain cross-racial and cross-ethnic connections.

In my assessment, it is more productive to acknowledge that music is a prominent focus in multiracial church services, racially framing the event and accentuating the emotional and symbolic significance of diversity in the service. Sociologists of music encourage looking at how shared musical practices both establish and transform social relations. Drawing on these insights, music is a social phenomenon in multiracial churches that plays a dynamic role in symbolically organizing a space as an expression of diversity, one that encourages an openly cross-racial personal identity and softer boundaries between ethnic identities.

"Diversity Congregations" Are Defined by Their Approach to Worship

The definition of a "diverse congregation" can be quite fluid. When we say "multiracial church," we are saying nothing about the church other than there is a presence of at least two distinct racial or ethnic groups within a common congregation. We imply nothing about the size of the church, the location of the church, the generational compositions of the church, or any other significant and highly valuable pieces of information for understanding a congregation. All we categorize is something abstract about the racial composition of a congregation when we label it multiethnic/multiracial. It is the work of scholarship for us to understand if there is something distinctive about these congregations in comparison with homogeneous ones.

I suggest that worship practices are becoming the core criterion for defining a new niche of congregations that I label "Diversity Congregations." Specifically, Diversity Congregations are creating new, unanticipated boundaries between themselves and homogenous congregations through racialized ritual inclusion. Following Stokes and his colleagues, I see "how music is used by social actors in specific local situations to erect boundaries, to maintain distinctions between us and them, and how terms such as 'authenticity' are used to justify these boundaries."[41] By suggesting that worship music is the means by which the intentional involvement of visible diversity through conspicuous color is accomplished, I am also suggesting a substantive, *qualitative* definition of multiracial congregations. The current definition of multiracial churches orients around quantitative proportions: specifically, that at least 20% of a church's attendance is different from the majority group.[42] Perhaps focusing on racialized ritual inclusion as a heuristic alternative fruitfully orients our criteria around the public, ongoing liturgical processes that affect multiracial congregations.

Music has always played a distinct role in American race relations, and now it is evident that multiracial congregations are using music in relation to their local "world-building" activities, creating a shared reality for what constitutes the values, identity, and mission of a diverse church. Amid the increasing conversations on diverse congregations, there is a growing level of institutionalized "world-building" activity that conforms to generalized expectations of how racial and ethnic diversity "works" within these congregations. Moreover, there is a growing sense of what constitutes a validly "diverse" congregation. In books, courses, workshops, and seminars, the understanding of multiracial/multiethninc/multicultural congregations are conforming to an ideal type of music and worship, which is being both propagated and commercialized.

We are now in a time when a sense of what multiracial worship *should* look like is taking root. In essence, a shared understanding of "multiracial/multiethnic/multicultural churches" is becoming more institutionalized around notions of proper worship. Multiracial church leaders are currently creating what Peter Berger and Thomas Luckmann called "plausibility structures," ways of making sense of the world.[43] Once a mental set of racial and ethnic categorizations exist in society, it directs our attention to those things and leaves us blind to the richness of the social world beyond them. If we are not careful, we will define racial phenomena in music as static cultural entities that must be "respected" and therefore socially bound instead of recognizing the ongoing, emergent dynamics that continually shape and reproduce social interactions. This is particularly so with the "Pluralist" approach to worship and music in multiracial churches.[44] Questioning the "common sense" notions of those actions is in part an attempt to allow, first, to recognize the contingent and non-deterministic manner in which racial and ethnic relationships are constructed and, second, to stimulate individuals to negotiate and re-shape those relationships in ways that enhance human freedom, dignity, and equality. Neither the Pluralist nor any other approach to music should be defined as the sole, legitimate, or truly "sacred" practice of multiracial worship. In the face of such cautions, there appears to be a generalized notion of legitimately diverse churches defined by their approach to music and worship.

Because worship is a highly situational, highly contextual, and highly interactive activity, situational theories of ethnicity help us to make sense of how worship helps create unity within a worship service or in particular places. This approach relies on Weberian developments from theorists who emphasize a dynamic understanding of race and ethnicity.[45] Drawing on scholars of race that reinforce the negotiated and constructed nature of racial categories, the observations of this study combine the "lived experience" of worship attenders with a careful understanding of racial dynamics in the United States today based on recent scholarly work. Moving away from quantitative surveys, this perspective acknowledges that "race" is more than the discrete categories established by the U.S. Census, but rather a negotiated and constructed phenomenon.[46] I agree with Martin Munro who emphasizes how ethno-racial identity is malleable, a "being in world, something born out of living, relating, changing, not a fixed category decided in advance" that is affected by music.[47] As William G. Roy states, "The racial dimension of music is intertwined in its use, in the kinds of social relations around doing music. Music and race are both constituted and become consequential in their doing."[48]

In this study, music is specifically examined within a liturgical framework, existing within congregational structures. DeNora reminds us that music exists within "a public stock of musical 'understanding.'" There are "kinaesthetic music-image associations."[49] Worship music is "framed" within services. I find Diversity Congregations particularly frame worship as having the character of public, visible racial-ethnic integration. Music is used to support and affirm those differences, whether through the accomplishing of the act of simply "worshiping" together or more elaborately performing various ethnically or racially targeted musical forms in the assumption that particular musical styles connect with specific racial and/or ethnic groups. In multiracial churches, music operates as a symbolic resource for the cultivation of a visibly diverse community.

While all multiracial churches are selective in their musical content as an aesthetic texture for the cultivation of their social environments, I suggest that Diversity Congregations go further in their music selection to universally assert racialized forms of authenticity and performativity. Legitimation as a

Diversity Congregation is based on having the proper physical representation of mixed heritages, leading congregations to exaggerate the level of diversity in their congregations through conspicuous color on the platform. In short, racialized ritual inclusion fundamentally defines diverse congregations.

Drawing together my observations of multiracial churches, I see a stabilization of the meaning of diversity occurring in congregations such that the ritual inclusion of visible racial and ethnic differences in musical worship is the sine qua non of Diversity Congregations. Churches want to create racially welcome atmospheres that are persistent in the face of fluctuating attendance, streams of guests and visitors, and turnovers in congregational leadership. A strong ethos is the goal. Through the incorporation of diversity in performance, worship music actualizes beliefs and serves to convince a congregation of the value and fulfillment of integration.

Research on music supports the use of ritual to stabilize and legitimate shared meanings. For example, Timothy Rommen writes that worship services "remain powerful drivers and markers of legitimacy."[50] DeNora commends the work of Richard Middleton in considering how "particular configurations of meaning (value, authenticity, affect) can be stabilized through ritual procedures and practices."[51] It raises the question of how multiracial churches are effective at cultivating and sustaining particular meanings of race and religion that can be held steady through the ongoing liturgical rituals of congregational services. Middleton states that "once particular musical elements are put together in particular ways, and acquire particular connotations, these can be hard to shift."[52] While the tone of Middleton's remarks seem negative ("hard to shift"), in relation to racial diversity, the robustness of promoting diversity-affirming beliefs and practices that counter mainstream views are persistent.

The institutionalization of musical practice to manipulate the attitudes and behavior of congregants in multiracial churches toward cross-ethnic and interracial relationships is similar to what DeNora finds in commercial businesses today. She writes, "At the locally based independent shops, music's role as a way of specifying store identity—and hence target consumers—is more overt." Similarly, I suggest that the manner in which worship music is performed in congregations today serves to distinguish churches from each other and proclaim certain type of market niche. DeNora also notes, "For retailers, these affective dimensions of agency are critical because 'point-of-purchase' or 'impulse' sales are typically transactions that involve consumers' emotions, for example, 'purchasing in response to moods.'"[53] For this reason, retailers are concerned, as noted above, to structure the aesthetic environment and, through this, the emotional conduct of consumers." Similar to shops, churches are engaged in structuring agency through music, creating a sense of the occasion and a type of scenic specificity as a site where racial and ethnic diversity "happens." To the degree that churches are places in which guests are potential consumers, religious music contains the ability to connect with potential members. DeNora again writes, "Music can be usefully conceived of as a device of scenic placement. It provides contextual cues that can be used to shape up the meaning of character and situation."[54] Thus, the cultivation of a multiracial liturgy through music is an opportunity to bring people to commit to a multiracial congregation.

For many, racial diversity in churches is an urban fantasy, and collective interests for fulfilling that fantasy can create places where diversity manifested through music can create a condition buttressing the existence of diversity. Grazian, for example, shows how the Chicago blues scene creates a particular form of racial and ethnic diversity where the production and consumption of music is central.[55] Could the success of multiracial worship be in part because of the manner in which it creates a safe place to fulfill the urban fantasy of interracial unity? I met several people who said in looking for a congregation, they were looking for "diverse church." Worship can be an important vehicle for signaling to potential members legitimacy and value for diversity.

Music can then be a tool for creating alternative, visibly diverse communities. DeNora writes, "Music may serve as a resource for utopian imaginations, for alternate worlds and institutions, and it may be used strategically to presage new worlds. As Pelle Ehn describes this role of 'sensuous knowledge' in the workplace, so, too, music provides a fund of materials that serve as paradigms, metaphors, analogues, hints and reminders of activity, practice and social procedure."[56] Music is "typically oriented to imagined communities and imagined (and often aspirational) scenarios—peer groups, idealized situations, conventional images and associations."

As we continue to investigate the dynamics of Diversity Congregations with greater sensitivity to liturgical processes, we can begin to look more carefully at how music is distributed and controlled, and "the social relations of how music is deployed within settings and the degree to which soundtracks for settings are negotiated." We begin to investigate "how actors come to connect with the musical resources which are agency's building materials and how this process transpires across a variety of social scenes and settings." We then ask, "How, then, are these structuring properties of music appropriated within institutions, organizations and situations so as to have organizing effects on social and embodied action? And how does music work at the interactive level where institutions, organizations and occasions are sustained and reproduced over time?"[57]

Looking carefully at the dynamics of the practice of worship in multiracial congregations, we can stop looking for a single, omnipresent manifestation of the workings of music and diversity. Rather, as DeNora states, "Music is a flexible but powerful interpretative resource." Musical forms can be used in many different ways in the ongoing achievement of congregational diversity. Congregational aesthetics are adaptable. The efficacy of aesthetics is not in the sound of the music but rather in the ability to actively recruit and include people of mixed racial and ethnic backgrounds. DeNora rightly says, "Music's role as a resource for configuring emotional and embodied agency is not one that can be predetermined (because it is a resource that must be appropriated by music consumers). Music is not an objective 'force' or a 'stimulus', but it is real in its effects and its specific properties provide mechanisms for achieving those effects"[58]

Among the congregations studied here, the process of racialized ritual inclusion—actively incorporating conspicuous color in the promotion of visible diversity in a church's liturgy—is emphasized as central. As music continues to change over time, a flexible, practice-based analytical framework as utilized here gives us the ability to further conceptualize new and unanticipated forms of connection and community associated with worship music. Further nuance in research will be crucial as the cultivation of racial and ethnic diversity continues to grow in importance among American congregations in the future.

APPENDIX

Research Methodology

This book is based on data collected from twelve successfully integrated churches in Southern California from 2005 through 2006 using participant observation, in-depth interviewing, and examination of available archived sources. My initial goal was to present a vivid understanding of the worship life of their attenders and the attempt (or lack of it) by leadership to cultivate a racially diverse congregation. Participation combined with in-depth interviews allows for a saturated understanding of particular sites that results in a more holistic understanding of the experiences of a group. I locate this understanding in the context of broader patterns of the "religious" streams in which they (knowingly or unknowingly) participate as well as the "secular" world in which they operate.

Rather than impose my understanding of the world onto these churches, I used qualitative research methods to earnestly attempt to uncover the understandings of leaders and attenders and bring conceptual order to what I find. By choosing a qualitative approach, I engage directly with people and understand through their "lived experience" how they appropriate, experience, and negotiate music in their church. In addition, interviews with decision makers and music performers allow me to understand the ongoing processes of musical construction. While the emphasis of this analysis is on those who regularly worshiped and provided leadership for worship in these diverse congregations, the implications about racial-ethnic groups not present or who fail to stay are addressed as well. Beyond what is said "officially" by leaders and attenders, I look at written records, observe ongoing interactions, and seek to discover the patterns of behavior rather than merely words and meanings. A picture is constructed that creates a whole out of the various pieces presented in my observation and the reported experiences of my respondents. When information does not match or is seemingly contradictory, I consider the source and weigh the evidence to obtain the best interpretive sense of what is happening sociologically. Using a combination of first-person narratives and my own observations of church ministries and their services, I pursue a plausible and coherent interpretation of the organizational dynamics to explain the operation of music and worship in these churches.[1]

I interviewed 172 people in these churches. The most fundamental division of social groups within each church was between (a) clergy, music directors, singers, musicians, and technicians involved in the regular construction of worship and music and (b) attenders who regularly "worship" in each church but did not participate in planning or programmatic discussions regarding the liturgical services of their church. I conducted a total of 49 interviews with decision makers/music performers and 123 interviews of worship service attenders. In addition, I attempted within each church to maximize the variation among long-time members and recent attendees, men and women, young adults and senior citizens, single and married people, and the various racial and ethnic ancestral heritages within each church (to preserve the anonymity of respondents and significant figures in the history of the congregations, all have been given pseudonyms).

I supplemented these interviews with field notes gathered during ethnographic observation of worship services in each congregation. I consulted my own field notes purposely taken from experience in services in each church 2005–2006. To gain experiential context, I attended at least two weekly worship services (and any available midweek services) in the main setting in which they typically occur. Interviews and field notes were transcribed, and qualitative software used to code and analyze data, seeking significant patterns of leader decisions and connections between respondent experience (like/dislike, stay/leave), music performance (music structure/structure of worship services), and racial/ethnic composition in diverse churches.

Finally, I pursued an understanding of each church's history (as short as two years to as long as over 150 years) based on the memories of long-term participants as they correlated with each other and with the few print resources available. Archived sources consisted of selected books, tapes given away or available for purchase, and pamphlets available from the church. I continued to collect data and provisionally interpreted it until a general picture emerged and was reaffirmed over and over again. I also made an attempt to be both descriptive and theoretical in the attempt to generate theory regarding congregational processes. The qualitative analysis software program NVIVO 8.0 was used to code and analyze data, seeking significant patterns of leader decisions and connections between respondent experience (like/dislike, stay/leave), music performance (music structure/structure of worship services), and ethnic composition. Coding and matrices were used to compare across interviews and field notes from different congregations. Competing explanations and discrepant data were especially noted.

PARTICIPANT OBSERVATION

Ethnographic sociological research enables an understanding of the use of music in certain space and among certain populations. On some occasions, I was able to take notes as if I were taking sermon or class notes; other notes were spoken into a tape recorder on my way home or typed into the computer once I arrived. Through participant observation, researchers gather information by interacting with and among the people they wish to study. "For many practical and theoretical problems, we want to take account of as much of an organization's complexity as our theory will allow."[2] I worked toward an understanding of music and worship through ongoing interactions with participants on their home ground. My research effort involved an ongoing effort to "share firsthand the environment, problems, background, language, rituals, and social relations of a more-or-less bounded and specified group of people."[3] The data I collected and the life experiences I pursued were those most directly involved with each congregation.

The work of the participant observer is constantly the attempt to see the researched community from an insider's perspective and grasp the subtle nuances in meaning and then situate these meanings in a broader societal context. A core assumption by researchers who use participant observation is that "in the course of daily life, people make sense of the world around them; they give it meaning and they interact on the basis of these meanings."[4] This belief is drawn from a history of theoretical considerations, including old-school phenomenologists like Alfred Schutz, prototypical symbolic interactionists like Herbert Blumer, and contemporary qualitative researchers like Norman Denzin. Of course, people can be quite wrong about the actual meanings, occurrences, and causalities of the "real" world, yet the "real" world is in some part shaped by the belief of its participants so that even "wrong" beliefs can become "right" out of the coordinated actions of believing individuals. W. I. Thomas famously said, "If men define a situation as real, it is real in its consequences." Moreover, people inhabit worlds of meaning that are very "real" such that different people in the same physical space can, and often do, live in very different "worlds" of meaning.[5] "Participant observation, in other words, is a very special strategy and method for gaining access to the interior, seemingly subjective aspects of human existence."[6]

The goal of the participant observer, then, is to make known the meanings people in a given social structure typically have, a world of meaning that is not typically understood or even sought to be understood by outsiders to that group. The concepts of the analysis emerge as much from the participants of the social setting as from the theoretical concepts of the investigators. Understanding of the setting is not limited to the viewpoint from the members of the group one wishes to study. They, like most human beings, do not seek to explain social interaction through systematic observation and comparative analysis. The great majority of people live routinized, ritualized lives that require little or no explicit analysis in order to live comfortably. Yet, the social scientist enters the study of a group (whether familiar or strange) with the explicit purpose to come to investigate the underlying, institutionalized patterns of social life and thus make a contribution to the general understanding of social life in other social structures.

The key is to seek the "ordinary, usual, typical, routine, or natural environment" of the social group in question. Written work of the researcher then provides an account of the community that emphasizes the unique cultural meanings with descriptive detail and embeds those details within a broad interpretive framework from which to understand the meaning of what is presented. The benefit of participant observation is that although some were aware of my research agenda, the overall activities and structure of the congregation superseded any concern for my observation. Leaders and attenders sang, swayed, clapped, stood, sat, listened, laughed, and left routinely in their meeting-to-meeting involvement in the congregation. Things happened because this is what it means to "do church" together.

In all instances, I remained concerned for the privacy and confidentiality of people and avoided notations that would indicate people by name or other identifying characteristics. I have made an earnest attempt to maintain confidentiality, including that of congregational leaders, unless they spoke publicly, in print, or on recordings freely made available either on site for purchase or online.

In each church, I was a sociologist interested in people's experience and involvement in music and worship. Most people agreed when I asked to interview them. Overall, people were very willing to tell me about their church experiences before arriving at their church, their first encounters with the church, and the nature of their music and worship experience with their church since then. I kept open with them about my research goals as motivating my presence at the church. When I was asked about my own religious commitment, I explained that I had been a member of a large multiethnic church in Los Angeles that was Protestant and written a book about it. Members and leaders treated me as a curious observer who would never join the church. I did not require conversion as I claimed to already be a Christian; and I did not need a church since I was a member of another one. That left a friendly ambivalence about my activities. Those who understood my project were willing to offer helpful information about continuing activities of the church and occasionally asked me how I was enjoying my research. Those aware of my study were glad to have me come to their church to learn and share what I learned with others. Although I did not know what the overall findings of my analysis would be, I knew that I was concerned to provide a sociological view on music and worship in diverse congregations and attempt to analytically describe it. Even though I was a marginal member of the group, I attempted to strike a balance between interacting with people who were deeply committed to the church and those who were on the fringes.

In each church, I participated in weekend worship services (often arriving early and/or staying late) in the main place and time institutionalized by the church and regularly attended by regular members, new guests, and those in the process of joining the church. Also, I was often able to attend mid-week services that included music and worship once I found out about them. I took time in observing and speaking with people. I lingered around churches; I relaxed in interviews. The work was by no means accomplished care-free. With questions and focus, I burrowed through the environment of data that I found myself in and sought to observe with purpose. I almost always found people to be warm, relationally open, and interested in my research project. Numerous conversations occurred with staff members, guests, regular attenders, and long-time members as I was around church offices and their services.

My familiarity with Southern California, the greater concentration of multiracial churches there, and a research affiliation with the Center for Religion and Civic Culture at the University of Southern California led me to focus on the Los Angeles region. With this choice, I was able to maximize a compressed data collection schedule and limited research funds. My church experiences (both charismatic and non-charismatic) gave me the opportunity to enter each community by understanding various subtle rites and rituals, religious lingo used among local believers, and theological distinctions. Nevertheless, I made an earnest attempt to expand the scope of my observations to churches with which I had no prior relationship and which come from denominational traditions different from my own past experience. Churches selected were already multiracial and explicitly committed to diversity. Using academic networks in California and then following up on connections made with church leaders over the past several years, I personally contacted twenty-eight congregations said to be multiracial (i.e., having at least 20% of regular attenders being a different race/ethnicity than the dominant group) through a combination of mail, email, and telephone. Four churches were not sufficiently diverse to be considered multiracial; another ten did not respond to my efforts to speak with their worship and/or pastoral leaders. In the end, I focused on twelve Protestant congregations from a broad spectrum of denominational and theological traditions with a variety of racial-ethnic compositions. These observations are supplemented by observations gathered in my previous ethnographies on Mosaic and Oasis.[7]

In each church, some saw me as an outsider; others saw me as an insider. Overall, I occupied an ambivalent position as a person who was acknowledged to be another "believer" but not necessarily a person who is the same as Christians at each church. The position of researcher consistently set me apart from others. There were a few occasions when a staff member would introduce me to another as a person doing research. On a few occasions, a pastoral staff member would invite me to come sit in the front row, a place that is held in honor for visiting guests. I would politely decline, partly because my observations were richer from the back of the auditorium versus the front and partly because I feared alienating any non-staff attenders who might associate me as someone "important" and aligned somehow with the pastoral leadership. Pastoral attention often helped me gain access and legitimacy because I was recognized as having a sense of "permission" to be observing and asking questions. That meant that I lost anonymity among a small circle of people, but not for most. The majority of my interactions at church were with strangers and brief acquaintances, and very few came to know me by face without my research "agenda."

An important question is whether the character of worship found in the racially/ethnically diverse churches I observed in Los Angeles is also found in diverse congregations elsewhere. Research shows that levels of segregation are not as high in Southern California as in the South and Midwest. We also know that diverse congregations are more common in the Western United States. Perhaps it does not take shared musical preferences to unite people in this region, whereas the need to overcome a racialized history in the South and Midwest may place a greater burden on the style of music.

How much is this a Los Angeles, southern California phenomenon? Qualitative researchers often balance the depth of exposure to congregations with the breadth of congregational experiences made possible. It is not unusual for broad samplings of churches to be limited to a region with the intent to uncover dynamics that would be true of all.[8] I chose the sample out of my understanding of Los Angeles and my ability to get to as many churches as possible within the constraints of time and money for research. My contribution has greater depth on worship processes within a range of churches. By focusing on the internal processes of a particular set of congregations, I can only speculate on more general dynamics across the nation. Although I only have anecdotal evidence of other multiracial churches (my own visits, talking with pastors around the country, phone calls from reporters regarding churches in their cities, conferences with clergy and congregational members of diverse churches), I speculate that the increased urbanization of cities across the nation leads to similar dynamics of that found in Southern California. My conversations and observations since completing my data collection give me some assurance that the dynamics described here have broader applicability across the United States.

IN-DEPTH INTERVIEWS

More data came from transcribed interviews. In-depth interviews allow researchers to solicit detailed life stories and life histories which cannot be gained by just observing or "hanging out." As Lewis Minkin writes in pursuit of getting close to "the real picture" to affirm his growing understanding of a peculiarity, "I interview a lot of people and talk informally to them, often on repeated occasions."[9] Interviews provide an opportunity to see how people make sense of their own beliefs and practices. This continues a tradition within sociology that includes Max Weber, Alfred Schutz, George Herbert Mead, and Peter Berger that the ways in which people make sense of themselves and their worlds is critical to understanding the dynamics of any social setting.

For this study, I conducted a total of 172 interviews with church participants. Since the worship leader or the lead pastor were critical entry points for coming into the congregation, they were instrumental in coordinating people to interview. In all cases, the church allowed me to conduct interviews on site; in addition, I met with people wherever was most convenient to them, which were in homes, restaurants, or coffeehouses. In all cases, I met with the worship leader/music director. In all cases, I also met with people with no understanding or involvement in the musical construction of the services. Interviews were usually about 45 minutes long. The shortest was 20 minutes, the longest was almost 3 hours. In all cases, I met with a representative mixture of racial/ethnic groups of people attending the church.

In the end, 42% were Caucasian, 32% African American, 13% Hispanic, 5% Asian, 2% Middle Eastern, and 6% with mixed heritages who identified themselves as "multiracial." The greater proportion of whites overall is due to the majority of staff and long-time members still in the congregation were white. In terms of educational background, 17% had completed high school, 6% had Master's and Ph.D. degrees, and the rest had Bachelor's degrees or some college. Among my respondents, 14% were original immigrants to America, 10% were second and third generation, and the rest had a long ancestral history in the United States. Eighty-four percent of my sample was active in some type of ministry at the church. Although I sought out guests and new attenders, four out of five interviewees were members. Twenty-five percent came from non-denominational Christian backgrounds (often multiple churches), 35% came from specifically charismatic backgrounds, 15% came from Roman Catholic backgrounds, and 20% had mixed religious backgrounds including no religious background at all. In terms of tenure, 20% of my respondents had been attending less than two years, and 40% had been at their church five years or more. About 12% of my respondents made first-time commitments to become "Christians" at their church. While the average age of my respondents was 38 years, the youngest person interviewed was 19 and the oldest person who would tell me their age was 57. In sum, my respondents demonstrated a wide range of social demographic characteristics and came from a variety of lifestyles and life experiences.

As the number of my interviews grew, I continued to interview until I approached a saturation of experiences. Themes were repeating, and I found patterns that organized the experiences of worshipers that were later affirmed in my structured analysis of transcribed interview texts using qualitative-analysis software. In each church, I spoke with a range of attenders with various levels of tenure and involvement and, as insights began to become repetitious, collected a reasonable sample of life experiences for my analysis. Overall, scheduling interviews was not difficult. Most were eager to share their worship experiences. Their church involvement was for most a critical aspect of their religious commitments, and such a personally vital topic was worth their time to describe. My discussions were appropriately private. Elite interviews occurred with pastors and staff members who had been at each church for many years. Overall, my goal was to try to approximate the racial proportion of the congregation in the people I interviewed.

Interviews with decision makers and music performers allowed me to understand the ongoing processes of musical construction. How do leaders of multiracial congregations decide on the content and performance of worship music? What ideologies, theologies, and philosophies of music characterize the musical choices of multiracial churches? How do concerns for diversity affect the construction of worship services? How flexible are leaders in their choice of music? How are congregational reactions to music processed? Interviews with attenders focused on their experience of music and worship. How important is music to the choice of joining/leaving a church? Where does music rank in importance in comparison with other factors in the decision to join/leave a church (pastor, sermon, children's and other specialized programs, church location, theological tradition, overall ambience)? Does the salience of music differ among people of different races/ethnicities? Beyond music (i.e., words or sounds), what shapes the musical worship of a service? What defines the "worship experience" in the congregation? Interviews with music leaders were pre-arranged by phone/email, and interviews with attenders were pre-arranged also by phone/email with the assistance of church staff. I was able to offer $50 to each research participant.

I had prepared an interview guide consisting of several core questions and then allowed myself the opportunity to explore experiences, connections, and implications through probes and follow-up questions as I learned more about my respondents and the congregation as a whole from the respondent within the interview and also, in later interviews. I assured each person of confidentiality and asked for the opportunity to share information gathered with scholars and church leaders interested in congregational diversity. All interviewees read a consent form and, if agreed, signed one copy for my records and a second copy for themselves. Every interview began with the question, "How did you get to your church?" With this question, every person had the opportunity to tell me their life history up to the point of their arriving at the congregation in their own terms. In telling me their story, most shared their family backgrounds, religious upbringing, church experiences, relationships both successful and unsuccessful, their schooling and occupational careers and other matters that explained their values and mindset. I asked about their first worship and musical experiences with the church. Regular attenders responded to questions regarding worship, while church leaders, music directors, singers, musicians, and any other person involved in the construction of church services responded to questions regarding their involvements and experiences in worship before, during, and after services. Some shared with me experiences with other members and leaders in the church. Some also shared important changes they have seen in the church throughout their tenure. While my core questions did not change in the course of interviewing people, later interviews included at the end of our time a few summaries of my gut reactions to findings at the churches that served as "member checks" of my initial conclusions. At the end of each interview, I asked whether there was anything else they wanted to share about their experience at of worship. Some did, while others said they did not think there was anything else they could add. I found most people to be quite open and willing to share.

People emphasized different aspects according to those things they found most relevant to understanding their worship and music experiences. Some talked at great length, while others were asked several follow-up questions for clarification. Although I followed an interview schedule, I changed my mode of exploration that consisted of dialogue as well as interrogation. These were "conversations with a purpose."[10] Minkin discusses interview flexibility when he writes,

> Flexibility in response to the conversation... allowed me to make the solid information-seeking enquiries on which the creative scholar depends, but also, on occasions to make detours down interesting byways where I saw a connection or a revealing insight. It permitted me to explore an emerging pattern of cases, and to react, there and then, to the sudden appearance of the peculiarities that my nose told me could fruitfully be followed. Thus, I was happy to allow the conversation to take unexpected courses and, at times, to meander

> along, risking that it would have its creative benefits, providing that I could, periodically and gently, return it towards the priority areas of enquiry.[11]

Therefore, while I had several critical things I needed to understand from them (where they grew up, previous religious experience, racial/ethnic affiliation), a more open-ended interview allowed me to learn about each person's own perceptions of their life experience.

Almost every interview was tape-recorded. I still asked explicit permission to share data from each person. I tried to maintain an attitude of being a student of their own life experiences, speaking as little as possible. In the process, a handful of people consisting between staff, lay leaders, and regular attenders were informants that called my attention to aspects of the procedures and settings that I may have otherwise overlooked.

In addition to my formal interviews, I conducted numerous informal discussions with attenders I came to know before, after, and during church services. This gave me glimpses into a wider range of guests and regular attenders than I was able to interview formally and hear about their experiences with the church.

ARCHIVED SOURCES

In addition to observation and interviews, other sources of data included various printed and recorded materials available through the churches. Some leaders have published books and maintain tape libraries of sermon series that are sold. I added to my data selected books and tapes in seeking "structural corroboration" described by Elliot Eisner as "a means through which multiple types of data are related to each other to support or contradict the interpretation and evaluation of a state of affairs."[12] The few documentary sources consisted of guest information pamphlets, new member guides, copies of notable tape series, copies of music resources, and the church's website. All of the material used for analysis is publicly accessible. I also asked leaders to indicate recordings, musicians, books, leaders, and other resources that were considered important to them, and the few that were mentioned revealed certain critical aspects of the congregation's values and beliefs. Finally, the text draws selectively on available historical materials to account for the development of worship and music in Christianity, especially in the American context.

Notes

CHAPTER 1

1. King, Jr. (1958:25, 207, 208).
2. For an overview of research on multiracial churches, see DeYoung et al. (2003), Emerson and Woo (2006), Emerson and Smith (2000), Garces-Foley (2007), and Marti (2005, 2008a, 2009a, 2009b, 2010a, 2010b).
3. For book-length studies of Mosaic and Oasis, see Marti (2005, 2008b). For comparisons between these two diverse churches, see Marti (2008a, 2009a, 2010b).
4. Courtney (2000:3).
5. Social scientists define successfully diverse congregations as those that have at least 20 percent of regular attenders being different racial and ethnic heritages from the dominant racial or ethnic group of the congregation. See Marti (2005:23–24).
6. Farahadian (2007:x).
7. Courtney (2000:5).
8. On ritual processes, see Bell (2009a, 2009b).
9. Since the advent of sound recording technology, it is difficult to consider words in a text as music; yet, careful hermeneutics confirms that music is embedded within scripture even if it is not marked off from the flow of the text in the original documents. Current English translations frequently use italics and offset lines in poetic verse form to indicate musical lyrics in the flow of a narrative.
10. McKinnon (1989).
11. The prohibition of congregational and individual singing resulted in the loss of any record of post-biblical music and contributed to the preference for Gregorian chant, a musical development which grew because it was given a particular space in which to develop.
12. Holloway (2000) notes that belief in the power of music is not found solely in Christianity. The social significance of music is also prominently found among political philosophers such as Plato, Aristotle and Rousseau for giving rise to

"political passions." Even so, these thinkers fail to agree on how best to utilize the influence of music. "The thinkers who have addressed this issue (music's relevancy to politics), while agreeing on music's power and political significance, disagree on what to do about it. Should we ignore it, as the early moderns suggest, use it to calm passion and awaken reason, as Plato and Aristotle recommend, or following Rousseau and Nietzsche, use it to excite passion and silence reason?" (Holloway 2000: 113).

13. Ratzinger (2000) describes the difference between Apollonian and Dionysian alternatives in sacred music. He (150–151) writes, "[T]he Apollonian/Dionysian alternative runs through the whole history of religion and confronts us today." Drawing on the writings of Plato and Aristotle, Apollo as the god of light and reason guides the development of humanity through music as it moves the flesh to the realm of the spirit. Music elevates and unites flesh with spirit. Yet, the Dionysian relation of music floods the senses and humanity revels in the music. Music is either a vehicle for moving people through enlightened reason to the transcendent, or it is an environment within which the spirit comes to fill and engulf the worshiper.
14. McNeil and Richardson (2004:62). See also Black (2000), DeYmaz and Li (2010), and Yancey (2003).
15. Francis (2002:25, 39, 52).
16. International Council of Ethnodoxologists (ICE), "International Council Of Ethnodoxologists: A Network for Culturally Appropriate Christian Worship" webpage, http://www.worldofworship.org/Ethnodoxology.php (accessed November 29, 2010).
17. Yancey (2003:72).
18. DeYoung et al. (2003).
19. Kujawa-Holbrook (2002:5, 2).
20. McNeil and Richardson (2004:27, 61, 28).
21. Emerson and Smith (2000:153, 18). See also Tranby and Hartmann (2008).
22. See Marti (2005, 2009a, 2009b) and Tranby and Hartmann (2008).
23. See Marti (2010b) as well as previous research found in Marti (2005, 2008a, 2008b, 2009a, 2009b, 2010a).
24. To explore more on the processes listed further, see Becker (1998); Christerson, Emerson, and Edwards (2005); DeYoung et al. (2003); Emerson and Smith (2000); and Marti (2005).
25. See Appendix: Research Methodology.
26. See Grazian (2003) for a recent example of the sociological study of music using ethnographic methods. My observations are supplemented by the preliminary data on worship gathered from my previous ethnographies on Mosaic (Marti 2005) and Oasis (Marti 2008b). In this analysis, I am sensitive to complex issues of "explanation" in the social sciences and particularly appreciate the perspective provided by Martin (2011).
27. See Marti (2005, 2008a, 2008b, 2009a, 2009b, 2010a, 2010b).

28. For more detail on the mechanics of data gathering and research methodology for this study, please consult the Appendix: Research Methodology.
29. DeNora (2000:163).
30. DeNora (2000:45). In the preface to her book, DeNora (2000:x) points out that "we have very little sense of how music features within social process" and "next to no data on how real people actually press music into action in particular social spaces and temporal settings." Certainly this research looks at the use of music in the racially diverse congregations with an ethnographic sensitivity to the range and types of divers congregations that exist in the United States.
31. See also Martin (1995).
32. DeNora (2000:21, 24).
33. DeNora (2000:6).
34. DeNora points out that in the development of what has been known as "the sociology of music," Theodore Adorno accentuated how music could be a "force" in social life, yet fail to provide mechanisms or more specific processes as to how music trains unconsciousness or the link between music and social action. Critical reactions to Adorno framed a core question about music: Does it reflect culture? Or does it lead to the formation of culture? Yet, both questions sidestep the more important questions of process: How is music implicated within social structures?
35. DeNora (2000:30, 31, 23, x).
36. DeNora (2000:5). See Willis (1978) and Frith (1978, 1981).
37. On music as a source of security and comfort, see the example of "Gary" in DeNora (2000:15–16).
38. More on the structure of the self in relation to music and worship is found in chapter 4.
39. DeNora (2000:5–6).
40. When thinking of music as a form of social control, it is important to note that church leaders who desire to diversify their congregations are seeking to enact this without the consent of the congregation. It is a form of coordination that does not require explicit assent or outright affinity. Research consistently shows that individuals left to their own choice and friendship networks remain within their own racial and ethnic groups. So, the capacity for congregations to diversify is in many ways something that is accomplished aside from the desires and interests of most people within a congregation. Music enables the ability for people to act in social concert. To the extent that music can be used to cultivate and even "lure" people to experience diversity, music becomes a means to accomplish a corporate structuring of a congregation in a manner guided by the desires of leaders to craft a congregation with diverse attendance; therefore, the actualization of diversity will be dependent on the level of social control achieved by organizational leaders to bring people into a common fellowship, even if they would prefer to not have that diversity in their own lives.

41. DeNora (2000:157, 19; see also 153).
42. Roy (2010).
43. Costen (1993) is an example of an analysis that includes an ideal worship outline presented as a model to be emulated rather than a description of actual occurrences.
44. While the focus on Protestant congregations may seem limiting at first, there is an intentional selection of a broad range of liturgical practices and worship experiences among the diverse churches included in the study. Moreover, the practice of soliciting data from a focused range of congregations is a common strategy among researchers (see Appendix: Research Methodology). After sharing my preliminary results at conferences, lectures, and workshops across the United States, I am confident that the range of investigation accomplished for this research allows for more general statements about dynamics within Christian churches from all traditions. Of course, I hope that by presenting my results, this book will stimulate even further research.

CHAPTER 2

1. McNeil and Richardson (2004:62).
2. See chapter 5.
3. DeNora (1986).
4. DiMaggio (1987). See also Clayton, Herbert, and Middleton (2003:245). It is helpful to read Burke (2008) who productively complicates simplistic distinctions between musical styles such as Dixieland, swing, and bebop. And since these styles were defined along racial lines, the music was itself a powerful challenge to racist ideology.
5. See chapters 3, 7, and 8.
6. See Marti (2005) and Marti (2008b).
7. Emerson, and Woo (2006). See also Chaves (2004).
8. Kimbrough (2000:23).
9. See Moreau, Netland, van Engen, and Burnett (2000:328).
10. Hawn (2003a:27–28). See also Nettle (1983:43, 75).
11. See chapter 6.
12. Doran and Troeger (1992:23).
13. Black (2000).
14. See chapter 6.
15. Yancey (2003:78, 67).
16. Yancey (2003:72, 75).
17. Aghahowa (1996:28).
18. Faus (1995:366–367).
19. Redman (2002:100).
20. Faus (1995:367).

21. Redman (2002:100).
22. For more on approaching multiracial worship as a process of "flavoring" and "spicing" ethnic styles, see chapter 6.
23. See Lornell and Rasmussen (1997).
24. Denisoff and Levine (1972).
25. Lewis (1977).
26. Schuessler (1980:3).
27. Maynard-Reid (2000).
28. For a more scholarly look at a "theology of discomfort," see Garces-Foley (2007).
29. Maynard-Reid (2000:24, 17).
30. Maynard-Reid (2000:61–62, 67, 69–70, 85, 70, 71, 78, 67). James Cone similarly asserted that the enthusiasm so often described in African American services "is the presence of the divine Sprit who accounts for the intensity in which black people engage in worship" (1978:140).
31. Maynard-Reid (2000:138, 141, 148, 149).
32. Maynard-Reid (2000:187, 183, 187).
33. Maynard-Reid (2000:187). See Villafañe (1993).
34. Maynard-Reid (2000:188–189). See also Burgos and Meltz (1989:16–18).
35. See Maynard-Reid (2000:192).
36. Maynard-Reid (2000:25, 53).
37. Here and elsewhere, the category "Asian" is problematic given the enormous differences between all the countries that are in Asia. Nevertheless, the current literature on racial and ethnic diversity in congregations has generally adopted a pan-Asian label (see Jeung 2004, Kim 2004, and Kim 2010). The same critique can be given to the category "Latino" (see Vasquez 1999).
38. Passion is an evangelically -based, non-denominational organization ministry that organizes worship concerts across the United States for younger adults.
39. Both chapters 3 and 7 show that despite the seeming affinity for "white music," Asian-led and Asian-dominated churches incorporate and perform black gospel music as a strategy for achieving diversity.
40. Redman (2002:113).
41. Kimbrough (2000:26, 29).
42. Tveit (2000:6, 11).
43. Donaldson (2001:4, 6).
44. Kimbrough (2000:25).
45. Kimbrough (2000:23).
46. Hawn (2003a:14).
47. Hawn (1999:45).
48. Hawn (2003a). See Bradshaw (1992).
49. Hawn (2003a:14).
50. See Clayton, Herbert, and Middleton (2003:271).
51. Metzler (1938); see also Bohlmann 2003 and Radano and Bohlman 2000.

52. See Brackett (2003:239).
53. See texts by Reck (1997), May (1983), and Titon (2002).
54. Appadurai (1990, 1996).
55. Shelemay (2001).
56. Rasmussen (2004:303–304).
57. Rasmussen (2004:305–306). See Taylor (2000).
58. The difficulty of attempting multiracial unity while keeping ethnic identities separate is recently explored by Kathleen Garces-Foley (2007) and will be explored further in chapter 6.
59. Redman (2002:107).
60. Vásquez(1999:620).
61. Hawn (2003a:27).
62. See Lincoln and Mamiya (1990).

CHAPTER 3

1. Burnim (1980).
2. Pinn (2002:56). See also Lincoln and Mamiya (1990: chap. 12).
3. Maynard-Reid (2000:68).
4. Yancey (2003:57).
5. Lincoln (1999:243–244).
6. Negro spirituals are seen as distinctive forms of expression among blacks, yet my interviews overemphasize how they dealt with misery and underemphasize that these songs were also an outlet for aggression and resistance.
7. DuBois ([1903] 1996:viii).
8. Bethea (1978:44). See also Pinn (2002) and Williams-Jones (1975).
9. Floyd (1995:5, 9).
10. For recent accounts of the history of gospel music, see Cusic (2002) and Darden (2004). More sources on the development of gospel music include Mays and Nicholson (1933), Nelsen and Nelsen (1975), Harris (1994), Helibut (1997), Jackson (1979), Spencer (1997), and Walker (1979). Most centrally, gospel is the type of music that represents a collective American black experience. Yet, the different styles and genres within African American gospel (traditional, contemporary, urban contemporary, inspirational) make a definitive statement of style difficult. Moreover, the orientation of gospel music changes over time. Jackson (1995:186) writes, "What we must not fail to remember is that gospel music is an evolving, dynamic, and vernacular art form."
11. Jackson (1995:198). See also Floyd (1995). While the emphasis here is on the co-development of gospel music and perceived notions of black worship, it is important to note that African Americans have a richer and more complex history of music in America both in its form and performance (see Brundage 2011).
12. Jackson (1995:198).

13. Dubois ([1903] 1996:155, 157). See also Pinn (2003).
14. Although race theories and all forms of biological determinism have been largely discredited in the twentieth century, especially through the work of Franz Boas and his influential students Ruth Benedict, Margaret Mead, Jacques Barzun, and Ashley Montague, nevertheless, the popular imagination even in the most "civilized" of nations continue to accentuate the belief in racially different traits. For a discussion focusing on the historical intertwining of African Americans and "black music," see Radano (2003).
15. The original work is titled *Essai sur l'inégalité des races humaines* and was translated by Josiah Nott (with Henry Hotze) for publication to American audiences in 1856 as *The Moral and Intellectual Diversity of Races: With Particular Reference to Their Respective Influence in the Civil and Political History of Mankind, from the French of Count A. de Gobinaeu.*
16. Painter (2010:197). See also Boissel (1993:129–130).
17. Painter (2010:197).
18. Evans (2008:166). Overall, Evans (2008) provides an excellent overview of understandings of "black religion" in American history.
19. Evans (2008:166).
20. Evans (2008:134).
21. Evans (2008:133).
22. Evans (2008:134).
23. Evans (2008:188).
24. Evans (2008:189).
25. Evans (2008:189).
26. From Bonheoffer's personal correspondence quoted in Schlingensiepen (2009:68).
27. Changes in musical education contributed to cultural sensitivity that allowed non-blacks to appreciate and assimilate black gospel into their musical repertoire. See Volk (1994) and Davis (1964).
28. Volk (1994).
29. Davis (1964:76).
30. See Heilbut (1978).
31. Frazier (1963:72–75).
32. Broughton (1985:48). Gospel music involves an antiphonal style, no predetermined length, call-reponse, leader-chorus, improvised text, time, melody with group responding with short repetitive phrase. See also Boyer (1979, 1987).
33. Boyer (1979:38).
34. Sanders (1996:71).
35. Jones (1974:81–82).
36. Anderson (2010).
37. Boyer (1979:34).
38. Quoted in Strauss (1965:583).

39. Pinn (2002:56).
40. Pinn (2002:54).
41. Lincoln and Mamiya (1990:380).
42. Frazier (1963:74).
43. Pinn (2002:55).
44. How much resistance was there of gospel music by the Black Church? The evidence seems to suggest that resistance to gospel music was only among a small minority, and the appeal of the music was great among the overwhelming majority. Lincoln and Mamiya (1990:377) isolate the resistance to exist among some segments of "newly black Baptist and Methodist churches" as well as some "traditionalists" who find the theology problematic and the lyrics and rhythms secularized.
45. Lincoln and Mamiya (1990:379). The neo-Pentecostal style of praise and worship is one that has grown nationwide with praise teams leading worship songs, visible movement in dance, and an energetic updating of gospel rhythms that included funk and R&B. The apparent success of such congregations in contrast with the worrisome decline of more traditionally styled churches has caused enough concern that it may threaten to create a permanent rift within the Black Church. Although Lincoln and Mamiya (1990:388) focus on the experience of neo-Pentecostalist worship within the A.M.E. churches, they go on to note that the style is spreading and that "the challenge which neo-Pentecostals imposes for the Black Church is real, and the issue of how to benefit from this potential church growth and spiritual revitalization without alienating the pillars of normative tradition . . . and without producing a crisis of schism is a challenge most want churches must inevitably address."
46. Pinn (2002:57).
47. Similarly, James Standifer and Barbara Reeder (1972:100) note that "the black performer makes a rendition strikingly 'black' by bringing himself and the black experience to that rendition."
48. Porter (2002:xiv).
49. Hutchinson, Rodriguez, and Hagan (1996:202).
50. DjeDje (1986:223).
51. Burnim (1985b:437).
52. Burnim (1980:68; see also 1985a).
53. Williams-Jones (1975:373).
54. Williams-Jones (1975:373, 376).
55. Including Mahalia Jackson, Clara Ward, James Cleveland, and Alex Bradford.
56. Williams-Jones (1975:384). See also Levine (1977:189) who concludes that gospel music is a significant factor in the "sustenance and identity and survival" of black people in America]. For her (383), it is connected with "Black speech," a significant aspect of the gospel performance idiom, a form of "Black linguistic elegance" that is equated with black poetry (383). She quotes from Stephen Henderson (1973:31).

57. Wong (1999) and Fettes (2000).
58. Jackson (1995:187, 198). Writers occasionally acknowledge the variety of music among African Americans: "Of course African-Americans do not have one uniform style of worship," (Maynard-Reid 2000:57). "Although African Americans share many common worship practices, one should not assume that all African American congregations will or should exhibit homogenous styles of worship. Different situations and circumstances under which exposure to Christianity took place for each congregation, denomination (history and theological orientation), geography, and social life-styles are significant determinants of worship," (Costen 1993:15–16). However, the overall thrust is to characterize the dominant style in a way that erases the understanding of variety. Maynard-Reid (57) also states, "Class structure determines the level of Afrocentrism in the denomination or congregation. The lower the class, the more Afrocentric the church; the higher the class, the more Eurocentric." Pentecostalism works with the middle-income strata (58), and he finds support for his findings in Lincoln and Mamiya (1990).
59. DjeDje (1986:223–224).
60. DjeDje (1986) describes how gospel is used to make the Catholic Church more relevant and responsive to needs of blacks. Liturgy was changed by the adoption of new forms of music out of developments in the broader society. Moreover, once it became known that one Catholic Church in Los Angeles had been successful in using gospel music in the liturgy, other Catholic groups began to experiment with the idea.
61. Asante (1988:9).
62. Philip Tagg (1989) finds the societal labels of "black music" and "white music" questionable. He cites that there are neither musicological nor ideological arguments for placing Afrocentric music opposite of Eurocentric music. Tagg and other musicologists seriously question defining boundaries of racial music and see this as a broader question of establishing genre. Gospel music now includes elements of jazz, blues, and modern dance, making it difficult to distinguish between genres. See also Brackett (2005).
63. Maultsby (1992:24) describes how radio became a popular source of mass entertainment in the 1920s at the same time that black churches broadcast their worship services featuring gospel music. By the 1930s, live performances of gospel choirs were available on the radio, initiating an important niche market for record producers. The commercial market for gospel music remains viable today; for example, satellite radio programming regularly includes gospel channels devoted to full-time gospel recordings feeding a demand for gospel music.
64. Frazier (1963:85).
65. Grazian (2003:59).
66. See chapter 7.
67. See chapter 7.
68. See Smith and Jackson (2005).

69. Wong (1999:103).
70. Hope for Life International, "The African American Pulpit: A quarterly journal that serves as a repository for the very best of African American preaching and provides practical and creative resources for persons in ministry," website, http://www.theafricanamericanpulpit.com/, accessed July 18, 2011; see also Jimmy Abington (2001).
71. Aghahowa (1996). See Troeger (1998).
72. See Edwards (2008) for a case study on the pressure on African Americans to accommodate worship styles to white-dominant practices in multiracial churches.
73. Edwards (2008).
74. More on this will be discussed in chapter 7.
75. A multiracial church where African American members describe their identities as "more than just black" is found in Marti (2010a, 2010b).

CHAPTER 4

1. On popular beliefs connecting race/ethnicity and worship, see chapter 2.
2. For more specific notions of worship among different racial and ethnic groups, see chapters 2 and 3.
3. DeNora (2000).
4. Rahn (1972:255).
5. Mark (1998:470). See also McPherson (1983).
6. See chapter 7 and 8.
7. More on the planning for worship is found in the analysis of worship leaders in Cchapter 6.
8. DeNora (2000:58).
9. Marti (2008b:160–162).
10. DeNora (2000:60).
11. DeNora (2000:78).
12. See Witkin (1974).
13. DeNora (2000:128–129).
14. Wolff (1999) similarly describes worship as involving concentration meaning a centering or focus. The initial orientating (Wolff's conforming) is followed by transformation, the time when the self is absorbed into a higher and distinctive activity in relation to both the self and the world.
15. For an earlier discussion of "letting go" in worship among multiracial worshipers, see Marti (2008b:160–162).
16. DeNora (2000:60–61).
17. Nelson (2005).
18. For a description of how notions of race structure the planning and performance of liturgy in multiracial congregations, see chapters 6 and 7.
19. DeNora (2000:45–46, 53, 61).
20. DeNora (2000:54, 85).

21. See Bocock (1993), Lash and Urry (1994), and Belcher (1997).
22. DeNora (2000:47).
23. DeNora (2000:53). See Hochschild (1983) and Nelson's (2005).
24. DeNora (2000:53).
25. DeNora (2000:95, 106).

CHAPTER 5

1. For more on congregations hiring black worship pastors, see chapter 7.
2. Waters (2001:63). See also Lash and Urry (1994).
3. See chapter 3.
4. For a discussion on worship and "letting go," see chapter 4.
5. DeNora (2000:96).
6. See Martin (1997), Whitson (1994), and Middleton (1990).
7. Jakobson (1960), Eco (1984), and Middleton (1990).
8. DeNora (2000:93).
9. See DeNora (2000:93).
10. DeNora (2000:93).
11. DeNora (2000:90).
12. DeNora (2000:91, 92, 102–103).
13. Middleton (1990).
14. DeNora (2000:90–91, 102).
15. DeNora (2000:94).
16. DeNora (2000:99–100, 102).
17. In liturgical studies, this term describes the priestly prayer occurring before the Eucharist in Roman Catholic and Eastern Orthodox services.
18. Callon (1986).
19. For more on the personal experience of corporate worship, see chapter 4.
20. Webber (1994).
21. DeNora (2000:101).
22. DeNora (2000:42–43, 53).
23. DeNora (2000:66).
24. This is the process of worship as "letting go" described in chapter 4.
25. For a description of the varied assumptions regarding what type of music should be included in multiracial worship services, see chapter 6.
26. DeNora (2000:95–96, 102).

CHAPTER 6

1. DeNora (2000:20).
2. Eventually, the growth of Spanish speakers in this congregation's "diversity service" resulted in creating a separate worship service led entirely in Spanish. The facilities

of the congregation allowed for two simultaneous services, and the congregation not only expanded staff for the new service but also gained around three hundred regular attenders. Larry said, "It was our purpose to stay as one church and one body even though we may have several services." Although the congregation celebrates this as an achievement, it also points to limits of "multicultural worship" with respect to linguistic differences. It appears that shared worship that incorporates different languages can become strained for both leaders and attenders and prompts both toward creating mono-linguistic services.

3. On the surface, research appears to support this. Perhaps there exists a musical space that allows greater potential for multiracial worship. For example, looking carefully at the chart that plots the worship style of congregations by level of ceremony and level of enthusiasm in Chaves (2004:chapter 5), I find that independent, nondenominational churches overlap with both white Baptist, black Baptist, and Pentecostal churches. This implies that the Baptist tradition of worship spiced by Pentecostal revivalist expressiveness creates a potential "space" for black-white congregational interaction. This cultural space represents a musically defined social area in which both black and white congregational members can find themselves in familiar and comfortable acoustic spaces. Nevertheless, the analysis represented in this book finds less support for specific musical styles and more for processes of recruitment for music ministries that accentuate diversity and the consequences of member involvement in music ministries (see chapters 7 and 9).
4. See Royce (1982).
5. Yancey (2003:78).
6. Yancey (2003:76, 78).
7. Kim (2006:115, 81).
8. Yancey (2003:67, 68, 117).
9. Kujawa-Holbrook (2002:2).
10. The concept of intentionality has a rich history in modern philosophy beginning with Jeremy Bentham and Franz Brentano, and continuing through Edmund Husserl and Martin Heidegger among others. While this is not the place to debate the relative merits of approaching the idea of intentionality, let it suffice to say that intentionality is a concept that implies perception of objects and an awareness of what one is doing in the process of accomplishment of human action.
11. Hawn (2003b:7).
12. For more on Oasis, see Marti (2008b).
13. For more on Mosaic, see Marti (2005).
14. On the musical stereotypes surrounding Asian Americans, see chapter 2.
15. Hawn (2003b:8).
16. Although incorporating Spanish appears reasonable in the context of Southern California churches, the Spanish language is introduced into services even when in churches where Latinos are absent. Indeed, the incorporation of Spanish songs

appears to be a trend in "Latino-less" churches across the United States who embrace a value for diversity.

17. Andrews (1916:7).

CHAPTER 7

1. On the expectations for racial authenticity and performance in multiracial worship, see chapter 3.
2. On the role of worship leaders in congregations and the musical choices they make, see chapters 5 and 6.
3. On African Americans and gospel music, see chapter 3.
4. Walker (2003:23).
5. Quoted in Walker (2003:24). See Dilling (1995).
6. DjeDje (1986).
7. On the iconic role of African Americans singing gospel music, see chapter 3.
8. In a fascinating book, Lewis (2010) writes that the formation of gospel choirs has been sweeping across the globe (including European countries, Anglophone nations like Australia and even Asian nations like Japan, and China) over the past two decades as a form of revitalization, motivating higher attendance and greater participation in churches.
9. The implication of visual presence can be drawn out from the work of Erving Goffman and the dramaturgical issues inherent to the visual presence of racial and ethnic difference.
10. Jessica Barron (2010) reports similar placement of colored bodies in her ethnographic research of a Chicago congregation.
11. Yancey (2003). Discussion of public placement of African Americans in church leadership in multiracial churches can also be found in Edwards (2008), Emerson and Woo (2007), and Marti (2010a).
12. See Evans (2008).
13. See Radano (2003).
14. See Stowe (2004:7).
15. For more on the iconic status of African Americans singing gospel music, see chapter 3.
16. Ammerman (2005).
17. DiMaggio and Mohr (1985).
18. Ammerman (2005:39).
19. Ammerman (2005:39).
20. Abbington (2001:31).
21. Chaves (2004).
22. Becker (1998).
23. For other examples of racialized ritual inclusion in multiracial churches, see also Marti (2005, 2008b).

24. For ethnographic studies of Mosaic and Oasis, see Marti (2005 and 2008b). Pettigrew (1985) writes that at the social-structural level, studies converge on the importance of social interactions for cross-ethnic/cross-racial relationships. For my past articulation of these processes as they operate in multiracial congregations, see Marti (2008a, 2009a, 2009b, 2010a, 2010b).
25. See Pattillo-McCoy (1998).
26. The process of "racialized ritual inclusion" is a counterpoint to the process of "ethnic transcendence" (Marti 2005, 2008a, 2009a, 2009b, 2010a). The first emphasizes recruitment and inclusion to liturgical structures on the basis of racialized differences. The second emphasizes affinity and camaraderie among members of a congregation who privilege a shared religious identity.

CHAPTER 8

1. For more on the variety of approaches to music in multiracial services, see chapter 6.
2. For more on music choices and the promotion of conspicuous color in multiracial services, see chapter 7.
3. See chapter 7.
4. Yancey (2003:67).
5. See chapter 3.
6. See chapter 7.
7. See chapter 7.
8. Connecting this insight to my previous research, it may be argued that the process here labeled "racialized ritual inclusion" is a means by which members have the opportunity to begin the process of finding relational affinities with each other which deepen as they are re-formed within a religious milieu. By participating in the liturgical music structures of their church, members come to build a shared religious identity within their congregation, a process I have labeled elsewhere as "ethnic transcendence." See Marti (2005, 2008a, 2009a, 2009b, 2010a, 2010b).
9. See Clawson (2011).

CONCLUSION

1. See Ashton (1947).
2. See also Calhoun and Sennett (2007) and Martin (1995).
3. Ammerman (2005:25). See also Becker (1997; 1999).
4. Ammerman (2005:25).
5. See Small (1998), Cook and Everist (1999).
6. DeNora (2000:103). See Ehn's (1988:399) discussion of Weizenbaum (1976).
7. DeNora (1986:89, 91, 92).
8. See DeNora (2000:41).
9. DeNora (1986:88) insists that music can be experienced as inherently meaningful, but this is not due to the structure of music but rather through the structure of

human interactions producing and consuming that music within particular social settings. Pointing back to Ludwig Wittgenstein's analysis of semantics, DeNora rightly states, "rather than comparing music to formal speech and grammatical rules it may be more productive to compare it to speech in practical contexts, to study meaning in *use*...."

10. DeNora (2000:110).
11. See DeNora (2000:61–62, 87).
12. DeNora (2000:109).
13. For an overview of recent debates on contemporary Christian music, see Basden (2004), Luhr (2005), Romanowski (1990, 2000), Howard and Streck (1996, 1999), Baker (1985), Miller (1993), and Webber (2004).
14. Hawn (2003a:15).
15. See Spencer (1995).
16. See Titon (1988).
17. Multiracial churches in this study using metered hymns had newer hymnbooks, either denominational hymn books that have been revised or updated or a widely distributed non-denominational hymnal. In one case, the congregation uses "blended worship" (Webber 2004), a style of worship arrangement that mixes established hymns with contemporary worship music.
18. See Hawn (2003a).
19. DeNora (2000:34).
20. DeNora (2000:33).
21. For example, research shows that a person's musical tolerance increases with their level of education. However, the same research shows that genres whose fans have the least education (gospel, country, rap, and heavy metal) are the most likely to be rejected by "musically tolerant" people (see Bryson 1996). In contrast to such "taste-based" findings, I find situational dynamics within multiracial churches encourage members to strongly favor gospel music (see chapters 3 and 8). Overall, my findings suggest that musical preference plays a subdued role in relation to the value for highlighting notions of racial diversity as well as the desire for individuals to connect with others in their church apart from the specific genre(s) of music played in the congregation.
22. From the perspective of technology studies, technology is not determinative of use. As Bruno Latour writes, "Artefacts do not *compel* users to behave in preferred or prescripted ways" (qtd in DeNora 2000:35). Latour critiques this as "technologism," a form of technological determinism (Latour 1991). See also Akrich (1991), Akrich and Latour (1991), Law (1994), Pinch and Bijker (1987), and Woolger (1997).
23. See Epstein (1994), Bennett (2000, 2001), Bennett and Peterson (2004), Fanarow (1997), Gaines (1991), Grazian (2003), Macias (2004), Malbon (1999), Stokes (1994), and Thornton (1996).
24. Silbermann (1963).
25. See DeNora (2000:44).

26. Stokes (1994), for example, turns analytic attention away from music "in a place" toward instead examining how "place" is constructed through music.
27. Turino (2008). This also finds resonance in the work of Émile Durkheim (1995; see also discussion of Durkheim and moral community in Marti 2008b).
28. Turnino (2008:1).
29. DeNora (2000:44).
30. Turino (2008:2).
31. Catchings (1952).
32. See Durkheim (1995) and subsequent commentary by Alexander (1988), Allen, Pickering, and Watts Miller (1998), Jones (1999), Lukes (1972), and Pickering (2002). My analysis of Oasis Christian Center also works with insights drawn from a neo-Durkheimian framework (Marti 2008b).
33. See Marti (2008b).
34. Whitely, Bennett, and Hawkins (2004:68).
35. DeNora (2000:123).
36. Anderson (1976).
37. Epstein (1994), Bennett (2001), and Stokes (1994).
38. For Stokes (1994:3), "The musical event... evokes and organizes collective memories and present experiences of place with an intensity, power and simplicity unmatched by any other social activity".
39. Bennett (2001) highlights the discussion on popular music culture as a mechanism to bring individuals together through shared tastes and lifestyles. For Stokes (1994:3), "The musical event... evokes and organizes collective memories and present experiences of place with an intensity, power and simplicity unmatched by any other social activity." (1994:3). Bennett discusses important social and political concepts such as localization and cultural exteriorization (see also Lull 1995; see Bennett 2001 for this).
40. Epstein (1994:xiii).
41. Stokes (1994:6).
42. See Emerson and Kim (2003).
43. Berger and Luckmann (1967).
44. See chapter 6.
45. For an application of Max Weber to understanding shared understandings of ethnic and racial groups, see Alba (1990), De Vos (1975), De Vos and Romanucci-Ross (1975), Gans (1979, 1994), Marti (2005, 2008a, 2010), Royce (1982), and Waters (1990).
46. See Marti (2008a).
47. Munro (2010:207).
48. Roy (2010:24).
49. DeNora (2000:13).
50. Rommen (2007:6).
51. DeNora (2000:32).

52. Middleton (1990:10).
53. DeNora cites Piron (1990, 1993), Rook (1987), and Rook and Hoch (1985).
54. DeNora (2000:136, 138, 143). DeNora also cites Gumperz (1977) and DeNora (1986).
55. Grazian (2003).
56. DeNora (2000:159). She cites Ehn (1988:449).
57. DeNora (2000:159, 152, 162-163, 108).
58. DeNora (2000:140, 107).

APPENDIX: RESEARCH METHODOLOGY

1. In constructing an "explanation" for the operation of music and worship in multi-racial congregations, I resonate with the approach to understanding social action described by John Levi Martin (2011).
2. Becker and Geer (1982:249).
3. Van Maanen (1988:3).
4. Jorgensen (1989:14).
5. Berger and Luckmann (1967).
6. Jorgensen (1989:21).
7. See Marti (2005, 2008b) as well as subsequent analysis found in Marti (2008a, 2009a, 2009b, 2010a, 2010b).
8. Two recent qualitative studies that utilize a broad sampling of congregations from a limited region include Bass (2006) and Ellingson (2007).
9. Minkin (1997:122).
10. Webb and Webb (1932:130).
11. Minkin (1997:149).
12. Eisner (1991:110).

Bibliography

Abbington, James. 2001. *Readings in African American Church Music and Worship*. Chicago: GIA Publications.

Aghahowa, Brenda Eatman. 1996. *Praising in Black and White: Unity and Diversity in Christian Worship*. Cleveland: United Church.

Akrich, Madeleine. 1991. The De-scription of Technical Objects. In *Shaping Technology/Building Society: Studies in Sociotechnical Change*, edited by W. E. Bijker and J. Law, 205–244. Cambridge, Mass.: MIT Press.

Akrich, Madeleine and Bruno Latour. 1991. A Summary of a Convenient Vocabulary for the Semiotics of Human and Nonhuman Assemblies. In *Shaping Technology/Building Society: Studies in Sociotechnical Change*, edited by W. E. Bijker and J. Law, 259–264. Cambridge, Mass.: MIT Press.

Alba, Richard D. 1990. *Ethnic Identity: The Transformation of White America*. New Haven, Conn.: Yale University Press.

Alexander, Jeffrey. C., Ed. 1988. *Durkheimian Sociology: Cultural Studies*. New York: Cambridge University Press.

Allen, N. J., W. S. F. Pickering, and William Watts Miller. 1998. *Durkheim's* Elementary Forms of Religious Life. London and New York: Routledge.

Ammerman, Nancy Tatom. 2005. *Pillars of Faith: American Congregations and Their Partners*. Berkeley and Los Angeles: University of California Press.

Anderson, Elijah. 1976. *A Place on the Corner*. Chicago: University of Chicago Press.

Anderson, Toni P. 2010. *"Tell Them We Are Singing for Jesus": The Original Fisk Jubilee Singers and Christian Reconstruction*, 1871–1878. Macon, Ga.: Mercer University Press.

Andrews, George Whitfield. 1916. Music as an Expression of Religious Feeling. *Musical Quarterly* 2, no. 3 (July): 331–338.

Appadurai, Arjun. 1990. Disjuncture and Difference in the Global Cultural Economy. *Public Culture* 2, no. 2 (Spring): 1–24.

———. 1996. *Modernity at Large: Cultural Dimensions of Globalization*. Minneapolis: University of Minnesota Press.

Asante, Molefi Kete. 1988. *Afrocentricity*. Trenton, N.J.: Africa World Press.

Ashton, Joseph N. 1947. *Music in Worship: The Use of Music in the Church Service*. Boston: Pilgrim Press.

Bainbridge, William Sims, and Rodney Stark. 1980. Networks of Faith: Interpersonal Bonds and Recruitment to Cults and Sects. *American Journal of Sociology*, 85, no. 6 (May): 1376–1395.

Baker, Paul. 1985. *Contemporary Christian Music: Where It Came From, What It Is, Where It's Going.* Westchester: Crossway Books.

Barron, Jessica. 2010. *The City Imagined: Race, Place and Identity in the Making of a Young Urban Church*. Paper presented at the annual meeting of the Association for the Sociology of Religion, Atlanta, Georgia.

Basden, Paul A., ed. 2004. *Exploring the Worship Spectrum: Six Views.* Grand Rapids, Mich.: Zondervan.

Bass, Diana Butler. 2006. *Christianity for the Rest of Us: How the Neighborhood Church Is Transforming the Faith*. San Francisco: Harper San Francisco.

Becker, Penny Edgell. 1997. Congregational Model and Conflicts: Identifying a Religious Logic in Local Congregations. In *Sacred Companies: Organized Aspects of Religion and Religious Aspects of Organization*, edited by Peter Dobkin Hall, N. J. Demerath III, Terry Schmidt, and Rhys H. Williams, 231–255. New York: Oxford University Press.

———. 1998. Making Inclusive Communities: Congregations and the "Problem" of Race. *Social Problems* 45, no. 4 (November): 451–472.

———.1999. *Congregations in Conflict: Cultural Models of Local Religious Life*. New York: Cambridge University Press.

Becker, Howard S., and Blanche Geer. 1982. Participant Observation: The Analysis of Qualitative Field Data. In *Field Research: A Sourcebook and Field Manual*, edited by R. Burgess. London: Allen & Unwin.

Belcher, Sophie. 1997. The Metropolis and Aesthetic Life: An Ethnography of London's Design Elite. MA thesis, University of Exeter.

Bell, Catherine. 2009a. *Ritual: Perspectives and Dimensions*. New York: Oxford University Press.

——— 2009b. *Ritual Theory, Ritual Practice*. New York: Oxford University Press.

Bennett, Andy. 2000. *Popular Music and Youth Culture: Music, Identity and Place*. Basingstoke: Macmillan / St. Martin's Press.

———. 2001. *Cultures of Popular Music*. Buckingham, England: Open University Press.

Bennett, Andy, and Richard A. Peterson, eds. 2004. *Music Scenes: Local, Trans-Local, and Virtual*. Nashville, Tenn.: Vanderbilt University Press.

Berger, Peter L., and Thomas Luckmann. 1967. *The Social Construction of Reality*. Garden City, N.Y.: Anchor Books.

Bethea, Joseph B. 1978. Worship in the Black Church. *Duke Divinity School Review* 43 (Winter): 44–53.

Black, Kathy. 2000. *Culturally-Conscious Worship*. St. Louis, Mo.: Chalice Press.

Bohlmann, Philip V. 2003. Music and Culture: Historiographies of Disjuncture. In *The Cultural Study of Music: A Critical Introduction*, edited by Martin Clayton, Trevor Herbert, and Richard Middleton, 45–56. New York: Routledge.

Bocock, Robert. 1993. *Consumption*. London: Routledge.

Boissel, Jean. 1993. *Gobineau: Biographie: Mythes et réalité*. Paris: Berg International.

Boyer, Horace C. 1979. Contemporary Gospel Music. *The Black Perspective in Music* 7, no. 1 (Spring): 5–11, 22–58.

———. 1987. Gospel Music. *Music Educators' Journal* 64, no. 9 (May): 34–43.

Brackett, David. 2003. What a Difference a Name Makes: Two Instances of African-American Popular Music. In *The Cultural Study of Music: A Critical Introduction*, edited by Martin Clayton, Trevor Herbert, and Richard Middleton, 238–250. New York: Routledge.

———. 2005. Questions of Genre in Black Popular Music. *Black Music Research Journal* 25, no. 1/2 (Spring–Fall): 73–92.

Bradshaw, Paul. 1992. *The Search for the Origins of Christian Worship*. London: SPCK.

Broughton, Viv. 1985. *Black Gospel: An Illustrated History of the Gospel Sound*. New York: Blandford.

Brundage, W. Fitzhugh. 2011. *Beyond Blackface: African Americans and the Creation of American Popular Culture, 1890–1930*. Chapel Hill, N.C.: University of North Carolina Press.

Bryson, Bethany. 1996. Anything but Heavy Metal: Symbolic Exclusion and Musical Dislikes. *American Sociological Review*: 61, no. 5 (October): 884–899.

Burgos, Celeste, and Ken Meltz. 1989. How Shall We Sing the Lord's Song in a Foreign Land? Theological and Cultural Implications of Hispanic Liturgical Music. *Faith and Forms* 22, no. 17 (Spring): 16–18.

Burke, Patrick Lawrence. 2008. *Come in and Hear the Truth: Jazz and Race on 52nd Street*. Chicago: University of Chicago Press.

Burnim, Mellonee. 1980. Gospel Music Research. *Black Music Research Journal* 1:63–70.

———. 1985a. The Black Gospel Music Tradition: A Complex of Ideology, Aesthetic, and Behavior. In *More than Dancing: Essays on Afro-American Music and Musicians*, edited by Irene Jackson Brown, 147–167. Westport, Conn.: Greenwood.

———. 1985b. Culture Bearer and Tradition Bearer: An Ethnomusicologist's Research on Gospel Music. *Ethnomusicology* 29, no. 3 (Autumn): 432–447.

Calhoun, Craig J., and Richard Sennett. 2007. *Practicing Culture*. London: Routledge.

Callon, Michel. 1986. Some Elements of a Sociology of Translation: Domestication of the Scallops and the Fishermen of St Brieuc Bay. In *Power, Action and Belief: A New Sociology of Knowledge*, edited by J. Law, 196–233. London: Routledge.

Catchings, L. Maynard. 1952. Interracial Activities in Southern Churches. *Phylon: The Atlanta University Review of Race and Culture* 13, no. 1 (First Quarter): 54–56.

Chaves, Mark. 2004. *Congregations in America*. Cambridge, Mass.: Harvard University Press.

Christerson, Brad, Michael O. Emerson, and Korie L. Edwards. 2005. *Against All Odds: The Struggle of Racial Integration in Religious Organizations*. New York: New York University Press.

Clayton, Martin, Trevor Herbert, and Richard Middleton. 2003. *The Cultural Study of Music: A Critical Introduction*. New York: Routledge.

Clawson, Laura. 2011. *I Belong to This Band, Hallelujah!: Community, Spirituality, and Tradition among Sacred Harp Singers*. Princeton, N.J.: Princeton University Press.

Cone, James H. 1978. Sanctification, Liberation and Black Worship. *Theology Today* 35, no. 2 (July): 139–152.

———. 1992. *The Spirituals and the Blues: An Interpretation*. Maryknoll: Orbis Books.

Cook, Nicholas, and Mark Everist. 1999. *Rethinking Music*. Oxford: Oxford University Press.

Costen, Melva Wilson. 1993. *African American Christian Worship*. Nashville, Tenn.: Abingdon.

Courtney, Craig. 2000. Humility in Worship. *Worship Arts* 46, no. 1:3–5.

Cusic, Don. 2002. *The Sound of Light: A History of Gospel and Christian Music*. Milwaukee, Wisc.: Hal Leonard Publishing Corporation.

Darden, Robert. 2004. *People Get Ready! A New History of Black Gospel Music*. New York: Continuum International Publishing Group.

Davis, John A. 1964. The Influence of Africans on American Culture. *Annals of the American Academy of Political and Social Science* 354, no. 1 (July): 75–83.

DeNora, Tia. 1986. How is Extra-Musical Meaning Possible? Music as a Place and Space for "Work." *Sociological Theory* 4, no. 1 (Spring): 84–94.

———. 2000. *Music in Everyday Life*. Cambridge: Cambridge University Press.

Denisoff, R. Serge, and Mark H. Levine. 1972. Youth and Popular Music: A Test of the Taste Culture Hypothesis. *Youth and Society* 4, no. 2 (December): 237–255.

De Vos, George. 1975. Ethnic Pluralism: Conflict and Accommodation. In *Ethnic Identity: Cultural Continuities and Change*, edited by George De Vos and Lola Romanucci-Ross, 5–41. Palo Alto: Mayfield.

———, and Lola Romanucci-Ross. 1975. Ethnicity: Vessel of Meaning and Emblem of Contrast. In *Ethnic Identity: Cultural Continuities and Change*, edited by George De Vos and Lola Romanucci-Ross, 363–390. Palo Alto: Mayfield.

DeYmaz, Mark, and Harry Li. 2010. *Ethnic Blends: Mixing Diversity into Your Local Church*. Grand Rapids, Mich.: Zondervan.

DeYoung, Curtiss Paul, Michael O. Emerson, George Yancey, and Karen Chai. 2003. *United by Faith: Multicultural Congregations as a Response to the Problem of Race*. New York: Oxford University Press.

Dilling, Margaret. 1995. Living the Life We Sing About: A Gospel Choir Challenges Academe. *College Music Symposium* 35 (Fall): 61–75.

DiMaggio, Paul. 1987. Classification in Art. *American Sociological Review* 52, no. 4 (August): 440–455.

DiMaggio, Paul, and John Mohr. 1985. Cultural Capital. Educational Attainment, and Marital Selection. *American Journal of Sociology* 90, no. 6 (May): 1231–1261.

DjeDje, Jacqueline Cogdell. 1986. Change and Differentiation: The Adoption of Black American Gospel Music in the Catholic Church. *Ethnomusicology* 30, no. 2 (Spring–Summer): 223–252.

Donaldson, Andrew. 2001. Singing Global Song: The Gifts are Many; The Body is One. *The Hymn* 54, no. 4 (October): 4–6.

Doran, Carol, and Thomas H. Troeger. 1992. *Trouble at the Table: Gathering the Tribes for Worship*. Nashville, Tenn.: Abingdon Press.

DuBois, W. E. B. [1903] 1996. *The Souls of Black Folks*. New York: Penguin Classics.

Durkheim, Émile. 1995. *The Elementary Forms of Religious Life*. Translated by Karen E. Fields. New York: The Free Press.

Eco, Umberto. 1984. *Semiotics and the Philosophy of Language*. London: Macmillan.

Edwards, Korie L. 2008. *The Elusive Dream: The Power of Race in Interracial Churches*. New York: Oxford University Press.

Ehn, Pelle. 1988. *Work-oriented Design of Computer Artifacts*. Stockholm: Arbetslivscentrum.

Eisner, Elliot W. 1991. *The Enlightened Eye: Qualitative Inquiry and the Enhancement of Educational Practice*. New York: Macmillan.

Ellingson, Stephen. 2007. *The Megachurch and the Mainline: Remaking Religious Tradition in the Twenty-First Century*. Chicago: University of Chicago Press.

Emerson, Michael O., and Karen Chai Kim. 2003. Multiracial Congregations: An Analysis of Their Development and a Typology. *Journal for the Scientific Study of Religion*. 42, no. 2 (June): 217–227.

Emerson, Michael O., and Christian Smith. 2000. *Divided by Faith: Evangelical Religion and the Problem of Race in America*. Oxford: Oxford University Press.

Emerson, Michael O., and Rodney M. Woo. 2006. *People of the Dream: Multiracial Congregations in the United States*. Princeton, N.J.: Princeton University Press.

Epstein, Jonathon S., ed. 1994. *Adolescents and their Music: If It's Too Loud, You're Too Old*. New York: Garland.

Evans, Curtis J. 2008. *The Burden of Black Religion*. Oxford: Oxford University Press.

Fanarow, Wendy. 1997. The Spatial Organization of the Indie Music Gig. In *The Subcultures Reader*, edited by Ken Glelder and Sarah Thronton, 360–372. London: Routledge.

Farhadian, Charles E. 2007. *Christian Worship Worldwide: Expanding Horizons, Deepening Practices*. Grand Rapids, Mich.: Eerdmans.

Faus, Nancy Rosenberger. 1995. Music of the World Church. In *Music and the Arts in Christian Worship: Book One*, edited by Robert E. Webber. Nashville, Tenn.: Star Song Communications Group.

Feld, Steven. 1984. Communication, Music, and Speech about Music. *Yearbook for Traditional Music* 16:1–18.

Fettes, Mark. 2000. Review of *Authenticity and Identity: Lessons from Indigenous Language Education* (In special issue, edited by R. Henze and K. A. Davis, *Anthropology & Education Quarterly* 30, no. 1:204–213) *Language and Education* 14, no. 2 (July): 143–145.

Floyd, Samuel A., Jr. 1995. *The Power of Black Music: Interpreting Its History from Africa to the United States*. New York: Oxford University Press.

Francis, Mark R., CSV. 2002. *Multicultural Celebrations: A Guide*. Washington D.C.: Federation of Diocesan Liturgical Commissions (FDLC).

Frazier, Edward Franklin. 1963. *The Negro Church in America*. New York: Schocken Books.

Frith, Simon. 1978. *The Sociology of Rock*. London: Constable.

———. 1981. *Sound Effects: Youth, Leisure, and the Politics of Rock 'n' Roll*. New York: Pantheon.

Gaines, Donna. 1991. *Teenage Wasteland: Suburbia's Dead End Kids*. New York: Pantheon Books.

Gans, Herbert J. 1979. Symbolic Ethnicity: The Future of Ethnic Groups and Cultures in America. *Ethnic and Racial Studies* 2, no. 1 (January): 9–17.

———. 1994. Symbolic Ethnicity and Symbolic Religiosity: Towards a Comparison of Ethnic Religious Acculturation. *Ethnic and Racial Studies* 17, no. 4 (October): 577–592.

Garces-Foley, Kathleen. 2007. *Crossing the Ethnic Divide: The Multiethnic Church on a Mission*. Oxford: Oxford University Press.

Grazian, David. 2003. *Blue Chicago: The Search for Authenticity in Urban Blues Clubs*. Chicago: University of Chicago Press.

Gumperz, John. 1977. Sociocultural Knowledge in Conversational Inference. In *Linguistics and Anthropology*, edited by M. Saville-Troike, 191–212. Washington, D.C.: Georgetown University Press.

Harris, Michael W. 1994. *The Rise of Gospel Blues: The Music of Thomas Andrew Dorsey in the Urban Church*. New York: Oxford University Press.

Hawn, C. Michael. 1999. The Fiesta of the Faithful: Pablo Sosa and the Contextualization of Latin American Hymnody. *The Hymn* 50, no. 4 (October): 32–45.

———. 2003a. *Gather into One: Praying and Singing Globally*. Grand Rapids, Mich.: Eerdmans.

———. 2003b. *One Bread, One Body: Exploring Cultural Diversity in Worship*. Bethesda, Md.: Alban Institute.

Helibut, Anthony. 1978. Black Urban Hymnody: Gospel. In *Brighten the Corner Where You Are: Black and White Urban Hymnody*. New World, NW-224.

———. 1997. *The Gospel Sound: Good News and Bad Times*. New York: Limehouse Editions.

Henderson, Stephen. 1973. *Understanding the New Black Poetry*. New York: William & Morrow.

Holloway, Carson. 2001. *All Shook Up: Music, Passion, and Politics*. Dallas: Spence Pub.

Hochschild, Arlie. 1983. *The Managed Heart*. Berkeley and Los Angeles: University of California Press.

Howard, Jay R., and John M. Streck. 1999. *Apostles of Rock: The Splintered World of Contemporary Christian Music*. Lexington: University Press of Kentucky.

———. 1996. The Splintered Art World of Contemporary Christian Music. *Popular Music* 15, no. 1 (January): 37–53.

Hutchinson, J. F., N. Rodriguez, and J. Hagan. 1996. Community Life: African Americans in Multiethnic Residential Areas. *Journal of Black Studies* 27, no. 2 (November): 201–223.

Jackson, Irene V. 1979. *Afro-American Religious Music: A Bibliography and Catalog of Gospel Music*. Westport, Conn.: Greenwood Press.

Jackson, Joyce Marie. 1995. The Changing Nature of Gospel Music: A Southern Case Study. *African American Review* 29, no. 2 (Summer): 185–200.

Jakobson, Roman. 1960. Closing Statement: Linguistics and Poetics. In *Style in Language*, edited by T. A Sebeok, 350–77. Cambridge, Mass.: Harvard University Press.

Jeung, Russell. 2004. *New Asian American Churches: The Religious Construction of Race*. New Brunswick, N.J.: Rutgers University Press.

Jones, Hettie. 1974. *Big Star Fallin' Mama: Five Women in Black Music*. New York: Viking.

Jones, Robert Alun. 1999. *The Development of Durkheim's Social Realism*. New York: Cambridge University Press.

Jorgensen, Danny L. 1989. *Participant Observation: A Methodology for Human Studies*. Applied Social Research Methods Series. Newbury Park, Calif.: Sage.

Kaufman Shelemay, Kay. 2001. *Soundscapes: Exploring Music in a Changing World*. New York: W. W. Norton.

Kim, Rebecca Y. 2006. *God's New Whiz Kids?: Korean American Evangelicals on Campus*. New York: New York University Press.

Kim, Sharon. 2010. *A Faith of Our Own: Second-Generation Spirituality in Korean American Churches*. New Brunswick, N.J.: Rutgers University Press.

Kimbrough, S. T., Jr. 2000. Practical Considerations for Promoting Global Song. *The Hymn* 51, no. 4 (October): 22–29.

King, Martin Luther, Jr. 1958. *Stride toward Freedom: The Montgomery Story*. New York: Harper.

Kujawa-Holbrook, Sheryl A. 2002. *A House of Prayer for All Peoples: Congregations Building Multiracial Community*. Bethesda, Md.: Alban Institute.

Lash, Scott, and John Urry. 1994. *Economies of Signs and Space*. London: Sage.

Latour, Bruno. 1991. Where are the Missing Masses? A Sociology of a Few Mundane Artefacts. In *Shaping Technology/Building Society: Studies in Sociotechnical Change*, edited by W. E. Bijker and J. Law, 225–258. Cambridge, Mass.: MIT Press.

Law, John. 1994. *Organizing Modernity*. Cambridge: Polity.

Levine, Lawrence W. 1977. *Black Culture and Black Consciousness: Afro-American Folk Thought from Slavery to Freedom.* New York: Oxford University Press.

Lewis, George H. 1977. Taste Cultures and Culture Classes in Mass Society: Shifting Patterns in American Popular Music. *International Review of the Aesthetics and Sociology of Music* 8, no. 1 (June): 39–48.

Lewis, Mark. 2010. *The Diffusion of Black Gospel Music in Postmodern Denmark.* Lexington, Ky.: Emeth Press.

Lincoln, C. Eric. 1999. *Race, Religion, and the Continuing American Dilemma.* New York: Hill & Wang.

Lincoln, C. Eric, and Lawrence H. Mamiya. 1990. *The Black Church in the African-American Experience.* Durham, N.C.: Duke University Press.

Lornell, Kip, and Anne K. Rasmussen. 1997. *Musics of Multicultural America: A Study of Twelve Musical Communities*. New York: Schirmer.

Luhr, Eileen. 2005. Metal Missionaries to the Nation: Christian Heavy Metal Music, "Family Values," and Youth Culture, 1984–1994. *American Quarterly* 57, no. 1 (March): 103–128.

Lukes, Steven. 1972. *Émile Durkheim; His Life and Work, A Historical and Critical Study*. New York: Harper & Row.

Lull, James. 1995. *Media, Communication, Culture: A Global Approach.* Cambridge: Polity Press.

Macias, Anthony F. 2004. Bringing Music to the People: Race, Urban Culture, and Municipal Politics in Postwar Los Angeles. *American Quarterly* 56, no. 3 (September): 693–717.

Malbon, Ben. 1999. *Clubbing: Dancing, Ecstasy and Vitality*. London: Routledge.

Mark, Noah. 1998. Birds of a Feather Sing Together. *Social Forces* 77, no. 2 (December): 453–485.

Marti, Gerardo. 2005. *A Mosaic of Believers: Diversity and Innovation in a Multiethnic Church*. Bloomington: Indiana University Press.

———. 2008a. Fluid Ethnicity and Ethnic Transcendence. *Journal for the Scientific Study of Religion* 47, no. 1 (March): 11–16.

———. 2008b. *Hollywood Faith: Holiness, Prosperity, and Ambition in a Los Angeles Church*. New Brunswick, N.J.: Rutgers University Press.

———. 2009a. Affinity, Identity, and Transcendence: The Experience of Religious Racial Integration in Multiracial Churches. *Journal for the Scientific Study of Religion* 48, no. 1 (March): 53–68.

———. 2009b. Preface to paperback edition. In *A Mosaic of Believers: Diversity and Innovation in a Multiethnic Church*. Bloomington: Indiana University Press.

———. 2010a. The Religious Racial Integration of African Americans into Diverse Churches. *Journal for the Scientific Study of Religion*. 49, no. 2 (June): 201–217.

———. 2010b. When Does Religious Racial Integration "Count"? A Caution Against Seeking Ideal Ethnographic Cases. *Journal for the Scientific Study of Religion*. 49, no. 2 (June): 224–230.

Martin, John Levi. 2011. *The Explanation of Social Action*. New York: Oxford University Press.

Martin, Peter. 1995. *Sounds and Society: Themes in the Sociology of Music*. Manchester: Manchester University Press.

Martin, Randy. 1997. The Composite Body: Hip-Hop Aerobics and the Multicultural Nation. *Journal of Sport & Social Issues* 21, no. 2 (May): 120–133.

Maultsby, Portia. 1992. The Impact of Gospel Music on the Secular Music Industry. In *We'll Understand It Better By and By*, edited by Bernice Johnson Reagon, 19–33. Washington, D.C.: Smithsonian Institution Press.

May, Elizabeth. 1983. *Musics of Many Cultures*. Berkeley and Los Angeles: University of California Press.

Maynard-Reid, Pedrito U. 2000. *Diverse Worship: African American, Hispanic, and Caribbean Perspectives*. Downers Grove, Ill.: InterVarsity Press.

Mays, Benjamin, and Joseph W. Nicholson. 1933. *The Negro's Church*. New York: Russell & Russell.

McKinnon, James W. 1989. *Music in Early Christian Literature*. New York: Cambridge University Press.

McNeil, Brenda Salter, and Rick Richardson. 2004. *The Heart of Racial Justice: How Soul Change Leads to Social Change*. Downers Grove, Ill.: InterVarsity Press.

McPherson, J. Miller. 1983. An Ecology of Affiliation. *American Sociological Review* 48, no. 4 (August): 519–532.

Metzler, Fritz. 1938. Dur, Moll und "Kirchentöne" als musikalischer Rassenausdruck. In *Zur Tonalität des deutschen Volksliedes*, edited by Guido Waldmann, 1–27. Wofenbüttel, Germany: Kallmeyer.

Middleton, Richard. 1990. *Studying Popular Music*. Milton Keynes, England: Open University Press.

Miller, Steve. 1993. *The Contemporary Christian Music Debate*. Wheaton, Ill.: Tyndale House Publishers.

Minkin, Lewis. 1997. *Exits and Entrances: Political Research as a Creative Art*. Sheffield: Sheffield Hallam University Press.

Moreau, A. Scott, Harold A. Netland, Charles Edward van Engen, and David Burnett. 2000. *Evangelical Dictionary of World Missions*. Grand Rapids, Mich.: Baker.

Munro, Martin. 2010. *Different Drummers: Rhythm and Race in the Americas*. Berkeley and Los Angeles: University of California Press.

Nelsen, Hart M., and Anne Kusner Nelsen. 1975. *Black Church in the Sixties*. Lexington: University Press of Kentucky.

Nelson, Timothy. 2005. *Every Time I Feel the Spirit: Religious Experience and Ritual in an African Church*. New York: New York University Press.

Nettle, Bruno. 1983. *The Study of Ethnomusicology*. Champaign: University of Illinois Press.

Painter, Nell Irvin. 2010. *The History of White People*. New York: W. W. Norton.

Pattillo-McCoy, Mary. 1998. Church Culture as a Strategy of Action in the Black Community. *American Sociological Review* 63, no. 6 (December): 767–784.

Pettigrew, Thomas F. 1985. New Black-White Patterns: How Best to Conceptualize Them? *Annual Review of Sociology* 11 (August): 329–346.

Pinch, Trevor and Wiebe Bijker. 1987. The Social Construction of Facts and Artifacts: Or How the Sociology of Science and the Sociology of Technology Might Benefit Each Other. In *The Social Construction of Technological Systems*, edited by W. E. Bijker, T. P. Hughes, and T. Pinch, 17–50. Cambridge, Mass.: MIT Press.

Pickering, W. S. F. 2002. *Durkheim Today*, New York: Berghahn Books.

Pinn, Anthony B. 2002. *The Black Church in the Post–Civil Rights Era*. Maryknoll, N.Y.: Orbis.

———. 2003. DuBois' Souls: Thoughts on "Veiled" Bodies and the Study of Black Religion. *The North Star: A Journal of African American Religious History* 6, no. 2 (Spring): 1–5.

Piron, Francis. 1990. Defining Impulse Purchasing. *Advances in Consumer Research* 18:509–514.

———. 1993. A Comparison of Emotional Reactions Experienced by Planned, Unplanned and Impulse Purchasers. *Advances in Consumer Research* 20:341–344.

Porter, Eric. 2002. *What Is This Thing Called Jazz: African American Musicians as Artists, Critics, and Activists*. Berkeley and Los Angeles: University of California Press.

Radano, Ronald Michael. 2003. *Lying Up a Nation: Race and Black Music*. Chicago: University of Chicago Press.

———, and Philip V. Bohlman, eds. 2000. *Music and the Racial Imagination*. Chicago: University of Chicago Press.

Rahn, John. 1972. Review of Coker's Music and Meaning. *Perspectives of New Music* 11, no. 1 (Fall): 255–257.

Rasmussen, Anne K. 2004. Mainstreaming American Musical Multiculturalism. *American Music* 22, no. 2 (Summer): 296–309.

Ratzinger, Joseph Cardinal. 2000. *The Spirit of the Liturgy*. San Francisco: Ignatius.

Reck, David. 1997. *Music of the Whole Earth*. New York: Da Capo Press.

Redman, Robb. 2002. *The Great Worship Awakening: Singing a New Song in the Postmodern Church*. San Francisco: Jossey-Bass.

Romanowski, William. 1990. Contemporary Christian Music: The Business of Music Ministry. In *American Evangelicals and the Mass Media*, edited by Q. J. Schultze, 143–169. Grand Rapids, Mich.: Zondervan Publishing House, Academie Press.

———. 2000. Evangelicals and Popular Music: The Contemporary Christian Music Industry. In *Religion and Popular Culture in America*, edited by J. H. Mahan and B. Forbes, 105–124. Berkeley and Los Angeles: University of California Press.

Rommen, Timothy. 2007. *"Mek Some Noise": Gospel Music and the Ethics of Style in Trinidad*. Berkeley and Los Angeles: University of California Press.

Rook, Dennis W. 1987. The Buying Impulse. *Journal of Consumer Research* 14:189–199.

———, and Stephen J. Hoch. 1985. Consuming Impulses. *Advances in Consumer Research* 12:23–27.

Roy, William G. 2010. *Reds, Whites, and Blues: Social Movements, Folk Music, and Race in the United States*. Princeton, N.J.: Princeton University Press.

Royce, Anya Peterson. 1982. *Ethnic Identity: Strategies of Diversity*. Bloomington: Indiana University Press.

Sanders, Cheryl J. 1996. *Saints in Exile: The Holiness-Pentecostal Experience in African American Religion and Culture*. New York: Oxford University Press.

Schlingensiepen, Ferdinand. 2009. *Dietrich Bonhoeffer, 1906–1945: Martyr, Thinker, Man of Resistance*. New York: Continuum International Publishing Group.

Schuessler, Karl F. 1980. *Musical Taste and Socio-Economic Background*. New York: Arno Press.

Silbermann, Alphons. 1963. *The Sociology of Music*. London: Routledge & Kegan Paul.

Small, Christopher. 1998. *Musicking: The Meanings of Performing and Listening*. Hanover, N.H.: University Press of New England.

Smith, Efrem, and Phil Jackson. 2005. *The Hip-Hop Church: Connecting with the Movement Shaping Our Culture*. Downers Grove, Ill.: InterVarsity Press.

Spencer, Jon Michael. 1997. *Protest and Praise: Sacred Music of Black Religion*. Minneapolis: Augsburg Fortress Publishers.

———. 1995. *Sing a New Song: Liberating Black Hymnody*. Minneapolis: Fortress Press.

Standifer, James A., and Barbara Reeder. 1972. *Source Book of African and Afro-American Materials for Music Educators*. Washington, D.C.: Contemporary Music Project, Music Educators National Conference.

Stokes, Martin. 1994. *Ethnicity, Identity, and Music: The Musical Construction of Place*. Providence, R.I.: Berg.

Stowe, David W. 2004. *How Sweet the Sound: Music in the Spiritual Lives of Americans*. Cambridge, Mass.: Harvard University Press.

Strauss, David. 1965. French Critics and American Jazz. *American Quarterly* 17, no. 3 (Autumn): 582–587.

Tagg, Philip. 1989. Open Letter: "Black Music," "Afro-American Music," and "European Music." *Popular Music* 8, no. 3 (October): 285–298.

Taylor, Timothy D. 2000. World Music in Television Ads. *American Music* 18, no. 2 (Summer): 162–192.

Titon, Jeff Todd. 1988. *Powerhouse for God: Speech, Chant, and Song in an Appalachian Baptist Church*. Austin: University of Texas Press.

———. 2002. *Worlds of Music*. New York: Schirmer.

Thornton, Sarah. 1996. *Club Cultures: Music, Media and Subcultural Capital*. Hanover, N.H.: University Press of New England.

Tranby, Eric, and Douglas Hartmann. 2008. Critical Whiteness Theories and the Evangelical "Race Problem": Extending Emerson and Smith's *Divided by Faith*. *Journal for the Scientific Study of Religion* 47, no. 3 (September): 341–359.

Troeger, Thomas H. 1998. Book Review: *Praising in Black and White: Unity and Diversity in Christian Worship* by Brenda Eatman Aghahowa. *Journal of Religion* 78, no. 2 (April): 280–281.

Turino, Thomas. 2008. *Music as Social Life: The Politics of Participation*. Chicago: University of Chicago Press.

Tveit, Sigvald. 2000. Hymnody and Identity. *The Hymn* 51, no. 4 (October): 6–11.

Van Maanen, John. 1988. *Tales of the Field: On Writing Ethnography*. Chicago Guides to Writing, Editing, and Publishing. Chicago: University of Chicago Press.

Vásquez, Manuel. 1999. Pentecostalism, Collective Identity, and Transnationalism among Salvadorans and Peruvians in the US. *Journal of the American Academy of Religion* 67, no. 3 (September): 617–635.

Villafañe , Eldin. 1993. *The Liberating Spirit: Toward an Hispanic American Pentecostal Social Ethic*. Grand Rapids: Eerdmans.

Volk, Terese M. 1994. Folk Musics and Increasing Diversity in American Music Education: 1900–1916. *Journal of Research in Music Education* 42, no. 4 (Winter): 285–305.

Walker, Linda B. 2003. Developing a Gospel Choir. *Music Educators Journal* 89, no. 3 (January): 23–28.

Walker, Wyatt Tee. 1979. *Somebody's Calling My Name: Black Sacred Music and Social Change*. Valley Forge: Judson Press.

Waters, Malcolm. 2001. *Globalization*. London: Routledge.

Waters, Mary C. 1990. *Ethnic Options: Choosing Identities in America*. Berkeley and Los Angeles: University of California Press.

Webb, Sydney, and Beatrice Webb. 1932. *Methods of Social Study*. London: Longman Green.

Webber, Robert E. 1994. *Worship Old and New*. 2nd ed. Grand Rapids, Mich.: Zondervan.

Weizenbaum, Joseph. 1976. *Computer Power and Human Reason*. San Francisco: W. H. Freeman and Co.

West, Cornel. 1999. Afro-American Music: From Bebop to Rap. In *The Cornel West Reader*, edited by Cornel West, 474–484. New York: Basic Civitas Books.

Whitely, Sheila, Andy Bennett, and Stan Hawkins. 2004. *Music, Space and Place: Popular Music and Cultural Identity*. Burlington: Ashgate Publishing.

Whitson, David. 1994. The Embodiment of Gender: Discipline, Domination and Empowerment. In *Women, Sport and Culture*, edited by S. Birrel and C. Cole, 353–371. Champaign: Human Kinetics Books.

Williams-Jones, Pearl. 1975. Afro-American Gospel Music: A Crystallization of the Black Aesthetic. *Ethnomusicology* 19, no. 3 (September): 373–385.

Willis, Paul E. 1978. *Profane Culture*. London: Routledge & Kegan Paul.

Wolff, Richard F. 1999. A Phenomenological Study of In-Church and Televised Worship. *Journal for the Scientific Study of Religion* 38, no. 2 (June): 219–235.

Witkin, Robert W. 1974. *The Intelligence of Feeling*. London: Heinermann.

Wong, Liana. 1999. Authenticity and the Revitalization of Hawaiian. *Anthropology & Education Quarterly* 30, no. 1 (March): 94–115.

Woolgar, Steve. 1997. Configuring the User: Inventing New Technologies. In *The Machine at Work*, edited by K. Grint and S. Woolgar, 65–94. Cambridge: Polity.

Yancey, George. 2003. *One Body, One Spirit. Principles of Successful Multiracial Churches*. Downers Grove, Ill.: IVP Books.

Index